Managing Misbehaviour
Strategies for Effective Management of Behaviour in Schools

Education titles from Macmillan:

The Caring Role of the Primary School
Editors: Kenneth David and Tony Charlton

Teacher Appraisal: A Practical Guide
Ted Wragg

Managing for Learning
Editors: John Buckley and David Styan

Norwood Was a Difficult School
Jean Lawrence and Margaret Tucker

Action Research: Principles and Practice
Jean McNiff

Assessing and Teaching Language: Literacy and Oracy in Schools
Editor: Mary Neville

Preventive Approaches to Disruption
Barry Chisholm, David Kearney, Grenville Knight, Howard Knight, Howard Little, Susan Morris, David Tweddle

Managing Misbehaviour
Strategies for Effective Management of Behaviour in Schools

Edited by **Tony Charlton** Cert Ed, BEd (Hons), MEd, PhD
and **Kenneth David** Cert Ed, BA

© Tony Charlton and Kenneth David 1989

All rights reserved. No reproduction, copy or transmission
of this publication may be made without written permission.

No paragraph of this publication may be reproduced, copied
or transmitted save with written permission or in accordance
with the provisions of the Copyright Act 1956 (as amended),
or under the terms of any licence permitting limited copying
issued by the Copyright Licensing Agency, 33-4 Alfred Place,
London WC1E 7DP.

Any person who does any unauthorised act in relation to
this publication may be liable to criminal prosecution and
civil claims for damages.

First published 1989

Published by
MACMILLAN EDUCATION LTD
Houndmills, Basingstoke, Hampshire RG21 2XS
and London
Companies and representatives
throughout the world

Printed in Hong Kong

British Library Cataloguing in Publication Data

Managing misbehaviour : strategies for
  effective management of behaviour in schools.
  1. Schools. Students. Behaviour problems.
  Treatment
  I. Charlton, Tony II. David, Kenneth
  371.8'1

ISBN 0-333-46928-3

Contents

The Contributors	ix
Introduction	1

PART I THE THEORETICAL BACKGROUND

1 The Development of Behaviour Problems — 11
Tony Charlton and John George

The complexity of behaviour	11
Behaviour problems: differing perspectives of causation	11
The complexity of causation: case studies	13
Factors associated with the development of behaviour problems	16

2 Behaviour Problems and the Teacher — 42
Ronald Davie

Problem children, or problem schools?	42
Assessing needs	43
Parallels with social services	44
Assessment as a continuous process	46
Where lies the problem?	47
Five models	48
The psychodynamic approach	49
Behaviour modification	50
Humanistic psychology	52
Behaviour and environment	53
A systems approach	54
Labelling theory	55
From individuals to systems	56
Which model to believe?	58
The practitioner's dilemma	58
An eclectic stance	59
Difficulties in eclecticism	61
A team approach	62

PART II THEORY AND PRACTICE IN CLASSROOMS

3	**Learning and Behaviour Problems**	67
	Hanne Lambley	
	Towards a definition of concepts	67
	Learning and behaviour problems – an interrelationship	69
	Children's emotional and cognitive performance	71
	The importance of the self-concept, expectancies and locus of control	72
	The nature of the interrelationship – a question of aetiology?	74
	Learning failure as a consequence of emotional problems	74
	Emotional problems as a consequence of learning problems	75
	Third-factor variables	76
	Intervention	77
	Implications for the teacher	79
	Access to the mainstream curriculum	80
	Pastoral care	81
	An unbalanced curriculum	82
	Some useful suggestions	82
4	**A Dynamic Approach to Understanding and Meeting Emotional and Behaviour Difficulties**	91
	John and Patricia Davies	
	Teacher interpretation and understanding of difficulty	91
	Conflicting philosophies?	93
	Trigger behaviours	95
	The classroom environment and learning task	101
	Attention, response and order	103
	Exploratory learning	103
	Social learning	104
	A whole-school approach and parental involvement	104
5	**Behavioural Approaches**	108
	John Presland	
	Behaviouristic, humanistic, behavioural?	108
	The behaviouristic standpoint	108
	The humanistic standpoint	111
	The behavioural standpoint	112
	The basis of a behavioural intervention	114
	The stages in a behavioural intervention	115

Range and scope of behavioural approaches	124
Learning to use behavioural techniques	125
Behavioural approaches and classroom management	127
Where next?	128

PART III CLASSROOM AND SCHOOL PRACTICES

6 Pastoral Care Practice — 133
Kenneth David
Pastoral care	133
The quality of teachers	135
Relations with young people	135
Selected critical viewpoints	136
Children's needs	139
Developments and changes	142
Improved pastoral practice	148

7 Working with Parents — 151
Kevin Jones, Mick Lock, and Martin and Terri Webb
The concept of a shared educational responsibility	152
Stages in the development of a shared educational responsibility	156
Factors affecting the successful outcome of educational partnerships	164

8 The Involvement of Outside Agencies — 173
Kenneth David
School Psychological Service	176
The Education Welfare Service	177
The School Health Service	177
Social Services Department	178
Other helping agencies	179

9 In-Service Training for Support Teachers — 187
Libby Falconer-Hall and Lawrence Harlatt
Background to making the additional provision in Wiltshire	189
Preparation	190
The in-service training	192
Planning training	193
Other courses	203
Future plans	204

10 Reflections and Implications	207
Tony Charlton and Kenneth David	
Teachers rule, OK?	207
The reality of the classroom	207
Guidelines to good practice	208
Index	235

The Contributors

Tony Charlton was a Director of English Studies and Head of Pastoral Care in a large comprehensive school, and taught in both primary and special schools before becoming a part-time tutor at University College, Cardiff. He is currently Principal Lecturer and Head of Special Needs in the Education Faculty at the College of St Paul and St Mary, Cheltenham. He has been published widely on a range of matters concerned with children's emotional and behaviour problems and is coeditor of *The Caring Role of the Primary School* published by Macmillan in 1987.

Kenneth David has taught in primary and secondary schools, as well as in colleges in UK and abroad. He became tutor-adviser in personal relationships in Gloucestershire, and then worked as a general adviser in Lancashire, with special responsibility for personal relationships. He has published numerous books and articles, a recent one being *Health Education in Schools* (2nd edition) edited with Trefor Williams (Harper and Row, 1987). He is coeditor with Tony Charlton of *The Caring Role of the Primary School*, and is now a freelance lecturer and writer.

Ronald Davie is Director of The National Children's Bureau, a body with a strong research record but unique in the world for the width of its corporate and individual membership in the children's field. The author of several educational books and numerous articles and papers, he was previously Professor of Educational Psychology at University College, Cardiff.

John Davies is coordinator of Special Needs at Oxford Polytechnic. He was previously headteacher of a residential special school for maladjusted children. In addition to contributing chapters to several books in the special needs' area, he has an impressive publication record in educational journals.

Patricia Davies is coordinator for the Special Needs Advisory and Support Teachers team in East Oxfordshire. She previously was a teacher at a residential school for maladjusted children and in primary schools in Wiltshire. She has published widely in a range of educational journals and books and is the joint editor of a book on support work for children with special needs in mainstream schools.

Libby Falconer-Hall has held varied teaching posts, including a head of department post in a large comprehensive school, providing for pupils with learning and adjustment difficulties. She has contributed to the development of Open University material on reading. Currently she is the Adviser for Special Needs in Wiltshire.

John George is Headmaster of Bettridge School, Cheltenham, which caters for the needs of children with severe learning difficulties. He previously worked in a variety of other special schools providing for pupils with physical and moderate learning/behaviour difficulties.

Lawrence Harlatt has been an educational psychologist in Wiltshire for ten years, having previously taught for twenty years. His experience includes both primary and secondary ages and subjects as diverse as Religious Education, Mathematics and Games.

Kevin Jones is a Senior Lecturer in Special Needs at the College of St Paul and St Mary, Cheltenham. Previously he taught in primary and secondary schools before being appointed as In-Service Training Officer in Service Children's Schools in North-West Europe.

Hanne Lambley worked in special and mainstream schools, both in Germany and the UK, prior to her appointment as an advisory teacher in Gloucestershire. Her present appointment is as Senior Lecturer with responsibility for Language in the Faculty of Education at the College of St Paul and St Mary, Cheltenham.

Mick Lock is an Educational Psychologist in the City of Nottingham. His work spans the 5–19 age range and covers both mainstream and special schools. Prior to his present appointment he worked as Head of House in secondary education. He has a particular interest in short-term problem-solving approaches towards problem behaviour which is conducted jointly with parents.

John Presland trained as an Educational Psychologist and worked for Warwickshire and Birmingham in that capacity before moving to his present post as Principal Educational Psychologist and Senior Adviser for Special Education in Wiltshire. He has published widely on a variety of educational and psychological topics.

Martin Webb is currently Headteacher of Roy First School, Dusseldorf (Service Children's Schools, North-West Europe). Throughout his teaching career he has developed an interest in working with parents and his contribution to this book, concerning children with behavioural problems, represents one aspect of this ongoing interest.

Terri Webb is presently working as a Special Education Needs Support Teacher in a primary school. She is particularly interested in the development of the support teacher role within schools and extends the concept of shared responsibilities towards the involvement of all people within and without schools who can participate in a planned contribution towards the education of children with special educational needs.

Introduction

The vulnerable teacher

Teachers are often assailed nowadays, not only by occasional physical assault and verbal abuse from pupils (and parents) but also by an unprecedented public challenge of their professional competence, as well as their moral leadership.

Arguably, as never before, teaching is becoming both more demanding and more difficult, and teachers need to be better equipped for the exacting tasks of caring and providing for, and exercising healthy control over, their clients: endeavours which are increasingly being subjected to evaluation and scrutiny.

This book is concerned with those tasks, particularly those which relate to teachers' management skills in efficiently directing classroom behaviour to help ensure that satisfactory learning can take place.

Prevention is better than cure

While this book is concerned with pupils' behaviour problems in schools and how schools can marshal and organise available resources to help ameliorate them, it is equally concerned with the prevention of such problems. We believe that the most effective way to manage behaviour problems is to prevent, or at least minimise, their occurrence. Support for this reasoning can be found in a number of studies such as the one undertaken by Kounin (1970). Attempting to differentiate between the characteristics of 'more' and 'less' successful teachers, the author reported that while he found no differences between the two groups in terms of their effectiveness in *dealing* with behaviour problems, successful teachers were noted to be far more adept at *preventing* them. In view of such findings it seems reasonable to contend that teachers' professional training should equip them with an understanding of a range of classroom management skills which help resolve problems when they arise and, more importantly, encourage the type of classroom setting which helps discourage the emergence of pupil misbehaviour.

Lawrence et al. (1984) provide a reminder that disruptive behaviour, for example:

> is frustrating, irritating and stressful, in extreme cases it may lead to complete breakdown of the classroom order and, more seriously, of the teacher's health. (p. viii)

Since dealing with problem behaviours can make considerable demands upon the teachers' time, energy and health, the skills of discouraging behaviour problems has an obvious 'survival benefit', as well as improving the likelihood of children benefiting from their schooling.

With reference to this last point HMI (1987) in their report entitled *Education Observed 5: Good behaviour and discipline in schools* stress that:

> Good behaviour is a necessary condition for effective teaching and learning to take place, and an important outcome of education which society rightly expects. (p. 1)

Behaviour problems: a wider definition

We argue that all children, to lesser or greater extents and in varying degrees, manifest behaviour problems at some time in their school lives, often requiring intervention. Too often, though, intervention is considered only in terms of the *application* of management strategies to eradicate, or suppress, *pupils'* behaviour problems. Our conception of intervention is not so naive. It suggests that the cause of problem behaviours may as often be located within the teacher (in terms of the teaching/management strategies being used) or aspects of the wider institution, as it is within the pupil or his/her peers. Intervention may therefore necessitate *changes* to eradicate existing conditions external to the pupil, for which the teacher or school holds some responsibility, which contribute towards the cause and maintenance of problem behaviours.

We, therefore, view behaviour problems in a more comprehensive manner than that used in most other books on this subject. In extending the parameter in this manner we are offering the following views:

(a) Except for a very small minority of the school population, there are only quantitative (rather than qualitative) differences between the behaviour problems which teachers are called upon to resolve during their day-to-day work in classrooms, and elsewhere in the school. These differences in 'degree', rather than 'kind', will often, though not always, reflect teachers' differing perceptions of a behaviour; perceptions which will be fashioned by a range of factors including individual teachers' tolerance levels, expectancies, temperament, emotional state and management competencies.
(b) The strategies, techniques and skills discussed later in this book can often be applied equally well in both a *curative* and *preventive* manner to help 'orchestrate' success for teachers and their pupils.
(c) Behaviour problems may present themselves as overt challenges (for example, aggression, abuse, defiance, and non-compliance), of varying magnitudes, to the teacher's classroom control. They may also challenge the teacher's skills in a more discrete, less obvious manner. Where pupils experience fears, anxieties or unhappiness their problems can be overlooked (or even ignored), especially where the teacher's skills are already being challenged to the limit by disruptive behaviour elsewhere in the class.

We are, therefore, emphasising in this book the effective *management* of behaviour in schools. In doing so we underline our belief that by effectively managing children's behaviour, competent teachers simultaneously help to prevent as well as resolve undesirable and unacceptable behaviour.

Schools make a difference

Schools, as never before, are now being challenged to examine the nature of what they offer, and how it is offered, in order to determine the extent to which they successfully meet the needs of all their pupils. Numerous studies have shown that most children tend to present behaviour problems either in school or at home; but not necessarily in both (Coleman *et al.*, 1966; Rutter, Tizard and Whitmore, 1970). Much behaviour is therefore *specific to situations*, which suggests that misbehaviour can best be understood – and prevented or resolved – within the setting where it may occur. Much evidence shows, quite clearly, that schools do affect their pupils' behaviour within schools (for example Hargreaves, 1967; Rutter et al., 1979; Galloway and Goodwin (1987). What schools offer, and how they offer it, helps determine whether pupils respond in desirable or undesirable ways. Factors which seem to affect this influence include:

- the calibre of the teaching staff and the quality of the school leadership
- the general school ethos (for example staffroom 'climate', expectations and attitudes offered to parents, as well as pupils)
- aspects of curriculum organisation (for example streaming/banding/mixed ability grouping)
- the nature and content of the curriculum
- how the curriculum is implemented (for example quality of classroom management and teaching strategies).

Drawing attention to school-based causes of behaviour problems Frude and Gault (1984) commented that:

Many of the incidents reported to us indicated some weaknesses in the school organisation, sometimes relating to the use of buildings, sometimes in the curriculum, or timetable, and sometimes in the teaching or pastoral context. (p. 36)

Along parallel lines Galloway et al. (1982) suggested that a:

knowledge of a school's policies and its teachers' attitudes is often as important in understanding disruptive behaviour as knowledge about family stress and intellectual weakness. (p. 63)

This reasoning does not imply that *all* behaviour problems in school emanate from within the school. We know only too well that pupils from disadvantaged or deprived homes can, understandably, bring their problems to school with them; though we must practise caution when linking disadvantaged and deprived homes with disturbed children. Stott (1972) reminds us that many well-adjusted pupils come from extremely adverse backgrounds, and some who are extremely disturbed come from good homes and have parents 'whom one has to rate not only as stable and affectionate, but as having shown almost superhuman patience and tolerance' (p. 43).

Difficulties with self-appraisal

Rabinowitz (1981, p. 6) cited the following caption in a cartoon which characterises the practice of, at least, a few teachers who become irrationally defensive when confronted by pupils' misbehaviour. A fearsome teacher is depicted towering over a miscreant, shouting:

> Some people will blame your genes, some people will blame your environment, some people will blame your teachers, but I blame you Wimpole, pure and simple.

If schools are willing to accept that they can favourably affect pupils' attitudes, values, feelings and actions when they are in their care, then they must accept that they can also influence such behaviour in unacceptable or undesirable ways. This responsibility is not always easy to accept and can generate great unease on the part of schools and their teachers for, as Lawrence *et al.* (1984) commented:

> Many teachers are understandably reluctant to acknowledge that the reasons for pupils' misbehaviour may be found as often in their teaching as in the pupils' inability or failure to learn. (p. 24)

A rationale for this book: schools make a difference

A great many schools and their staffs have made concerted and successful efforts to improve the quality of the education that they make available to all their pupils. Others, for a variety of reasons, have been less able or willing to initiate informed innovation. While many of the changes that have taken place – and a few of these are described in later chapters – have been at the institutional level, much of this book has chosen to focus upon the classroom – and the teacher's role in particular.

Initial teacher training is rarely as concerned with enhancing students' classroom management techniques as it is with other aspects of their professional or curriculum studies.

Sadly it appears to us that at present, when there is a clear recognition in schools that staff are becoming increasingly concerned about the demands being made upon them by pupils' behaviour problems, there is little evidence of a positive response within teacher training to help meet identified needs in this area.

This book then is a contribution to the continuing debate on the quality of education in classrooms and schools. It attempts to offer readers opportunities to consider their understanding of theoretical perspectives of children's behaviour development, and the associated management skills which derive from them.

We are attempting to help practising and student teachers:

(a) to enhance and reflect upon their knowledge and understanding of factors within, and outside, the pupil which may affect behaviour in school, and

(b) to develop techniques, strategies, skills and attitudes which can be used effectively and sensibly to successfully manage pupils' behaviour in school.

Our contributors have been invited to reflect, with us, from their considerable experience and knowledge on these aspects of pupil behaviour. Their presentations gradually move away from a mainly theoretical stance in the earlier chapters to a more practical one in the later ones.

Throughout the book the writers make wide-ranging and valuable contributions to our understanding of possible causes of behaviour problems in school, and the ways in which teachers, as individuals and collectively as a staff, can create classroom and school climates which help deter problems, and successfully and healthily manage them if they do arise.

As we have stated earlier, the chapter contents in this book are for the most part directed towards the behaviour of *all* children in mainstream primary and secondary schools; though on occasions some discussions may be more pertinent to primary than secondary schools, and vice versa. This does not imply that special schools, and the pupils who attend them, are ignored. All of the theoretical viewpoints referred to, the biological and environmental factors examined, and the management techniques/attitudes/policies/practices discussed, have as much relevance for those pupils experiencing emotional/behaviour problems – and deemed to have special educational needs (with or without formal statements) – as for their more adjusted peers. Arguably, parts of some chapters have even greater relevance for special education. In one important way this diversity or breadth is a desirable one. The traditional, artificial divide between children with special educational needs and others is gradually being eroded both in terms of policy and practice. The once distinct and divisible populations are now much more amalgamated (though not necessarily more integrated), and mainstream teachers – in line with their colleagues working in the special sector – have become both more sensitive to individuals' emotional/behavioural needs, and their professional responsibilities in making appropriate provisions for them.

We have greatly valued the cooperation of our expert colleagues in the fresh review of behaviour in schools, and in the final chapter, after considering their varied experiences, standpoints and recommendations we have attempted to offer a personal and tentative set of guidelines for practising and student teachers.

References

COLEMAN, J., CAMPBELL, C., HOBSON, C., McPARTLAND, J., MOOD, A., WEINFIELD, F., and YORK, A. (1966) *Equality of Educational Opportunity* (Washington, D.C.: US Government Printing Office).

FRUDE, N. and GAULT, H. (1984) *Disruptive Behaviour in School* (London: Wiley).

GALLOWAY, D., BALL, T., BLOMFIELD, D. and SEYD, R. (1982) *Schools and Disruptive Pupils* (London: Longman).

GALLOWAY, D. and GOODWIN, C. (1987) *The Education of Disturbing Children* (London: Longman).

HARGREAVES, D. H. (1967) *Social Relationships in a Secondary School* (London: Routledge and Kegan Paul).

HMI REPORT (1987) *Education Observed 5: Good Behaviour and Discipline in Schools* (Stanmore: DES).

KOUNIN, J. (1970) *Discipline and group management in classrooms* (New York: Holt, Rinehart and Winston).

LAWRENCE, J., STEAD, K. and YOUNG, L. (1984) *Disruptive Schools: Disruptive Pupils* (London: Croom Helm).

RABINOWITZ, A. (1981) 'Schools for Children or Children for Schools', *New Growth*, 1, 2, 3–10.

RUTTER, M., TIZARD, J, and WHITEMORE, K. (1970) *Education, Health and Behaviour* (London: Longman).

RUTTER, M., MAUGHAN, B., MORTEMORE, P. and OUSTON, J. (1979) *Fifteen Thousand Hours: Secondary Schools and their Effects on Pupils* (London: Open Books).

STOTT, D. H. (1972) *The Parent as Teacher* (London: University of London Press Ltd).

PART I
THE THEORETICAL BACKGROUND

In Chapter 1 Tony Charlton and John George emphasise the intricate interaction between factors, internal and external to pupils, which may affect their behaviour in some aspects of their lives. Having argued for the effect of specific situations on much behaviour they then discuss a range of biological and environmental factors which have been shown to influence pupils' behaviour at home, in school and elsewhere. Particular attention is given to school influences upon behaviour.

They are setting a theoretical basis for behavioural problems, which is developed by Ronald Davie in Chapter 2. He begins by questioning whether assessment can be divorced from the process of dealing with behaviour problems in the classroom, the school or elsewhere, and considers the implications of this issue for schools and for their relationship with the other agencies involved. He then introduces some of the major theoretical models which provide explanations of children's behaviour problems. Many of these are already familiar to practitioners in the field in one form or another but are rarely made explicit. He questions how far they are mutually inconsistent and incompatible, and asks how far this matters from a practical standpoint. Can they inform and help structure everyday decisions about individual children and about school systems? Finally he examines the advisability and efficacy of basing one's practice on a single theoretical model or on a more eclectic approach, and explores the practical advantages and limitations of both approaches.

Chapter 1

The Development of Behaviour Problems

Tony Charlton
and John George

The complexity of behaviour

The more we investigate human behaviour the more we appreciate its complexity, and how difficult it often is to explain precisely why individuals behave as they do. We know only too well that the manner in which and extent to which children and adults learn behaviours, and whether (and, if so, which of) those behaviours will be practised, are affected by a whole range of variables, usually in combination.

These variables can be usefully construed as being either internal or external to the individual. *Internal* variables include biological factors such as the state of the nervous system and certain glandular functions, heredity and other genetic considerations. They also encompass psychological factors which refer to aspects of the individual's affective and cognitive states (for example levels of self-concept, anxiety, intelligence and motivation). *External* ones are represented by an array of environmental influences of which the family, school, and peer group appear to be the most influential. It is the intricate interaction amongst, and between, such variables which affects how (and what) we think, feel and act.

Behaviour problems: differing perspectives of causation

Where behaviour problems arise in school, or elsewhere, it may be difficult to determine precisely which – or how – internal and external factors combined to generate them. One way of helping to clarify the complexity of this difficulty is to think in terms of predisposing, precipitating and reinforcing causes.

Research findings, although not conclusive, have suggested, for example, that particular types of temperament may *predispose* young children to later maladjustment (Thomas and Chess, 1977). Predispositions of this type include under- and over-activity, poor adaptability, tendency to withdrawal, irregularity of sleeping and irritability. Such patterns of 'aggravating' behaviour – particularly where they persist into adolescence – are more likely to arouse negative than positive responses from caregivers, and others. Responses of this kind may create unhealthy feelings within the child (for example of rejection, lowered self-esteem) as well as generate overt responses of a kind unlikely to improve the situation (for example hostility, aggression). It is fairly conclusive, also, that certain adverse temperamental characteristics may render children more vulnerable to environmental stress (Graham *et al.*, 1973).

On other occasions behaviour problems may be *precipitated* by certain happenings in the environment. Teachers preoccupied with berating pupils when they misbehave, yet ignoring them when they behave, may be precipitating the very behaviours they are attempting to eradicate. Children, like adults, need attention. It is unfortunate that some pupils find that their only route to secure this attention is to misbehave. Problems become compounded when children learn that such attempts are successful; for their subsequent misbehaviour is often then *reinforced*, though unintentionally, by the teacher.

Unfortunately for those who try to assist in the prevention and resolution of children's behaviour problems, the subject of causation is often far more complex than the previous paragraphs perhaps imply and involves intricate interactions amongst a host of contributory factors (as the later case studies illustrate).

However complex the cause-and-effect association may be, a paramount task confronting teachers is to determine ways in which appropriate management skills can be directed towards the amelioration or prevention of behaviour problems. On many occasions this can only be accomplished where teachers are sensitive to the differing causal mechanisms which may be operating in a given instance. Without this knowledge the assessment 'picture' may be incomplete and any action taken unlikely to be effective.

Another perspective on causation refers to the particular theoretical model within which the behaviour is examined (for example psychodynamic, humanistic, behavioural). Different models not only hold disparate perspectives on the aetiology (causation) of behaviour problems, but also on the skills which are required to address them. There are, of course, many models of human behaviour which speculate about how behaviour is fashioned. However, of the major theories referred to in Chapter 2, the three upon which later chapters primarily focus are the *behavioural, psychodynamic* and *humanistic* models. These are selected for purely practical reasons; arguably, of all the theories they are of most use to classroom practitioners in helping them to understand causes of problem behaviours as well as acquire the skills to manage them. Nevertheless, for reasons which Ronald Davie makes clear in the next chapter, both the systems approach and labelling theory are taken into account when discussing the other three theories.

The complexity of causation: case studies

The following extracts from case histories highlight how numerous factors (some related, others seemingly not) may combine to create, or exacerbate, behaviour problems which young children and teenagers experience or present

> CLIVE, a fifteen year old, attended a residential special school for children with emotional/behaviour problems. His unmarried mother had abandoned him when he was two. During the next ten years he spent time in two children's homes, and with three sets of foster parents before transfer from a day special school to one with residential provision. As he became older his behaviour progressively deteriorated. Adults in both the children's and foster homes, and the teachers in the day school, found his behaviour increasingly disruptive, and disturbing to the other children around him. When he was twelve an educational psychologist's report showed him to be seriously underfunctioning in all basic skills' areas, frequently depressed, and experiencing difficulties building – with even greater difficulties sustaining – relationships with peers and adults.

> CLAIRE, born with both cleft palate and a double cleft lip, did not receive the last of the corrective surgery until she was in her late teens. In the primary school her poor articulation elicited hurtful comments from her peers. In response she rarely spoke in class and, where practicable, gradually withdrew from all social situations. Despite repeated attempts by teachers, parents and more helpful peers to involve her with her peers she became more and more withdrawn. When the teacher attempted to involve her in group discussions, or other group work, she became embarrassed, highly anxious and reluctant to become involved. As a result she found it difficult to make friendships, became both more and more isolated, and increasingly unhappy.

RICHARD came from a large family. Shortly after Richard's eighth birthday, his father (a violent character with a long history of convictions – and prison sentences – for GBH and burglary) left home to live with his wife's sister. When Richard was nine the mother, unable to cope with her seven children, sent Richard to live with aged maternal grandparents some miles away. Right from the start teachers at his new school found him almost impossible to contain. While occasionally he was affable, on most occasions he was not. At the age of nine he had a reading age of 6.1. Apart from being boisterous and aggressive with his peers – to such an extent that most of the children became frightened of him – he also had a short attention span and quickly became frustrated when confronted with problems in his academic work. In such instances he would fling his books away, storm out of the room and then out of the school. Usually it took the headmaster to entice him back within the school, when he would spend the rest of the day quietly working in the Head's study. On following days, however, the pattern was likely to repeat itself.

According to his mother, STEWART, who was asthmatic and suffered from eczema, had always been difficult; even his birth had been difficult and prolonged. As a baby he had irregular sleep patterns, did not feed properly, was rarely quiet and constantly active. At primary school the teachers found him pleasant, but highly distractful, and easily distracted. He was rarely able to work quietly, and his boisterous and hyperactive behaviour frequently upset his peers. After transfer to secondary school, Stewart became increasingly agitated before going to school where he was frequently referred by teachers to the Head of House, because of his poor attention span and habitual bouts of disruptive behaviours.

The parents of JANE were adamant that her transfer to the local comprehensive school was the cause of all her problems. At the small village primary school she made reasonable progress in all school subjects, was quiet but friendly, never seemed worried and always enjoyed going to school. When she was seven it was discovered that she suffered from petit mal, although the seizures seemed infrequent and slight. Upon transfer, matters soon changed. Each morning the mother had to contend with persistent tantrums during which Jane screamed that she wasn't going to school. Towards the end of her second term at secondary school her attendance became, at first, erratic and then was followed by more prolonged absences. Letters from the school and visits by the educational welfare officer, initially failed to improve the situation. Only finally, at the end of her second year at school, when the local education authority threatened legal action, did her attendance improve slightly. Her behaviour, however, deteriorated. At school she became insolent and disobedient and was finally suspended from school, pending the outcome of a case conference, for stealing money from a member of staff. In the home she became sullen, uncooperative and eventually beyond the control of the parents.

The case studies emphasise a number of points. *First*, they indicate that when more serious problems become manifest in school it is more than likely that whatever intervention is required will need to refer to a range of so-called causal factors. Additionally, a number of the helping professionals outlined in Chapter 8 may need to become involved. These professionals will be equipped with the expertise and experience to deal with aspects of the problem which the school can not.

Second, because more serious problem behaviours usually demand more time, energy and greater expertise than lesser ones, it seems more sensible, wherever practicable, to prevent problems arising, or less serious ones escalating. Just as there is much that can happen in classrooms and schools which increases the likelihood (and severity) of problems arising, so there is much that can be done to help problems from occurring or escalating. This latter point is a recurrent theme in the chapters within Parts II and III of this book.

Third, within any case description (and even with access to the complete files) it is difficult – if not impossible – to isolate a *single* factor which was the sole cause of *all* the problem behaviours. While it may be possible to point to one particular factor which triggered the problem initially, others were certainly contributory.

Finally, how the problem is rationalised, or explained, in terms of causation, will depend upon which theoretical perspective is used. Each perspective focuses upon differing facets of the case histories, and explains the behaviour problems in differing ways. In Richard's case the behaviouristic model could see problems in the context of maladaptive behaviours being learned (for example through reinforcement or modelling of undesirable behaviours) and adaptive behaviours or competencies not being learned. The psychodynamic model would be more concerned with Richard's inner experiences; the extent to which a succession of rejections (by father, mother and other adults) posed as a threat to his ego, and generated anxieties; and the manner in which he handled those anxieties. Similarly, the humanistic model's focus would be upon the manner in which he perceived those experiences and the impact of the perceptions upon his developing 'self' (that is, self-concept, self-esteem) and consequent behaviour.

Factors associated with the development of behaviour problems

In the rest of this chapter the intention is to look at some examples of factors, internal and external to the individual, which:

- are often associated with behaviour problems, and
- may exert adverse influences (either separately or in combination) upon children's behaviour.

BIOLOGICAL FACTORS

While it has long been recognised that the individual is the product of genetic inheritance, sociological and psychological influences, it is the nature of biological differences among people which, until recently, has received the least attention. One difficulty is the complexity of analysing biological factors and the consequent shortage of research. Another problem is that some biological abnormalities may not be visually apparent and the observer has no immediate clues to their existence, other than the abnormal behaviour of the child. For example, the child with a visual defect may be immediately recognisable by his performance, whereas the child with a specific food intolerance may pass undetected except for concern over his abnormal behaviour.

We can start to explore the biological influences on human behaviour by examining the nature of the building blocks of the human body, for any imperfections which occur at the foundation level are likely to have far reaching consequences as development proceeeds.

Nervous systems. One of the most important underlying features in determining behaviour is the integrity, or quality, of both the central (nerves in the brain and spinal cord) and peripheral (nerves from the brain and spinal cord to other parts of the body) nervous systems. Inevitably, *serious* damage to either system usually manifests itself in gross physical and/or performance abnormalities, the effects of which can be quite marked.

The young child's developing brain is particularly sensitive and vulnerable to damage from a number of agencies. Damage may occur during pregnancy as a consequence of the mother's exposure to certain diseases, for example rubella, toxoplasmosis, AIDS and syphilis, the effects of which may be transferred to, and affect the nervous systems of, the unborn child. More recently, attention has focused on the harmful nature of certain drugs, alcohol abuse, smoking and excessive radiation during pregnancy. Similarly, placenta insufficiency, toxaemia and poor maternal nutrition may cause conditions of low birth weight which, in turn, may increase the vulnerability of the very young child.

Complications during the birth process itself can result in direct damage to the brain or may limit or prevent the flow of oxygen. As brain cells are particularly sensitive to a lack of oxygen, any interruption of supply may result in widespread and irreparable damage.

Infections of the brain such as meningitis and encephalitis can also have a marked effect on the performance and behaviour of the victims as can any direct or severe injury to the head. Not surprisingly Barker (1981) suggests that from evidence provided from research there is an increased incidence of a wide variety of behavioural disturbances in children following such traumas. However, more subtle or minimal damage to the nervous system may create conditions in children which, at first, are not so obvious and may include auditory and visual perceptual disturbances which disrupt the processing of information and form the basis of cognitive and psychomotor learning problems.

Clumsy children constitute such an enigma. Some researchers see such a problem as a consequence, primarily, of a developmental disorder and outline several factors including genetic and environmental influences which may produce the atypical clumsy child (for example Gordon and McKinlay, 1980). Difficulties may appear in large-muscle activities and balance or equally as an impairment of fine motor movements. Exposure of such children to situations which amplify their problems, such as the games field or PE lesson, may lead to the development of secondary emotional problems and increasing social isolation.

Endocrine glands. The nervous system does not work in isolation to other body functions and its total coordination is assisted by the secretion of various hormones into the bloodstream by the endocrine glands. Such hormones are important in determining levels of growth, motivation and response, emotional behaviour and some aspects of personality.

Of the two most important glands, *adrenal* glands play a vital role in neural functioning and in preparing the body to tolerate the effects of stress, and the *pituitary* gland which produces a large number of different hormones also controls the activity of several other endocrine glands, such as the thyroid, sex glands and those which control the timing and amount of body growth. It therefore follows that any malfunction in the operation of these glands can have far-reaching effects on individual development.

Heredity. All behaviour is the result of the complex *interaction* between heredity and environment. The characteristics of each parent are passed on to their children by a special code – the genetic code, a blueprint for the child which is carried in each cell of the body and which plays a specific role in psychological, emotional and physical development. While inherited physical characteristics are perhaps some of the first features to draw comment from the parents of newborn infants, later developing intelligence and special abilities, such as musical or artistic talent, also appear to have a hereditary component and some differences in temperament appear to be innate. It follows, therefore, that any errors which occur in the transmission of inherited information can have a direct effect upon the quality of development and behaviour.

Chromosomes. Most of the body cells have a nucleus in which there are special filaments called chromosomes. Each of these cells contains 46 chromosomes arranged in pairs. One chromosome of each pair comes from each parent in a system of automatic reduction as the cells divide into twenty three pairs. Twenty two of these pairs are perfectly matched, but the twenty third pair determines our sex and are known as the sex chromosomes. In the female they are perfectly matched (XX), but in the male they are unequal (XY). Occasionally, something goes wrong with the process of reduction and each cell may contain an extra chromosome or 'trisomy' which may be linked to certain developmental or behavioural features. For example, an extra chromosome on pair 21 results in the condition known as Down's Syndrome (1.8 per 1000 live births).

Very rarely only some of the cells have an extra chromosome which is known as 'mosaicism', and partial trisomies may exist where extra chromosome material is present. In these cases the abnormal chromosome pattern may cause low intelligence rather than bring about emotional disturbance, although an emotional disorder may also be present.

Some conditions exist, however, where abnormal chromosome formation may produce a deficiency in the ability to absorb essential vitamins and minerals. In Down's Syndrome, for example, the changes in the structure of the wall of the intestine brought about by the presence of the trisomy create a condition of poor absorption. In recognition of this biological abnormality, the prescription of vitamin supplements to complement the diet of such children has received considerable support in recent years.

Sex chromosome abnormalities also occur on rare occasions where, for example, the female may have only one X chromosome (Turner's Syndrome) or where the male may have an extra Y chromosome (XYY). Attempts have been made in the past to suggest a causal relationship between sex-linked chromosome abnormalities and certain behaviour disorders, but the evidence has been lacking and inconclusive. It does seem reasonable to suggest, however, that some basic features of personality are genetically determined.

Genes. Each chromosome is made up of hundreds of small units known as genes, each of which plays a specific role in the development of the body. In some cases a single abnormal gene can arise spontaneously and have a marked effect on the way in which development proceeds. In others, two abnormal genes may be present, one from the father and one from the mother. These are known as recessive genes. A number of syndromes associated with intellectual retardation are due specifically to abnormal genes (for example Rubinstein-Tabi's syndrome, tuberous sclerosis, microcephaly).

Gene defects can also cause errors in metabolism such as phenylketonuria, in which there is an error of amino acid metabolism characterised by an abnormal build up of damaging chemicals which requires treatment with a diet low in phenylalanine. Untreated, phenylketonuria has strong associations with severe intellectual retardation.

Recent research into autism includes an exploration of the rules of essential fatty acids and the secretion of hormones in the creation of this condition which, with an incidence of 4:10,000, is a mental handicap which affects the ability to use senses to the full. Although theories of the causation of autism are so far only tentative, it has been noted that by adulthood a number of autistic people show definite signs of neurological abnormalities, and early research by Folstein and Rutter (1977) strongly suggested the involvement of a genetic factor.

Similarly, it has been suggested by Stevenson (1987) that dyslexia has genetic causes, which may be treated by the use of certain drugs. Excess of the hormone testosterone appears to facilitate the growth of ectopias (brain warts) which have been found in abnormal quantities in the brains of deceased people known to have had reading and writing difficulties.

What is clear at this point is that researchers are becoming far more aware of the need fully to explore the biological bases of many conditions in the increasing knowledge that subtle biochemical imbalances, whether genetically or environmentally initiated, do have a significant effect upon individuals' behavioural performance.

Hyperactivity. Many children are hyperactive from birth (often also *in utero*). They present as restless and fidgety, sleep for only 3–4 hours in 24 and cry incessantly. They will not feed properly and may also suffer from asthma and eczema. As they grow older, such children may destroy furniture and toys, have poor communication and may resort to self-injurious behaviour. Parents are often exhausted by the stress and continual crises of coping with the excessive demands of such a child, as are teachers when these children enter schools.

Several attempts have been made to isolate factors which may cause such a condition to occur. Feingold (1975) was one of the first to focus international attention on the relationship between diet and behaviour. Prior to this there had been too great a willingness to ascribe a psychosocial aetiology to children's behaviour disturbances when often the cause stemmed from adverse responses to environmental factors such as food, or chemicals. Crook (1980) contended that on the basis of 'reports that have appeared in the literature during the last 60 years and my own clinical experience, I am absolutely certain that what a child eats can make him dull, stupid or hyperactive' (p. 285). However, Vass and Rasmussen (1984) suggested that foods are not the only environmental factors implicated in allergy, but that many other products of modern technology are commonly incriminated (for example pollution).

Allergic responses in young children are thought by some researchers to stem from a vulnerability to foreign chemicals at a time when the mechanisms that provide protection against these substances are absent or not fully developed. The lower efficiency of young children in metabolising some chemicals may cause them to accumulate such chemicals to excessive levels at a time when sensitivity to toxic effects is critical, and therefore most detrimental to balanced growth. In a review of possible causes of hyperactivity, Shreeve (1982) suggests that hyperactive children have abnormally low levels of essential fatty acids, and are in this respect biologically different to non-hyperactive children. Such a defect in metabolism allows hyperactive children to become extremely susceptible to certain substances, the result of which is an observable deterioration in behaviour.

Morley (1985) describes those whose behaviour is affected by food as having a 'food intolerance', and she distinguishes between a non-allergic mechanism or food idiosyncrasy, and a good allergic disease, where there is a measurable *allergic* response.

More recently, attention has been paid to the quality of the daily diet, not so much from the perspective of restricting artificial additives, but from a realisation that many young people eat huge amounts of 'junk food' much of which is deficient in vitamins and minerals which are essential for healthy living and efficient mental functioning. The results of early pilot studies in Britain and America indicate that children who receive a sufficient daily intake of vitamins and minerals are in a better position to profit from learning experiences than their peers, who languish almost daily in a state of dietary deficiency.

A general and positive spin off from such research can be seen by the increasing efforts being made to produce healthy eating habits across the nation and in particular by the schools' catering services and an awareness of the dangers of eating and drinking indiscriminately. However, Swinson (1988) warns against the danger of believing that, when faced with a badly behaved child, all that needs to be done to improve his behaviour is to change his diet. His message directs teachers and parents to improve their behavioural management rather than merely rely on restricting the consumption of additives.

Epilepsy. The exact size of our epileptic population is not easily determined but it is suggested by the British Epilepsy Association that over 100 000 children and young people in the UK have some form of epilepsy, the majority of whom receive their education in ordinary schools. Less than 1 per cent actually attend the six schools for children with epilepsy.

Epilepsy is caused by brief disruptions in the normal electro-chemical activity of the brain which can affect people of all ages and intellect. It is not a disease or illness but may be a symptom of some physical or metabolic disorder which, although not always obvious, is an elusive condition, the existence of which many individuals and families may choose to conceal. It has been suggested by Stedman (1973) that social rejection of children with epilepsy is still apparent in many schools and, coupled with the risk of overprotection and anxiety by parents and staff, can create a climate in which the child is prevented from fulfilling real potential.

Epilepsy causes people to have fits or seizures which fall into broadly different categories according to their nature and severity. Major fits or *grand mal* seizures often last for several minutes during which the child may fall to the ground and lose consciousness, salivate, jerk violently and may pass water. Minor fits or *petit mal* seizures may easily pass unnoticed by adults. The child may blink his eyes or appear to be day dreaming or staring inattentively. Often during this confused period, sensory messages are not received by the child and learning may be seriously impaired. For example, if a teacher says to a child, 'Andrew, sit down here and (put those books away before you) go to the toilet', and Andrew has a petit mal fit for the duration of the words in the bracket, the teacher's communication will make little sense and could provoke a quite disturbing reaction from the child.

Psychomotor fits or *temporal lobe* seizures occur when only part of the brain is affected and may lead to a child making involuntary movements such as twitching, and being unable to communicate although conscious. Unobserved fits or sub clinical seizures may be suspected if a child's attention, work or attainment level suddenly drops for no apparent reason. Such fits impair a child's ability to receive, retain and recall information and can have a devastating effect upon progress and learning. Small 'absences' and 'blank spells' should arouse the suspicion of teachers who should then seek professional support and advice.

Medication given for the treatment of epilepsy is designed to build up chemical resistance to stimuli that can trigger or precipitate a fit. When correctly balanced with need, the use of medication can be most effective. Surprisingly, however, little is known about the side effects of medication given to children with epilepsy and imbalances sometimes occur which manifest themselves in the child by drowsiness or an increase in seizures. Such changes should be closely monitored, and reported.

There is evidence to suggest a higher incidence of behaviour disorders among epileptic children than among normal children but, as long ago as 1957, Halstead concluded that there was no such thing as the 'Epileptic Personality'. However, Stedman (1973) identified an unusual scattering of abilities from the results of intelligence tests on epileptic children with a particular imbalance on subtests concerning language and spatial skills. This can lead to very uneven educational profiles compounded by the fact that on some occasions epileptic children may be unteachable for days at a time due to fluctuations in their ability to attend and respond to their environment.

Further information about epilepsy is available in the form of a schools information pack from The British Epilepsy Association, Anstey House, 40 Hanover Square, Leeds LS3 1BE.

Asthma. A number of children attending both ordinary schools and special schools suffer from varying degrees of asthma. Asthma is a non-infectious disease of the chest which causes a narrowing of air passages of the lungs with resulting difficulty in breathing and wheeziness. Attacks may be brief, occasional and mild or may be more severe, resulting in the need for absence from school and, in extreme cases, treatment in hospital. The start or 'trigger' of an attack may be different for individual children and occurs because of the extreme sensitivity of the air passages to environmental changes. Such changes may be physical such as exposure to strong winds or very cold dry weather, or may be related to emotional strains such as excitement or prolonged laughing. Alternatively, infections and activity which is too vigorous or prolonged, may also induce an asthmatic attack.

Allergy is a special form of sensitivity in which substances normally innocuous to most people provoke attacks of wheezing in asthmatics. Allergens may be airborne such as pollen, dust, hair or fur and therefore inhaled, or may be taken as food where, for example, there may be a measurable allergic response to cheese, eggs, milk etc. Such allergens may not always produce wheezing but instead may cause other responses such as running eyes and nose, sneezing and itching. It is not uncommon to find that some asthmatic children also have eczema, the condition of which can also be affected by similar factors.

Minor attacks are usually coped with by the child ceasing the activity in hand, and administering one of the medical treatments available. Once this treatment has proved effective the child may continue with normal activities. Severe attacks usually occur after treatment that is normally effective fails to work and the child becomes acutely distressed, often blue around the lips and finds it extremely difficult to exhale. At this stage urgent medical attention should be sought without delay as the need for additional treatment is required immediately.

Two different forms of medication are available to help control the effects of asthma and to help affected people to live a normal life:

(a) Preventive treatments (usually sprays or tablets) taken regularly attempt to increase the resistance to factors which may trigger attacks, by reducing the sensitivity of the air passages.

(b) 'Bronchodilators' (often taken as a spray) open up the narrowed bronchial tubes of the lungs to give immediate relief.

Teachers should ensure that they have a thorough knowledge of the child's condition, preferably by contact and discussion with parents, and that within the classroom setting asthmatic children are not exposed directly to animals, materials, foods etc. which are known to cause problems for them, and that sympathetic consideration is given to the child's individual needs in matters relating to games and PE.

It is often possible for all but the most severely affected asthmatic children to participate in a wide range of physical activities, but the type of sport and level of participation will be critical. Most asthmatic children will prefer to cope with short bursts of moderate exercise in an atmosphere which is warm and moist and may need to take additional doses of inhalant before they start. It is important for teachers to take seriously the need for a child to have an inhaler constantly available, and not to dismiss the condition as merely a nervous disorder.

This information, and more, is readily available for teachers from The Asthma Society and Friends of the Asthma Research Council, St. Thomas' Hospital, Lambeth Palace Road, London SE1 7EH.

ENVIRONMENTAL FACTORS ASSOCIATED WITH BEHAVIOUR PROBLEMS

Behaviouristic, psychodynamic and humanistic models of behaviour all recognise that the *environment* affects human behaviour; although, as mentioned earlier, they have differing ways of conceptualising how that influence works. The major environments which exert this influence are the *home*, the *peer group*, and the *school*.

(I) FAMILY FACTORS

Of the major environments within which children grow and develop the parental home (in most instances) generates the earliest influences upon their behaviour. Consequently, the range, duration and quality of family experiences are likely to make significant contributions, adversely or otherwise, to children's behaviour.

Separation experiences is one such area which has attracted much interest and some controversy. As early as 1946, Bowlby contended that early and prolonged separation of young children from their mothers was a prime cause of 'delinquent character development and persistent misbehaviour' (p. 41). His contention derived from his observations of institutionalised children, most of whom were denied the facility to develop close interpersonal relations with a care-giver. Similar discoveries were later reported by Beres and Obers (1950) with their sample of 38 adolescents who had been institutionalised between the ages of three weeks and three years. At the time of their enquiry all but 7 per cent of the adolescents were diagnosed as psychotic, having a character disorder, neurotic or mentally retarded.

Underpinning the concern of studies in this area has been the 'disruption of bonding' between mother and infant; a concept which has been criticised by Rutter (1972). He argued that bonding need not take place only with the biological parent (whether father or mother) but can take place with a surrogate parent, or care-giver. What appears to be of primary importance where protracted periods of separation take place, is that the child has someone available with whom he/she can form stable relationships. Along these lines Upton (1983) makes the valid point in his summary of the research that:

neither separation per se nor separation from the biological mother or 'permanent mother substitute' are key factors. Rather, it seems that the quality of substitute care is of major importance.   (p. 49)

Bowlby's findings also generated concern about the effects of other separation experiences, such as *hospitalisation*, upon young children's later behaviour. While Rutter (1980) argued that although emotional distress may arise from such experiences it was unlikely to persist, others showed that the impact of hospitalisation experiences seems to depend upon the child's age upon admission, length and frequency of stays, temperamental characteristics, and prior relationships with the mother (Stacey *et al.*, 1970; Douglas, 1975). Stacey *et al.* confirmed earlier findings that the crucial time is between six months of age and the child's fourth or fifth birthdays, and suggested that children who were under stress at home, highly dependent upon their mothers, or who felt insecure upon admission were the most vulnerable. The two previously mentioned studies also found that repeated admissions and more long-term stays were associated with increased risks of later behaviour problems.

Parental deprivation as a consequence of the *bereavement of a parent* may also have an impact upon children's emotional and behavioural functioning. The extent, duration and levels of severity of any consequent problems seem to depend upon a range of factors including the age of the child when the bereavement occurred (Rutter, 1966), the manner in which the remaining parent discusses the death with the child (Marsden, 1969), and the quality of prior parental relations (Anthony, 1973). The post-bereavement 'health' of the family is also an important factor (see Finer Report, 1974).

During the past twenty years or so there has been a rapid increase in *divorce* rates. In 1961 25 000 divorces were granted; a figure which rose to 74 000 in 1972, and 180 000 in 1986. With the majority of divorces taking place during the early years of marriage a considerable number of young and vulnerable children are involved. Rutter (1971) found that children between the ages of two and three seem to be particularly vulnerable to the separation of their parents; particularly to the loss of the parent of the same sex. In line with a number of enquiries Douglas (1975) found a significantly higher risk of later delinquency among boys, and illegitimate births among girls, where parental separation occurred before they were six. Experiences leading up to, and those following, separation may precipitate stress, feelings of rejection and insecurity within offspring (Mitchell, 1987). However, it must be noted that not all children of divorced parents develop behaviour problems; indeed, as Jobling (1976) noted in her research review, behaviour problems are often not generated by the divorce itself but by prior turbulent parental relations, and the act of separation 'may actually benefit the child by bringing relief from inconsistent discipline, constant quarrelling and tension' (p. 1).

While the types of separation referred to so far are indicative of one type of deprivation (that is, that resulting from permanent or temporary separation from parents, the death of a parent, or the loss of a parent consequent to divorce), another is concerned with *inadequate parenting*. An enquiry by Bullard *et al*. (1967) identified a 'failure to thrive' syndrome; a condition arising from 'parental neglect and variable forms of maternal "deprivation"' (p. 689). A follow-up study completed after neglected children had been removed from the home revealed that two-thirds of the children evidenced growth failure, mental retardation, or emotional disorder. Ribble's (1944; 1945) earlier studies had already shown that children who were exposed to maternal rejection, indifference and frequent punishment, later became tense, unsatisfied and negativistic. In a similar vein Rutter and Madge (1976) found that symptoms of emotional disturbance were most common in children who had failed, in early childhood, to form stable attachments with an adult.

Coleman (1976) made reference to children's behaviour problems which he perceived as being consequential to adverse influences arising from conditions existing *among* the family, as well as their *relationships with* either or both of the parents. He perceived problem behaviours stemming from inadequate, disturbed, and antisocial families; though these categories are by no means exclusive. The *inadequate family* (for a number of reasons including immaturity, lack of education, and mental retardation) lacks the competencies to cope with ordinary day-to-day living and the responsibilities and problems associated with them. Any neglect which children incur in these instances derives from the parents' inability, rather than unwillingness, to exercise reasonable care over them. A characteristic of the *anti-social family* is a set of values inconsistent with those held by the wider community. These values often lead to marital and other family problems as well as conflict with the law, and similar circumstances which lead to the presence of unsatisfactory models for children and youngsters. Loyalty *within* such a group, usually contrasts with its *absence* to the wider society. Members of the *disturbed family*, because of personal instability, interact with the people around them in ways which are destructive to themselves as well as the others. The constant quarrelling, bickering and conflict within the family unit is additional to the tension and anxiety which it generates.

Concern about *child abuse* has been well documented in recent years in both research investigations (for example Furniss, 1987) and the wider media. The NSPCC (1974) showed that children from violent families often manifest withdrawn or disruptive behaviour which retarded their development and impeded their progress in school. While some children become withdrawn 'to keep themselves inconspicuous in a situation of conflict' (Hart, 1976, p. 1), others model parental behaviours and become aggressive themselves. In these latter instances there is the distinct likelihood that, in time, abused children become abusers of their own children (Rutter and Madge, 1976). This modelling characteristic is emphasised by Jones (1976) who wrote that:

> There is increasing evidence from retrospective data on the backgrounds of parents who abuse their children, husbands who seriously assault their wives, and murderers, that physical violence featured prominently in their childhood experiences. (p. 10)

Addressing the consequences of child abuse in a wider context, Kempe (1981) identified three categories of possible long-term effects upon children who were victims of child abuse:

> ... namely, psychological problems such as neurosis, psychosis, depression and low self-esteem; problems in sexual adjustment including dysfunction during intercourse, promiscuity, prostitution,

homosexuality and sexual molestation of children; and interpersonal problems such as conflict with marital partner, parents or in-laws, and social isolation. (p. 111)

Clearly, research evidence supports the notion that children with more serious behaviour problems often come from homes characterised by parental conflict, psychiatric illness, or family disturbance:

> that often eventuates in divorce, absence of prosocial standards of behaviour in the parents as evidenced by high rates of parental delinquency, and a failure to communicate standards of behaviour to the child. (Suran and Rizzo, 1979, p. 344)

While most of the families referred to so far represent a minority of troubled or troublesome family groups, there are other occasions when, perhaps for the very best of reasons, parents in otherwise healthy families act in ways which generate emotional problems within their children. Teachers are often well aware of pupils whose anxiety has been caused by parents demanding 'perfection' from their children. By holding *unrealistic expectations* about their offsprings' performance in school, and elsewhere, by being continually dissatisfied with their performances and habitually telling them that they should do better, they may precipitate fears and anxieties within them which cause untold misery and unhappiness.

Overpermissive parents can also create anxieties in their children. Children require boundaries, or guidelines, within which they can act, and feel secure. Homes which fail to provide reasonable structure and where 'environmental predictability is lessened and uncertainty heightened' (Clarizio and McCoy, 1983, p. 63) may leave children feeling insecure and anxious.

Social class differences. Inconsistencies are evident amongst studies investigating the association between social class and behaviour. While some reports have indicated that behavioural difficulties are found more frequently in children from families in the lower social classes (Davie *et al.*, 1972; Rutter *et al.*, 1970), others have either found no such differences (Newson and Newson, 1976; Miller *et al.*, 1974) or have reported a greater incidence of problems amongst children from social class I groups (Moore, 1966). Some writers have drawn attention to the imbalance between upper and lower class children attending special schools for children with behaviour problems. In a study by Ford *et al.* (1982) it was noted that the overwhelming majority of children on roll at four schools for the maladjusted came from social classes IV or

V. Similarly, Galloway and Goodwin (1987) concluded that 'While it would be an overstatement to say that children from middle-class and professional homes are never placed in special schools or units, it is certainly true that this happens very seldom indeed' (p. 45).

In his review of the literature Upton (1983) added a cautionary comment which emphasised that 'the relationship between social class status and behaviour problems is neither consistent nor proven' (p. 35). Additionally, he explains the contradiction (though not inconsistency) between findings in the following way:

> Explanations of a higher proportion of problems amongst lower class groups have commonly focussed on the extent to which criteria of adjustment and problem behaviour are based on middle class norms. Conversely, a greater proportion of behaviour problem children amongst higher social class groups can be explained in terms of an increased interest among upper class groups in psychiatric problems . . . . . . and greater strains of brittle middle class nuclear family existence. (p. 35)

Social disadvantage. The National Child Development Study has made major contributions to our understanding of the impact of home characteristics upon children's health, educational progress and behaviour. Wedge and Essen's (1982) study, for example, revealed that 5.8 per cent of children were socially disadvantaged at either 11 or 16 years of age. The criteria for this group were that children grew up in families which:

1   had a single parent/large family, *and*
2   were poorly housed, *and*
3   had a low family income.

The writers questioned what it must:

> be like for a child in the late twentieth century to have grown up in a family that lives on the poverty line and is overcrowded? Or to have lived with only one parent in a household which lacks basic amenities and depends on a subsistence income provided by the state? (p. 27)

Later in the book the writers give a graphic account of some of the answers to these questions. They talk of the children, at the time of birth, as 'already facing substantially diminished prospects of normal development' (p. 48) and progressing through childhood experiencing (compared to their non-disadvantaged peers) more health problems, increased rates of accidents requiring medical treatment, weighing less and being shorter, behaving less acceptably – as well as performing academically less well – in school, leaving school earlier and holding lower aspirations for further education.

Lask and Lask (1981) made the pertinent comment that:

> Poverty is likely to be associated with other socio-cultural factors such as poor housing and unemployment, family factors such as increased tension and disharmony, and such biological factors as poor nutrition, inadequate ante-natal care, and increased susceptibility to disease. (p. 19)

More recently, Graham (1988) has provided a similar, and cogent explanation of the association between overcrowding/lack of sufficient living space and housing amenities/low income and both emotional and behaviour problems in childhood as well as later delinquency.

While the notion that children from such homes *will* develop behaviour problems must be expunged, they clearly are exposed to conditions and experiences which may render them more vulnerable to the onset of such problems than their more advantaged peers.

(II) PEER GROUP INFLUENCES

As children grow older so the influence of their peer groups becomes stronger and more pervasive. As they attach themselves to a group it usually becomes incumbent upon them to accept, and behave according to, what Frude (1984) refers to as, the 'consensus attitudes of the peer group' (p. 32). Peer groups often have their own sets of values and norms and where these conflict with, or are radically different from, those of the individual's family or the wider society, he/she has to determine which of the conflicting or differing expectations to adhere to. The behaviour of children who come from home backgrounds where little concern or interest is expressed about their 'out of home' activities, and who find satisfaction from becoming involved with a high status delinquent group, is likely to be more strongly influenced by the peer group than the home. Similarly, in school pupils are likely to:

> form small sub-cultures with shared views about school, teachers, and attitudes to discipline and disruption. The existence of such groups is widely recognised by the children themselves and, to a lesser extent, by those who teach them. (Frude, 1984, p. 32)

Hargreaves (1967) suggests that 'pressures towards conformity to the peer group will be especially powerful after the third year in secondary school with the onset of the 'adolescent syndrome' (p. 183). Similarly, Morris (1976) talks of school as:

a place where only the fittest survive socially. Those who don't measure up find themselves left out, and pressure to be 'in' and fear of being 'out' can cause far greater emotional strain than the academic pressure parents typically worry about. (p. 103)

The outcomes of Hargreaves' (1967) enquiry in a Manchester boys' secondary school suggested the existence of two distinct pupil-cultures linked to social class (one conformist and the other oppositional). The school's policy and organisation seemed responsible for helping to differentiate the two groups whereby the oppositional, or delinquent, subculture became status deprived and were allocated poorer teachers. Conscious of their inferior status within the school the subculture established its own 'autonomous and independent peer culture' (p. 172) which Hargreaves claimed:

is unlikely to encourage a boy to strive towards academic goals, since the pressures within the peer group will confirm and reinforce the anti-academic attitudes . . . and the climate within the low streams will be far from conducive to academic striving. (pp. 169/170)

(III) SCHOOL FACTORS

Only in recent years have research enquiries, to any great extent, begun to explore the impact of school-based experiences upon children's behaviour. The findings from these enquiries have tended to confirm what most teachers have always believed: that the range and quality of these experiences (in varying ways and to differing degrees) affect not only children's academic performances and attainments but also their social and emotional functioning. This is hardly surprising. Numerous studies had already shown that much behaviour is determined by, and confined to, specific situations. This is not to deny that occasions do arise when children endure experiences (usually traumatic in nature) which adversely affect their behaviour across all, or at least most, of the areas of their lives. Most of us can recollect unpleasant happenings (at home, school or elsewhere) which generated anxieties, unhappiness, or fears which were omnipresent within us for short, or more protracted, periods of time.

As teachers we sometimes find it difficult to accept that there are limitations to the extent to which we can intervene, directly or indirectly, to improve the quality of our pupils' experiences at home. We can derive some comfort, however, from research which provides strong indications that there is much that we can accomplish to enhance the range and quality of services which we make available to children in school. This optimism is stressed within the comment by Galloway and Goodwin (1987, p. 135) that:

> the consistency with which behaviour at school has been found to be relatively independent of the pupils' families and social backgrounds could be seen as extraordinarily encouraging for teachers.

The study by Burt and Howard (1974), for example, listed a number of school experiences or conditions significantly associated with *maladjustment*, including:

1. teachers who were uncongenial, unsympathetic or lacked understanding
2. uncongenial pupils; a reference to pupils who bullied, teased or generally made life difficult for their peers
3. absence from, or a change of, school
4. placement in a class where the work was too difficult.

In support of their contention that the above factors, separately or collectively, help precipitate or exacerbate pupils' problem behaviours, they referred to a large number of their own case studies, spanning a period of twenty years, where transfer to another school or class (and in most instances a change to a more congenial teacher) was 'followed by a complete and apparently permanent disappearance of every overt sign of maladjustment' (p. 130).

Some writers have cited an *inappropriate curriculum* as a major source of pupil disaffection (Hargreaves, 1967; Charlton, 1986; Reynolds, 1988). Reynolds (1988), for example, referred to two large comprehensive schools both of which offered their pupils a traditional academic, grammar school curriculum which had adverse 'consequences on the bottom two-thirds of the ability range who entered a pressured, academic and alienating school atmosphere' (p. 68). Understandably, it is difficult for (and unreasonable to expect!) pupils to engage in, and sustain, good behaviour when their school days are filled with material and presentations which fail to arouse their interest and industry.

Other enquiries have focused upon variations in schools' *delinquency* rates. As early as 1967 Power *et al.* reported large differences between the delinquency rates of a London borough's twenty secondary schools: differences which they contended could not be accounted for in terms of variations between the schools' catchment areas, selection processes, intake characteristics such as ability, sex or ethnic composition, school size, or the age and type of buildings used. Their findings, supported by later studies (for example Gath et al., 1977; Rutter et al., 1979), pointed to 'within school' factors which help determine delinquency rates and led to their suggestion that:

> some schools may be successful in protecting children from the risk of delinquency, though they live in neighbourhoods where many children come before the courts. Conversely, other schools may be exposing children who live in delinquency-free neighbourhoods to such a risk. (p. 542)

For some time a strong association has been recognised between *truancy*, or *persistent school absenteeism*, and behaviour problems (Tattum, 1982; Galloway et al., 1982). In more general terms Rutter et al. (1979) found that secondary schools varied markedly with regards not only to their pupils' behaviour, examination successes and delinquency rates, but also to pupils' attendance rates, even after 'taking into account differences in their intakes' (p. 205). Understandably the incidence of truancy has been a major concern shared by local education authorities, the police as well as a range of other professionals. Thornbury (1978) provided an indication of the magnitude of the problem in one region, Lambeth, where 'police estimated that one-third of all secondary school children in the locality played truant' (p. 183). The remarkable expansion of special provision for truants in both mainstream schools and elsewhere provides a salient indication of local authorities' current concern.

An indication of the link between truancy and behaviour problems is given by Reid (1984) who revealed that one in three of his sample of absentees in a South Wales comprehensive were rated as disruptive (anti-social) by their teachers. A similar – though hardly scientific – finding was found by the first of the present two writers when meeting the staff of another comprehensive school in South Wales. Staff reported that on any one school day they anticipated one in three of the children on roll being absent; they then declared that if the 'missing' third (many of whom they regarded as disruptive) returned *en bloc*, then the staff would walk out.

Some studies have attempted to explore reasons for the truancy/behaviour problem link and have noted that schools which have fewer behaviour problems also tended to have more favourable school attendance patterns. Others have reported differences between secondary schools' truancy rates which were not a consequence of variations between their intakes (Reynolds, 1976; Rutter *et al.*, 1979; Gath *et al.*, 1977). The consensus of opinion seems to be that many absences from school are for neither medical nor other acceptable reasons, but a response to unpleasant or unattractive conditions or experiences within school. It is worth noting that while some pupils may be absent from school because they are fearful of attending, others elect not to go because they have found alternative less arduous and less boring activities to engage in away from school. Jones (1980), for example, argues that absenteeism is often a response to an unstimulating curriculum administered through the use of boring and uninteresting teaching methods. Supportive to this reasoning was Charlton's (1986) comment that those:

> who are disinterested in, or disenchanted and dissatisfied with the educational programmes schools offer to them, may well direct their interest and energies away from school tasks towards a variety of maladaptive behaviours (e.g. non-involvement in academic work, truancy, abuse towards teachers) which facilitate an excitement and involvement unavailable elsewhere in school. (p. 56)

In a similar vein Reynolds (1984b, p. 15) stresses truancy 'may be the rational reaction of a psychologically normal child to an institution which is not using his talents'. Additionally, he points out that schools often fail to investigate the 'root' cause of poor attendance rates by restricting their efforts mainly to 'get the truants to attend, rather than attempt to see if the child is being misused by the institution' (op cit, p. 15). Reid (1984) gives a salient reminder of negative school practices of this type where there is a tendency to punish non-attenders rather than give positive attention to attenders.

While ten years ago Rutter (1976) was stressing that little was known about *specific school factors which encouraged and discouraged desirable pupil behaviours*, considerable increments have been added since then to our knowledge and understanding. Gradually research enquiries are assembling useful pointers towards good practice.

Rutter *et al.* (1979), for example, concluded in their major study that children:

> benefit from attending schools which set good standards, where teachers provide good models of behaviour, where they are praised and given responsibility, where the general conditions are good and where the lessons are well conducted. (p. 204)

Similarly, Lawrence *et al.* (1984) drew attention to a range of characteristics of a difficult school in which she had taught: characteristics likely to evoke and maintain problem behaviours. Among them she made reference to an unstructured environment, poor home–school liaison, insufficient use of support services, faulty curricula, and poor morale. More specifically she drew attention to a number of teachers who seemed:

> 'bad' for all children but especially disturbed children. Blatantly racially prejudiced staff teaching immigrant children. A number of neurotic or otherwise disturbed staff. Teachers with weak personalities, with abnormally low professional standards (e.g. fail to arrive, or are absorbed in themselves, neglecting their teaching functions).
> (p. 153)

While these comments are subjective they have a 'ring of truth' about them. A more recent study by Reynolds (1984b) presented a portrait of the high-vandalism and high-disaffection school, and referred to factors such as:

1. a highly coercive regime where control was more concerned with physically punishing, than seeking the root cause of, deviant behaviour; where many rules prevailed and were inflexibly enforced
2. relationships between teachers being marked by friction
3. the headteacher and staff apportioning the blame for school problems upon each other
4. a high turnover of staff
5. a paucity of pupil involvement in the running of the school
6. classroom management practices which included public ridicule of miscreants, and the administration of class punishment for individual rule-breaking
7. an unwillingness to welcome parents to school
8. an iniquitous investment of staff expertise, time, energy and other resources into A streams; and a consequent low, or inferior, investment into other classes
9. negative staff perceptions of pupils who were seen as '"irredeemable" and as having irremedial problems, stemming from apparent deficiencies in primary socialization'. (p. 174)

In contrast, other writers (for example Rutter *et al.*, 1979; Lawrence *et al.*, 1984; Galloway and Goodwin, 1987; HMI, 1987; Reynolds, 1988) have suggested that characteristics of more successful schools seem to include:

1. good leadership by senior management in consultation with colleagues, and sensitive to opinion of parents and pupils
2. shared staff policy on academic and behaviour expectations, which are meaningful to pupils, and consistently (though not necessarily inflexibly) enforced
3. a curriculum which is matched to pupils' present and future needs
4. academic expectations which are high, though not unreasonable
5. an emphasis upon effective use of rewards for good behaviour and good work, rather than the application of punishments
6. high professional standards by staff in terms of planning, setting and marking of work; starting and ending lessons on time
7. pedagogical skills which arouse pupils' interest in the subject material, and motivate them to work well
8. classroom management skills which help prevent problem behaviours from arising
9. healthy supportive and respectful relationships amongst teachers, between teachers and pupils, amongst pupils, school and parents, and school and outside agencies
10. opportunities for pupils to become involved in, and share responsibilities for, the running of the school
11. an effective system of pastoral care.

In a more specific context Kounin (1970) provided cursory indications of specific teacher behaviours which may prevent, or encourage, the emergence of behaviour problems. He found significant differences between the managerial skills of *successful* and *less successful teachers* in terms of preventing behaviour problems arising in the classroom. Successful teachers were more able than their less successful counterparts in keeping their pupils on task, better organised at setting and monitoring work, wasted little time when changing activities, maintained high levels of pupil interest, were able to do two or more things at once (for example controlling misbehaviour while continuing teaching), and displayed more 'withitness' (for example being aware of, and continually monitoring, what was happening around them). Additionally, Kounin noted that the less successful teachers committed a number of cardinal mistakes such as:

timing errors (they permitted minor problems to escalate).
target errors (failed to recognise culprits, and blamed others who were not involved. This minimized pupil accountability and allowed culprits to 'get away with it' and harmed student/teacher relationships when students were unfairly blamed).

overreactions (shouting, becoming hysterical or otherwise overreacting emotionally when calm control was called for).

Conclusion

In this chapter discussion focused upon examples of a range of factors located within – as well as outside – the child, which may interact to affect his or her behaviour in unhelpful or unhealthy ways. It was stressed that where problems arise it may be necessary to search for problem causes from a multifactorial perspective. A failure to understand this could result in an incorrect assessment of a child's needs and, consequently, the formulation and implementation of intervention stategies unable to meet those needs satisfactorily. Attention was drawn, also, to varying ways of conceptualising the impact of those factors upon behaviour, with particular reference being made to the differing causal, and intervention, perspectives of behavioural, humanistic and psychodynamic models.

The latter part of the chapter was preoccupied with school effects upon pupil behaviour, and concluded in an optimistic vein by noting that whilst aspects of school organisation and classroom experiences have been shown to be strongly associated with a range of pupil misbehaviours, there is evidence available strongly suggesting that schools and their teachers can do much to minimise the occurrence of behaviour problems, and successfully help manage them when they do arise.

References

ANTHONY, E. J. (1973) 'The syndrome of the psychologically invulnerable child' in Anthony, E. J. and Koupernik, C. (eds) *The Child in his Family: Children at Psychiatric Risk* (New York: John Wiley and Sons).
BARKER, P. (1981) *Basic Child Psychiatry* (London: Granada Publishing).
BERES, D. and OBERS, S. J. (1950) 'The effects of extreme deprivation in infancy on psychic structure in adolescence' in Eissler, R. S. *et al.* (eds) *The Psychoanalytic Study of the Child* Vol. 5 (New York: International University Press).
BRITISH EPILEPSY ASSOCIATION, Wokingham, Berks. RG 11 3AY.
BULLARD, D. M., GLASER, H. H., HEAGARTY, M. C. and PIVCHEK, E. G. (1967) 'Failure to thrive in the neglected child', *American Journal of Orthopsychiatry*, 37, 680–90.

BOWLBY, J. (1946) *Forty-four Juvenile Thieves: Their characters and home lives* (London: Ballière, Tindall and Cox).

BURT, C. and HOWARD, M. (1974) 'The Nature and Causes of Maladjustment among Children of School Age' in Williams, P. (ed.) *Behaviour Problems in School* (London: University of London Press).

CHARLTON, T. (1986) 'A special need in the curriculum: Education for life' in Charlton, T., Lambley, H. and Jones, K. (eds) *Educating Children with Learning and Behaviour Problems: Some Considerations* (Faculty of Education Monograph No 1: College of S. Paul and S. Mary, Cheltenham).

CLARIZIO, H. F. and MCCOY, G. F. (1983) *Behaviour Disorders in Children* (New York: Harper and Row).

COLEMAN, J. C. (1976) *Abnormal Psychology and Modern Life* (Dallas: Scott, Foresman and Co).

CROOK, W. G. (1980) 'Can what a child eats make him dull, stupid or hyperactive?', *Journal of Learning Disabilities*, 13, 53–58.

DAVIE, R., BUTLER, N. and GOLDSTEIN, H. (1972) *From Birth to Seven* (London: Longman).

DHSS (1974) *Report of the Committee on one-parent families* (Finer Report) (London: HMSO).

DOUGLAS, J. W. B. (1975) 'Early Hospital Admission and Later Disturbance of Behaviour and Learning', *Developmental Medicine and Child Neurology*, 18, 358–68.

FEINGOLD, B. F. (1975) *Why is your child hyperactive?* (New York: Random House).

FERRI, E. (1976) *Growing up in a One-Parent Family* (Windsor: NFER).

FINER REPORT (1974) *Report of the Committee on One-Parent Families.* (London: HMSO).

FOLSTEIN, S. and RUTTER, M. (1977) 'Infantile autism: a genetic study of 21 twin pairs', *Journal of Child Psychology and Psychiatry*, 18, 297–321.

FORD, J., MUNGON, D. and WHELAN, M. (1982) *Special Education and Social Control: Invisible Disasters* (London: Routledge and Kegan Paul).

FRUDE, J. (1984) 'Frameworks for Analysis', in Frude N. and Gault H. (eds), *Disruptive Behaviour in Schools* (Chichester: John Wiley and Sons).

FURNISS, T. H. (1987) 'An integrated treatment approach to child sexual abuse in the family', *Children and Society*, 1, 2, 123–35.

GALLOWAY, D., BALL, T., BLOMFELD, D. and SEYD, R. (1982) *Schools and Disruptive Pupils* (London: Longman).

GALLOWAY, D. and GOODWIN, C. (1987) *The Education of Disturbing Children* (London: Longman).

GATH, D., COPPER, B., GRATTONI, F. and ROCKETT, D. (1977) *Child Guidance and Delinquency in a London Borough* (London: Oxford University Press).
GORDON, H. and MCKINLAY, I. (1980) *Helping Clumsy Children* (Edinburgh: Churchill Livingstone).
GRAHAM, P., RUTTER, M. and GEORGE, S. (1973) 'Temperamental Characteristics as Predictors of Behaviour Disorders in Children', *American Journal of Orthopsychiatry*, 43, 328–39.
GRAHAM, P. (1988) 'Social Class, Social Disadvantage and Child Health', *Children and Society*, 2, 1, 9–19.
HALSTEAD, H. (1957) 'Abilities and Behaviour of Epileptic Children', *Journal of Mental Science*, 103, 28–45.
HARGREAVES, D. H. (1967) *Social Relationships in a Secondary School* (London: Routledge and Kegan Paul).
HMI REPORT (1987) *Behaviour and Discipline in Schools. Education Observed 5.* (London: DES).
HART, S. (1976) *Violence, Disruption and Vandalism in Schools – A summary of research* (London: National Children's Bureau).
JOBLING, M. (1976) *The Abused Child: An Annotated Bibliography* (London: National Children's Bureau).
JONES, A. (1980) 'The school's view of persistent non-attendance', in Hersov, L. A. and Berg, I. (eds) *Out of School* (Wiley: Chichester).
JONES, C. (1976) 'Children in Violent Families', *Therapeutic Education*, 4, 2, 8–12.
KEMPE, H. (1981) 'Recognition of Child Sexual Abuse in the United Kingdom', in Mrazek, P. and Kempe, H. (eds) *Sexually Abused Children and Their Families* (London: Pergamon Press).
KOUNIN, J. (1970) *Discipline and group management in classrooms* (New York: Holt, Rinehart and Winston).
LASK, J. and LASK, B. (1981) *Child Psychiatry and Social Work* (London: Tavistock Publications).
LAWRENCE, J., STEED, D. and YOUNG, P. (1984) *Disruptive Children – Disruptive Schools* (London: Croom Helm).
MARSDEN, D. (1969) *Mothers alone: Poverty and the fatherless family* (Harmondsworth: Allen Lane Penguin).
MILLER, F. J. W., COURT, S. D. M., KNOX, E. G. and BRANDON, S. (1974) *The School Years in Newcastle-upon-Tyne* (London: Oxford University Press).
MITCHELL, A. (1987) 'Children's Experience of Divorce' *Children and Society*, 1, 2, 136–47.
MOORE, T. W. (1966) 'Difficulties of the Ordinary Child in Adjusting to Primary School' *Journal of Child Psychology and Psychiatry*, 7, 17–38.

MORLEY, C. M. (1985) *Food and Behaviour*, Paper given at a one day conference on Nutrition and Behaviour on 13 July 1985 at John Radcliffe Hospital, Oxford.

MORRIS, C. G. (1976) *Psychology: An Introduction* (Englewood Cliffs, New Jersey: Prentice Hall).

MORTIMER, P. (1980) 'Misbehaviour in Schools', in Upton G. and Gobell A. (eds) *Behaviour Problems in the Comprehensive School* (Faculty of Education, University College, Cardiff).

NEWSON, J. and NEWSON, E. (1976) *Seven year-olds in the Home Environment* (London: George Allen and Unwin).

NSPCC School of Social Work (1974) *Yo Yo Children. A study of 23 Violent Matrimonial Cases* (London: NSPCC).

NSPCC (1986) *The Forgotten Children* (London: NSPCC).

POWER, M. J., ANDERTON, M. R., PHILLIPSON, C. M., SHOEBERG, E. and MORRIS, J. N. (1967) 'Delinquent Schools?', *New Society*, 10, 542–3.

REID, K. (1984) 'Disruptive Behaviour and Persistent School Absenteeism', in Frude, N. and Gault, H. (eds) *Disruptive Behaviour in Schools* (Chichester: John Wiley and Sons).

REYNOLDS, D. (1976) 'The delinquent school', in Hammerslee, M. and Woods, P. (eds) *The Process of Schooling* (London: Routledge and Kegan Paul).

REYNOLDS, D. (1984a) 'The School for Vandals: A Sociological Portrait of a Disaffection-prone School', in Frude, N. and Gault, H. (eds) *Disruptive Behaviour in Schools* (Chichester: John Wiley and Sons).

REYNOLDS, D. (1984b) 'Creative Conflict: The Implications of Recent Educational Research for those concerned with Children', *Maladjustment and Therapeutic Education*, 2, 1, 14–23.

REYNOLDS, D. (1988) 'Changing Comprehensive Schools', *Children and Society*, 2, 1, 68–77.

RIBBLE, M. A. (1944) 'Infantile experience in relation to personality development', in Hunt, J. McV. (ed) *Personality and the behaviour disorders* (Vol. 2) (New York: Ronald).

RIBBLE, M. A. (1945) 'Anxiety in infants and its disorganizing effects', in Lewis, N. D. C. and Pacella, B. L. (eds) *Modern Trends in child psychiatry* (New York: International University Press).

RUTTER, M. (1966) *Children of Sick Parents: An Environmental and Psychiatric Study*, Maudsley Monograph No. 16 (London: Oxford University Press).

RUTTER, M., TIZZARD, J. and WHITMORE, K. (1970) *Education, Health and Behaviour* (London: Longman).

RUTTER, M. (1971) 'Parent-child separation; Psychological effects on the children', *Journal of Child Psychology and Psychiatry*, 12, 233–60.

RUTTER, M. (1976) 'Sociocultural influences', in Rutter, M. and Hersov,

L. *Child Psychiatry: Modern Approaches* (Oxford: Blackwell Scientific Publications).
RUTTER, M. (1972) *Maternal Deprivation Reassessed* (Harmondsworth: Penguin).
RUTTER, M. and MADGE, N. (1976) *Cycles of Disadvantage* (London: Heinemann).
RUTTER, M., MAUGHAN, B., MORTIMORE, P. and OUSTON, J. (1979) *Fifteen Thousand Hours: Secondary Schools and their Effects on Children* (London: Open Books).
RUTTER, M. (1980) *Changing Youth in a Changing Society* (Oxford: Nuffield Provincial Hospitals Trust).
SILVA, P. A., KIRKLAND, C., SIMPSON, A., STEWART, I. A., WILLIAMS, S. M. (1982) 'Some Developmental and Behavioural Problems Associated with Bilateral Otitis Media with Effusion', *Journal of Learning Disabilities*, 15, 7, 417–21.
SHARRON, S. (1987) 'Asthmatic children: Victims of ignorance', *Special Children*, 13, 8–9.
SHREEVE, C. M. (1982) 'A state of perpetual motion', *World Medicine*, 17, 15, 87–93.
STACEY, M., DEARDON, R., PILL, R. and ROBINSON, D. (1970) *Hospitals, children and their families* (London: Routledge and Kegan Paul).
STEDMAN, J. (1973) 'Epilepsy: A Barrier to Learning', *Times Educational Supplement*, 3.3.73.
STEVENSON, J. (1987) 'Report of a one day conference', *Special Children*, 8, 5.
SUDDABY, A. (1987) 'A temporary phenomenon', *Special Children*, 8, 22–3.
SURAN, B. J. and RIZZO, J. V. (1979) *Special Children: An Integrated Approach* (Dallas: Scott Foresman and Co).
SWINSON, J. (1988) 'In praise of chemical food', *Special Children*, 18, 6–7.
TATTUM, D. (1982) *Disruptive Pupils in Schools and Units* (Chichester: John Wiley and Sons).
THOMAS, A. and CHESS, S. (1977) *Temperament and development* (New York: Bruner/Mazel).
THORNBURY, R. (1978) *The Changing Urban School* (London: Methuen).
UPTON, G. (1983) *Educating Children with Behaviour Problems* (Faculty of Education, University College, Cardiff).
VASS, M. and RASMUSSEN, B. (1984) 'Allergies: the key to many childhood behaviour abnormalities', *Elementary School Guidance and Counselling*, 242–50.
WEDGE, P. and ESSEN, J. (1982) *Children in Adversity* (London: Pan Books).

Chapter 2

Behaviour Problems and the Teacher

Ronald Davie

Introduction

This chapter tackles three broad questions which are at the centre of the professional task of meeting the needs of pupils with behaviour problems. First, we examine the concept and process of assessing pupils' needs. Second, we look at some of the major theoretical models or explanations of children's behaviour problems. The answers to some of the questions which arise lead on to the third issue, namely, the advisability and efficacy of basing one's practice on one theoretical model versus a more eclectic strategy, which seeks to use in the particular case whichever model appears likely to be the most relevant.

Problem children, or problem schools?

In assessing the needs of children with behaviour problems we need to be especially careful not to imply that the problem is somehow seen to be located within the child. Such an implication should *not* be assumed here. Indeed, it will become a substantive issue for us to consider, as we explore later the models for explaining children's behaviour.

Nevertheless, the assumption that it is the pupil who has the problem – rather than, say, the school which is creating it – is very prevalent in our educational system. This is very understandable when for most other kinds of special educational need (for example hearing and visual impairment, physical handicap) the assumption is much more justifiable. Even there, however, when one is considering the handicap rather than the disability (see Davie, 1976), the situational factors can be very powerful. For children with behaviour problems in particular, though, the last twenty years have seen a growing realisation that some children may be disturbing rather than disturbed and that the system in which they are embedded, especially the school, may itself be creating the apparent deviance (Galloway and Goodwin, 1987). Even clinicians and psychotherapists are now very much readier to accept this possibility than once they were (for example Holman and Coghill, 1987).

Let us then accept that the term 'pupils with behaviour problems' has a potentially misleading connotation and treat it simply as a shorthand for what is a more complex notion.

Assessing needs

We now return to the concept of assessment, which is normally taken in this context to refer to the process of predicting, diagnosing or explaining children's behaviour. It is often assumed that the outcome of this process will be a recommendation or decision about some form of 'treatment', perhaps a new educational programme or a different school placement. The group of professionals usually at the centre of this process in educational settings are educational psychologists, perhaps working in collaboration with child psychiatrists and psychiatric social workers. Until quite recent years psychologists saw themselves largely in this role (Chazan *et al*. 1971; Gillham, 1978). Their emergence into a wider role than this has been somewhat set back by the pressure of work arising out of the 1981 Education Act, in particular the necessity to prepare a 'statement' of need in respect of those pupils requiring extra provision or support (Dessent, 1987).

If, then, educational psychologists have tended to see themselves, and be seen, as assessors, teachers on the other hand normally view their contribution as responding to the recommendations which emerge from the assessment. This may take the form of using different teaching materials in the classroom, or handling the pupil differently, or else considering a change of class or school. Furthermore, not only do psychologists and teachers differentiate their roles in this way, there is often the implicit assumption that the former play a more skilled part in the process, whereas teachers are on the whole following the guidelines set out by the psychologists, and therefore are less expert. This relationship may be reflected in the professional status which each group perceives itself to have in this context.

Parallels with social services

Interestingly, a parallel situation in some respects can be seen in the social services field in Britain. The traditional way of arriving at a judgement about especially difficult or problematic cases in statutory care has been to refer them to residential 'observation and assessment' (O and A) centres, where 'experts' have compiled a report making recommendations about the young persons' future. These recommendations have then been put into effect by residential care staff or field social workers (Fuller, 1985).

The similarities between education and social services in this field lie not at the structural or procedural level but in the underlying assumption that assessment and treatment for children or young people whose behaviour is giving cause for concern are separate functions or events. The former involves finding out about the nature of the problem, while the latter involves taking action in the light of the insights thus revealed.

The fact that the education and social services systems are based upon a similar assumption or model may seem unsurprising. After all, they represent, at least in a British context, two departments of the same local authority, ultimately responsible to the same body of elected members. However, their shared assumption has little or nothing to do with the matching of their functions and responsibilities. On the contrary, their two systems operate largely in isolation from each other and in almost complete ignorance of each other's operation – and this despite the fact that in this particular context they are dealing not only with a similar range of problems but in many cases with the same children.

The shared assumption by education and social services about the relationship between assessment and treatment in respect of children's behaviour problems is almost certainly because both services are still drawing upon a medical, or pathological, model in construing the situation. The terms we have found ourselves using in discussing this issue above have tended to derive from this model, for example diagnosis, treatment, etc. In other words, the child is assumed to have something wrong with him, which needs, first, understanding and explaining and then dealing with.

Of course, the picture above has been presented more starkly than one may always find it. Furthermore, the two systems have in recent years been moving in a similar direction, albeit for reasons which have to do with broad tendencies affecting all the 'personal' services (that is, social, educational, medical) rather than any explicit understanding between them. Thus, social services departments have since their original formation in the early 1970s taken an ever increasing interest in community work. This has led them amongst other things to review the appropriateness of 'O and A' centres and to explore the possibilities of 'non-residential assessment', following the 'Tutt Report' (DHSS, 1981). Social services' assessment procedures and systems in Britain at present, then, are much more varied; many do not assume that assessment needs to be carried out in a residential setting and some are breaking away from the notion that it needs to be undertaken in a particular place by a particular group of people.

Nevertheless, the Tutt Report itself (op. cit.) seemed at times to be using the old model, for example, when it set out the aims of assessment in the following terms:

(i) To describe the problems presented or experienced by the child;
(ii) to make a judgement about the nature of the problems for which the child is referred;
(ii) to make recommendations about the form of intervention, if any, required to resolve or alleviate the problem.

It should be conceded that the committee chaired by Tutt point out that assessment must be seen as a continuous process and not one tied down in space or time. Furthermore, the committee stressed that assessment itself involves intervention. Fuller (op. cit.), however, in reviewing the committee's report, pointed to the importantly different perspective given on assessment in a report produced earlier from a different source (MIND, 1975). The definition here was:

> The formulation of a coherent but flexible plan of action in which both short-term and long-term goals are stated, points of disagreement or conflict made explicit, and the child and family as fully and genuinely involved as possible.

This latter definition, leaving aside the participatory elements introduced at the end, has a rather more provisional, open-ended ring to it. It stresses flexibility and seeks to make explicit any alternative explanations or perceptions. Even so, it shares with other, official, reports (for example the 'Warnock Report', DES 1978; DHSS, 1981) an apparent commitment to 'continuous assessment' without, one feels, the concept having been fully thought through. In other words, these reports have accepted that assessment should not be viewed as a once for all event in the educational (or other) career of a child and urge that the position should remain flexible and be reviewed from time to time. However, their concept seems at times only to envisage a series of events in place of the single one; it does not present the situation as a dynamic, ongoing, interactive relationship between assessment and 'treatment', which is implicit in the idea of continuous assessment. We may note, for example, that the Tutt Report (op. cit.) speaks of children being 'referred' and of the resulting 'recommendations', presumably to the referring agency. This certainly smacks of an occasion or event, which is difficult to reconcile with the concept of a 'continuous' process.

Assessment as a continuous process

What seems clear is that assessment cannot be continuous unless it is seen as inextricably linked with treatment; these two facets have to be viewed as 'indivisible parts of a continuous cyclical process' (Davie, 1983). Thus:

> The model used is rather like that used in the empirical sciences, namely, data gathering, hypothesis and experiment. The experiment yields further data on the basis of which the hypothesis is sustained, rejected, modified, etc.
>
> In an educational context, the data gathering may be seen as the production and collation of information from reports, interviews, tests and observations. On the basis of this information, certain provisional conclusions are reached about the possible causes of any difficulties and/or the best way of proceeding (the hypothesis). The next phase (experiment/action) might in some circumstances appropriately be called 'experimental teaching' (see Leach and Raybould, 1977) in the sense that we do not yet know whether it is the correct response, or whether our 'hypothesis' is valid. However, the 'experimental' phase, carefully monitored, throws further light on the validity of the original formulation, i.e. either it works or it doesn't. In the light of the success or otherwise of our action, we may accept the hypothesis (and continue the action) or reject the hypothesis and put forward another one, thus changing the action.

The above may appear a little too neat and tidy; real life situations are rarely like that. This is true, of course, but real life situations in their untidiness confirm the underlying point even more strongly. It is virtually impossible in life to respond at all to another person's behaviour without making some kind of assessment of what is called for, what is appropriate. The other person involved is reacting in the same way, of course. This is why such situations are described as interactive. Each person is assessing and then responding in turn.

The more structured process of assessment in education and in other professional contexts is thus but a special instance of a universal phenomenon. Or rather it should be. But whereas in a normal, interactive, social situation, the feedback is inevitable and continuous, in the formality of an assessment procedure, there may be either no subsequent feedback, or it may be episodic, or else the feedback may not relate at all to the significant issues. This latter possibility is especially likely if the person or people involved in assessing a child's needs are different from, and seen as separate from, those whose major responsibility is to help meet those needs. The principal shortcoming, even danger, in any of the above situations is that the formal system involving several different kinds of professionals gets split off from, and may become totally irrelevant to, what actually happens with the child. It does not mean that the process of assessing the child's behaviour and reacting to it will not go on; as we have seen, that interaction is inevitable at the one-to-one level. However, at this informal level the process is often covert and because it typically involves only one professional, often a class teacher, the feedback loop may constitute a self-fulfilling prophecy rather than a self-correcting mechanism.

In summary, then, on this first major question, assessment and one's response in the light of that assessment are seen to be normal, interactive elements of day-to-day, even minute-by-minute social relationships. Thus, *they are at the centre of every teaching situation*. Assessment and response (or treatment) in a wider, more formal, context must mirror that interactive process if it is to be effective. Certainly, the class teacher – and residential child care worker, etc., as appropriate – needs to be seen as a vital part of the assessment process; and those professionals who may play a less direct role in the day-to-day treatment should nevertheless become involved in this, wherever possible, if only at the level of observation.

Where lies the problem?

Before moving on to the second major part of this chapter, it is perhaps worth reminding ourselves once more that no assumption is being made that if a behaviour problem exists in this context, it is a problem which in some sense the child has and which the professionals and parents have to treat, or cure. It is now well established that a large proportion of pupils whose behaviour is a cause for concern at school are not causing any problem at home, and vice versa (for example Rutter *et al.*, 1970). There is a number of explanations for this phenomenon, which are not mutually exclusive, but one of them must be that for some children the context or situation is either causing the problem or else exacerbating it. This general point is reiterated here, as it was in Chapter 1, because discussion on the previous issue, at times, used some of the terminology of what has been described as the 'medical model'; that is, one that assumes a condition which has an aetiology and needs to be diagnosed (or assessed) and treated (for example Upton, 1980). Again, the parallel drawn with the empirical sciences in the preceding discussion implied a 'positivist' model (Bullock and Stallybrass, 1977) and this, too, raises a number of issues, which are considered shortly.

Five models

We now turn our attention to a brief review of five of the major theoretical models encountered in this field, which are used to understand or explain children's behaviour problems. Many of these models are dealt with in some detail in the following chapters, so that our purpose here is to set them out in broad outline and to make some initial comparisons.

The order in which they are presented is not fortuitous. It happens largely to be a chronological order. More importantly, however, it follows a trend which has been evident and gathering momentum over the past twenty to thirty years in our thinking about children and about the structuring of our services for them, discussed elsewhere by Davie (1982). In the context of children's behaviour and development, this period has seen a movement from a narrow, psychological perspective to a broader, contextualised, at times sociological, approach. It might be characterised as a 'movement from an individualised to a systems approach, from the atomistic to the holistic, occasionally from the micro to the macro' (Davie, 1986).

At the professional level, one can see this movement in most of the relevant sectors. Educational psychologists, for example, saw themselves until the 1970s largely as psychometricians, dealing mostly with the assessment of individual pupils, albeit having an important role as a link between the child guidance team and schools. Since that time, however, they have increasingly seen themselves as working in a consultative capacity, perhaps as 'agents of change', with teachers and with whole schools (see Gillham, 1980 and 1985).

A not dissimilar trend can be seen in social work over the same timescale. The concept of 'community social work' emerged in and around the time of the Seebohm Report (DHSS, 1968) and was extensively discussed in the Barclay Report (1982). This concept did not replace the idea of individual or family casework but it moved the profession towards a wider view of its role. Another example of this trend was the emphasis given in the Court Report on child health services to the role of the community paediatrician' (DHSS, 1976).

These parallels cannot be coincidental, although no one as yet has attempted to analyse in depth the common factors which lay behind them. It is clear nevertheless that the movement was – and is – not confined to professional development but is to be traced in academic writing both in Britain and in the USA (Davie, 1982).

The psychodynamic approach

Hence, in reviewing the theoretical models we shall start with arguably the most individual of them all, namely, the one which originated with Sigmund Freud. Strictly, we should be speaking of models here rather than a single model because of the number of important differences of approach within this general orientation (for example Adler, Bowlby, Erikson, Klein, Redl, Winnicott, etc.). However, for present purposes within this chapter we can group them together as sharing certain common features and beliefs; and we shall refer to this common ground as the 'psychodynamic model'.

Brown and Pedder (1979) distinguish five common features or assumptions which can be found in the work of all theorists and practitioners adopting this model, namely: unconscious processes; anxiety and psychic pain; defence mechanisms; motivational drives; and developmental phases. Both the general framework of the psychodynamic model and the significance of these five principles are so familiar as to require no substantial restating here. They are now part of western cultures, appearing frequently in art, literature and drama as well as in everyday language and allusions.

Perhaps the most central and the most widely known feature of this model is the assumption of the unconscious: that inner, psychic world, not normally accessible to conscious thought but exerting a powerful influence upon our feelings and our behaviour. Much of this unconscious material, it is assumed, has been repressed because it is associated with feelings of guilt, conflict or anxiety, too painful to be held at the conscious level. If this inner conflict or pain becomes intolerable for the individual, it can emerge as unacceptable or sometimes debilitating behaviour. However, it will be noted, this overt behaviour is essentially a symptom of the underlying, unconscious conflict (see Chapter 4). Thus, to concentrate on removing or suppressing the symptom without tackling the underlying problem can be seen as at best of limited value, because some other symptom may take its place; at its most dangerous, it can be thought to be taking away the safety valve which alone is safeguarding the individual's mental health. Thus, 'the aims of many of the psychodynamic procedures in teaching and therapy are primarily concerned with the provision of opportunity for acceptable outlets of the internal pressures ("letting off steam", "getting it off your chest") ... In addition to finding release, it is also seen as important to gain understanding of some of the causes of the internal pressures and problems' (Gobell, 1980).

Behaviour modification

The second model for us to consider goes back almost as far as the psychodynamic one but comes from a very different stable. While Freud, as we all know, developed his theory and his practice out of his work with patients, our second model has its modern origins in the laboratories of experimental psychologists working largely with animals. These 'behaviourists' developed in a much more rigorous and scientific way, a body of empirical evidence which was subsequently brought together as a theory of learning.

Although it has quite a long history, this behavioural model has only in more recent years had any major impact or practical relevance for work with people. In this context it is usually referred to as social learning theory; and the clinical techniques employed are known as behaviour modification. The principal and most obvious contrast with psychodynamic theory is that the behavioural model makes no assumptions about unconscious or inner processes. Its quintessential principle is that behaviour which is reinforced, whether by accident or design, tends to recur or gain in strength, while behaviour which is not reinforced tends to disappear (see Herbert, 1987, for a good general introduction.)

The simplicity and universality of this principle is one of its attractions both in relation to its practical uses and also in theoretical scientific terms, where the law of parsimony applies. Furthermore, there is no room for doubt about the effectiveness of the approach in changing behaviour. Indeed, its effectiveness has given rise to some ethical concern about its use, not unlike the anxiety sometimes expressed about the use of drugs to help modify or influence behaviour. The difficulty about sustaining ethical objections to behavioural techniques is that parents and teachers have been utilising the same basic principles since time immemorial, albeit with less success!

The behaviourist, then, is concerned largely with the here and now and the observable rather than with any distant aetiology or unconscious mental conflicts. He does not therefore assume that the behaviour problem is a symptom of some underlying mechanism. It would be wrong to say that he actively rejects that possibility; it just does not enter his scheme of things. As far as he is concerned, the behaviour in question must have been learned, which implies that it must have been, and still is being, reinforced. His first concern is to carry out a 'behavioural analysis', which is a precise and detailed description and analysis of the behaviour which is causing concern. How does it manifest itself? What circumstances precede it and accompany it? Who else is involved and in what way? The second stage of the analysis is to identify what it is that is reinforcing the behaviour. Paradoxically, the attention which a behaviour problem may attract from adults attempting to deal with the problem can be the reinforcement for an attention-seeking child. The teachers' or parents' current solutions therefore may actually be making the position worse! The third stage is to seek ways of changing the situation so that the problem behaviour is not reinforced and – if at all possible, too – so that some more acceptable pattern of behaviour is reinforced.

This is a very simple description of what can be quite a complex and time-consuming process. In fact, the time involved can be an important inhibiting factor in considering the use of this approach, especially in mainstream schools. However, this has to be weighed against the time taken, disruption and distraction caused and pressure exerted by even a single pupil with a significant behaviour problem. Furthermore, an understanding of the basic principles involved can often help teachers prevent a problem occurring, or assist them to analyse a situation in a way which will suggest a constructive way forward without any elaborate and time-consuming programmes.

Humanistic psychology

Our third theoretical model is much less well known than the first two, discussed above. It could be said, as we shall see below, to be a reaction against earlier models. It is usually referred to as humanistic psychology or, when related to the education process, as humanistic education. Its principal proponents and architects in the 1950s and 1960s were the Americans Carl Rogers (for example 1961) and Abraham Maslow (for example 1968).

The model is in some ways more difficult to characterise than the others included in this chapter but in other ways it is simpler. Humanistic psychology can be seen as a reaction against the positivism of the empirical sciences. It therefore rejects 'mechanistic' explanations of human behaviour or generalisations about causal processes. For the humanistic psychologist, the individual is unique. At the centre of this theoretical model, therefore, is the individual's perception of himself (his self-image) and his unique perception of others and of the world around. The model also stresses the relevance and the integrity of the whole person and resists attempts to split off and deal with bits of behaviour or life experience.

Writers and practitioners espousing this model tend to stress empathy, in the same sense of being able to put or feel oneself in someone else's place (Visser, 1983). Hence, they emphasise the validity of a person's perception or interpretation of events rather than any attempt at an 'objective' description of the events themselves.

Gobell (1980) emphasises the above points as central to the humanistic model and highlights some of the practical implications for teachers. Worster and Bird (1980) in the same publication usefully describe a number of specific techniques emanating from this model which can be utilised in schools. They highlight the value of working in small groups in a pastoral care group situation, developing the interpersonal skills of listening and sharing. The benefits of such activities, they claim, are cognitive as well as affective. The overall objective is to encourage respect for others' perceptions, others' points of view, others' feelings. In the process of doing this, pupils gain in respect for their own perceptions, points of view, etc. because of the positive feedback they are obtaining from other group members. Hence, their self-image is improved, they benefit as a whole person and this is reflected in their behaviour and their school work.

Humanistic education seeks to involve the students in experimental learning and self-discovery methods. Also 'the teacher is characterised as a helper who provides a climate in which the student can feel free to develop emotionally' (Burns, 1982).

Behaviour and environment

At this point, we pause briefly to consider a group of researchers who have much in common with each other but are not sufficiently close theoretically to be described as adopting the same model in the way in which we have been using that term in this chapter. Nevertheless, their evidence is often cited in the literature on behaviour problems, so they should be mentioned.

This group shares the same scientific paradigm and its members are all broadly interested in the relationship between behaviour problems in children and environmental factors in the home, the school and beyond. Most of them could be described as epidemiologists. Amongst the factors they have measured, analysed and correlated with behaviour problems (as you will already have noted in Chapter 1) are social class, family size and composition, family pathology, sex, poor housing and overcrowding, educational attainment, birth factors (including maternal smoking in pregnancy) and parental–child relationship. Upton (1983) in reviewing these workers' findings points to the considerable degree of agreement in their results. At the same time their methodology is mostly designed to establish correlations rather than to prove causation. Their principal values for the practitioner, therefore, is to increase his general awareness of the range of environmental factors which may be impinging upon the behaviour and adjustment of individual pupils.

Best known amongst this group in Britain is Rutter (for example 1983) whose work since the 1960s has included most of the above variables and whose later research has also examined the relationships between school characteristics and pupils' behaviour and adjustment (Rutter *et al.* 1979).

At the outset of this second section of the chapter we foreshadowed moving along a continuum in terms of the models we are examining, both chronologically and also from the psychological to the psycho-social perspectives. Of course, such directional movements are never exact. As we have seen, the humanistic model was something of a reaction against prevailing approaches and could be said to be the most individually based of all the models we are reviewing. However, as we move to our penultimate model, we reach well past any notional centre point of the continuum.

A systems approach

The model we now examine is rooted in systems theory, implicitly or explicitly, and therefore in an educational context embraces 'whole-school' approaches and institutional change strategies, while on the therapeutic front it includes family therapy. In essence, the systems model takes the view that each individual child is embedded in a number of systems, notably family and school, and that the individual's behaviour can only meaningfully be viewed in that sort of context. There are some elements of this in all of the models we have reviewed, of course. From the psychodynamic standpoint, the context is largely historical, although it is the present inner state which is of central concern. The behaviourist on the other hand is interested in the immediate context, the precipitating factors, the reinforcers and so on. The humanist is perhaps furthest from this position in that he tends to reject any notion of the individual being caught up in a system outside of himself. However, it is notable that the techniques described by Worster and Bird (op. cit.) involve working in groups, developing listening skills and a respect for others' perceptions.

Nevertheless, the systems model is a far cry from these other perspectives. From a theoretical viewpoint, the model like most others can become quite complex and the practical or treatment techniques, too, are often elaborate, but the central core of the approach is simple. Man is a social animal and his behaviour is essentially defined in social terms. Therefore, if a child's behaviour is a cause for some concern, it is highly likely to be related in some way to the matrix of relationships around him. It is a familiar concept that a child may be 'scapegoated', for example, and there are many other circumstances where behaviour may be clearly seen to be directly related to some external factor. Even where the genesis of a problem is found to be an identifiable medical condition, the way in which the problem manifests itself, the reactions to it by others and the child's reaction to those reactions are often influenced by the pre-existing relationships in a particular system. Furthermore, the nuclear systems (family, school, peer group, etc.) are related to each other in ways which may be important in understanding an individual child's problem.

In discussing family therapy, for example, Speed (1983) explains that 'working with families . . . . . . is not an adjunct to the main business in hand (treating the individual), rather it is central to the whole enterprise of therapy'. A similar movement can be discerned in educational circles. Thus, Davie (1980a, 1980b) describes and later evaluates (Davie et al. 1984 and 1985; Phillips et al. 1985) an in-service course for experienced and senior teachers which is concerned with institutional change in schools as a way of responding to behaviour problems. This approach has subsequently gathered momentum nationally in different forms and has also widened to cover the whole field of special educational needs. Muncey and Ainscow (1986), for instance, describe a scheme developed in Coventry which involves the selection and training of a teacher in each school who is responsible for assisting the school as a whole to respond to its pupils' special educational needs.

Labelling theory

The final model for us to consider shares with systems theory a rejection of the idea that individual behaviour (or problems) can meaningfully be viewed out of context. However, this last model goes further in challenging the very concept of individual deviance. The theory is usually attributed to the American sociologist Becker (1963). He argued that deviance is not something intrinsic to the individual; it is created by society. Thus, our social system sets up certain rules or has certain expectations of people; when these rules are broken or expectations confounded, deviancy is created. Another concept and term which forms part of this theoretical model is that of labelling (hence, 'labelling theory'.) It is pointed out, for example, that the same overt acts carried out by, say, Oxbridge undergraduates and young football club supporters may be seen as boisterous high spirits in the former and hooliganism in the latter.

Labelling theory represents, like humanistic psychology, a rejection of the determinism and positivism of conventional empirical science. Both models also place great emphasis upon the personal, subjective perspective as against attempts to measure objective reality. The former is often referred to as a 'phenomenological' approach. Hargreaves *et al.* (1975) contrast the difference between the kinds of questions posed by empirical scientists and labelling theorists. The scientists set out to establish measurable criteria by which, say, a 'behaviour problem' may be identified and classified. They then ask about causal factors and associated relationships. Finally, they seek to find out how to predict, prevent, control or cure the condition. The labelling theorists on the other hand ask what the circumstances or conditions were which led to a pupil being categorised as a behaviour problem. How have other people's (and pupils') attitudes or actions changed as a result of that categorisation? How has the pupil reacted to being cast in that role? and so on.

In educational contexts this model – sometimes also called the interactionist approach – would lead the practitioner to ask whether the pupil was a problem all of the time and with all teachers. If not, the practitioner would further explore the nature of the interactions which were presenting the difficulty. He would also be especially vigilant to ensure as far as possible that the mere attribution of a label was not itself adversely affecting the situation. The dangers of self-fulfilling prophecies are well known.

From individuals to systems

We have now reviewed five different theoretical models. Each of them offers a different way of understanding, explaining or construing children's behaviour problems. In consequence, each of them may suggest different ways of responding to, or treating, such behaviour. We shall return to the implications of these differences shortly. Before doing this, however, we should spend a moment to consider any implications of the broad direction which the models are taking, namely, the suggested continuum from an individual/psychological perspective to a social/sociological one.

First, we may note, as we did earlier in another context, that the reality in such things is often not neat and tidy. The idea of a continuum does not imply a straight line without deviations; nor should it be taken to mean that there is only one dimension to the issue. Furthermore, the swing from a micro to a macro perspective is by no means new in the history of knowledge. In many fields, one has seen, and can see, movements which focus more narrowly or in a more detailed fashion on particular areas of knowledge, followed by subsequent movements to broaden the knowledge, sometimes for the purpose of generalising it, or else to temper it in the light of a wider perspective.

To take an educational example of this phenomenon, there are periods when schools and education generally seem very concerned with curricular matters, with standards or teaching methods in literacy and numeracy, with the training of teachers and so on. In contrast, at other times the field appears much more outward looking with talk of 'whole school approaches', of community schools and of partnership with parents and with other services. Although such trends are much more evident at a national level and in the area of policy developments and debate, they can also be discerned in the individual school.

No doubt, then, there is an element of this general phenomenon in the directional trend identified in the continuum along which our five models are ranged. This is not to seek to reduce the significance or importance of the trend but to place it in a wider context. Furthermore, although in many of these movements, there is often an element of fashion – a 'bandwagon' effect – there is also a serious, underlying reason for the trend. The pendulum may swing back but it rarely returns to its former position.

In terms of the perspectives we have been examining in this chapter, the directional trend is an important area to consider. If the individual professional is to be in full command of his professional situation or task – rather than be blown by winds of change he does not recognise, far less understand – he needs to grasp the significance of this movement. The major implications are twofold. First, there has been some tendency in the past to concentrate on the individual child and his personal history without fully taking into account the potential relevance and importance of external forces and perceptions and systems. On the other hand, there is also the danger of ignoring the individual and overstressing the system. The danger – in both directions – exists to some extent in the construction of theoretical models but, more importantly for most professionals, it exists in terms of how a particular child or situation is perceived or handled.

The second major implication is the impact of the trend on professional training and professional roles. Most teachers enter their profession – as do psychologists and psychiatrists, for example – because of an interest in individuals. It is not a difficult step for them to grasp, accept and utilise the concept that the child's immediate contexts to a greater or lesser extent affect his behaviour, his performance, etc. However, the wider the contextual view becomes, the more difficult it is for an individual teacher or school to pursue it in any practical sense.

If he does try to pursue it, there are twin dangers. Let us take, for example, poverty, poor housing and unemployment. All of these factors, as we know, impact upon educational performance, if not directly then in the consequential effects on the morale, aspirations, mental and physical health, etc. of families and communities. A teacher faced with these consequences may be tempted to blame families or the local authority or central government for the performance or behaviour of children in the school. This is especially dangerous if, as a result, he ignores what the school could or should be doing.

The opposite temptation is for a teacher within and outside school to spend an inappropriate amount of time and energy on welfare matters and on community work to the detriment of his pedagogic role. For some teachers, political or industrial action is seen as a relevant and appropriate response to the wider, contextual view.

This leads us into issues beyond the scope of this chapter, or this book. Suffice it here to put a marker by this more distant terrain because when one opens up the more social and societal perspectives, it becomes ever more difficult to draw a firm line around the professional role.

Which model to believe?

We now reach the final section of our chapter and confront the issues raised by having a variety of different models. Each of them has an extensive literature and, albeit in varying degrees, a strong following. More problematically, they are in several important respects mutually incompatible. Does this matter?

To those who are concerned primarily to build theories and/or to carry out scientific research, the discrepancies are not problematic. On the contrary, they could stimulate experimental work designed to test alternative hypotheses, drawn from different theories. In reality, this potential advantage is not often seen because most researchers have insufficient familiarity with a range of theoretical models and their associated research literature to be able to design such critical experiments. They tend instead to confine their work and their interest to one model. Where any kind of comparative work is attempted, the results are not definitive enough to permit the rejection of a major theoretical tenet. Therefore, in summary, the incompatibility between theoretical models does not pose a problem for the theorists, mostly because they are not often interested in theories other than their own except perhaps to use them as straw men! Potentially, the discrepancies could be valuable scientifically, although this seems rarely to happen.

The practitioner's dilemma

Experienced practitioners in the specialised field of emotional and behaviour difficulties have often tended to take a position similar to the theorists, namely, they have espoused one model and eschewed the others. Indeed, some of the most distinguished practitioners have themselves written extensively on theoretical aspects.

However, this position has been changing in recent years for a number of reasons. First, the number of credible, well-documented theoretical models with their associated practical skills and techniques has increased. Behaviour modification, for example, and family therapy have both made giant strides in the past twenty years. Their impressive results are difficult for intelligent, uncommitted new entrants into the professions to ignore. Second, there has been a tendency over a similar period to move towards multi-disciplinary teams in this context as in many others; and this, too, has led to significant erosion of the single-model approach. It is true, of course, that child guidance and child psychiatric teams were quite common fifty years ago and more but they were on the whole dominated by the psychiatrist or medical director who would determine the treatment model. Today's clinical teams are much less hierarchical professionally, therefore allowing different approaches to be introduced more readily. Furthermore, non-clinical teams (that is, without a medical base) are now much more common in this area; and the 1981 Education Act with its movement towards integration in mainstream schools and the growth of a community orientation in social services will continue that trend.

What might at first sight, then, appear to be a dilemma for the practitioner is on further scrutiny much less so. The problem only remains if the question to be answered is: which of the theories is right? As we have already seen, the definitive evidence to validate one model and discredit another is not in sight; and it is unlikely ever to emerge in quite that way. Much more probable will be some formulation which incorporates two or more of the models together within an overarching framework.

The answer to the above question may therefore be that all of the theories may be right in their own way. Each one takes a different point of departure in terms of its mainspring: its conceptual, or professional framework; the evidence it seeks in order to verify or modify its direction; and the outcomes it expects, which will justify its continued existence. Thus, to say that each model gives us a partial glimpse of the truth, is not to imply that they are all deficient but merely that in the present state of our knowledge the truth appears to have a number of faces, which shine in a certain light, as it were.

An eclectic stance

Without wishing to venture further down this metaphysical path, we can accept from a practical standpoint that there is no necessity to make any absolute choice between different, and even conflicting explanations. The range of possible interpretations in the individual case, or situation, may readily be scanned in order to determine which is likely to be the most productive. However, this is not seen as a process of attempting to assemble a number of possible *solutions*. For example, for an individual child with a prima-facie problem, we might start by asking whether we are quite sure that there really is a problem. Does everyone who interacts with him see him as a problem? And does everyone have the same perception of the situation? If not, why not, and how do they differ? How does the 'problem' manifest itself? Is it specific to, or different in, different situations? What appears to trigger the difficulties? What could be reinforcing this particular behaviour? Would it be useful, or practical, to bring the whole of the child's family together, or all of his teachers, etc., to consider the situation? Is the behaviour likely to be a symptom of some underlying problem in the family? Is it therefore a cry for help? Is it attention seeking?

By concentrating on the questions, one is in a sense trying out different formulations of 'the problem' in order to judge which of them may suggest further enquiry or action. The great virtue of such an approach is that options are kept open, and several possible lines of enquiry or action usually emerge. Furthermore, no assumption is made that somewhere, somehow *an* answer will be found. This is because in the individual case more than one of the theoretical models may very well be relevant.

Thus, it is not difficult to conceive of a child who, because of some changed situation at home (a new baby arrives, mother remarries), is feeling unwanted or rejected. Whether that situation were to be fairly straightforward, or complex, it could result in some attention-seeking behaviour at school. If misbehaviour proved to be the only – or easiest – way of obtaining that attention, it would be reinforced. Furthermore, if he were new to the school, he might be identified (labelled) as a 'difficult' child. This might become self-fulfilling if the school were to complain to the parents, who then were to chastise the child, making him feel further rejected, and so on.

The example is a facile one, but it illustrates the point. Several of the questions suggested earlier would have thrown some light on such a situation. It also illustrates that there is no single 'cause', which can necessarily be identified and removed, thus providing a solution. It further demonstrates that if, in this hypothetical instance, the child's teacher had intuitively sensed some need for attention and provided this, the whole 'problem' might have melted away in months if not weeks.

Difficulties in eclecticism

The adoption of this kind of eclectic stance is, however, not entirely without difficulty. Its first potential shortcoming might be the creation of a shallow, professional dilettantism, which would militate against sound judgement from an adequate knowledge base. This might best be prevented by structuring the professional situation on a team basis. This, as we have seen, is a growing trend anyway but a structured, eclectic approach would perhaps necessitate different members of the team electing to familiarise themselves with particular models, if there were significant gaps in the team's collective expertise. Beyond this, it is difficult to generalise because the detailed structure and level of expertise needed would be very different, depending on the institutional context, for example mainstream school, special unit, day or residential special school, clinic team, etc.

However, there is one other potential difficulty which has particular relevance to special schools and units. There has been some tendency, as was mentioned earlier, for special schools to base their whole ethos on one theoretical approach. The psychodynamic model in particular has provided a framework in which many of the best known residential schools or communities for children with emotional and behavioural difficulties have operated and this still applies to a lesser extent. Behaviourism, too, more recently has been the model on which a number of schools have based their education and care.

Dealing with disturbed and disturbing children in a segregated setting, especially if this is residential, is recognised to be extremely demanding and stressful work. Perhaps these demands incline some practitioners to develop a strong identification with, and faith in, a particular set of beliefs about children's behaviour and adjustment. If this is the case, eclecticism may be found wanting on this plane. It is rather more cerebral than inspirational. In difficult and stressful situations there is great comfort and support to be derived from an inner conviction that one knows the way, the truth and the light! Indeed, religion in some circumstances may provide that support. Eclecticism, however, explicitly demands a rejection of such an approach. There is no royal road. Judgements need to be weighed options kept open.

A team approach

The special school context, of course, especially the residential situation, applies only to a minority of children who need professional help. However, whatever the context, there is growing evidence of the efficacy and attractions of the multi-disciplinary team approach (e.g. ILEA, 1979; Woodcock and Frances, 1981; Hollins, 1985), and although this is not synonymous with eclecticism, there must be a great deal of common ground in terms of group dynamics and team building. It is no easy option, but it offers a way forward which can be adapted to many different situations – including the use of outside consultants, for example, to a school – and which has much to commend it.

References

BARCLAY, P. (1982) 'Social workers: their role and tasks', Working Party Report (London: Bedford Square Press).

BECKER, H. (1963) *Outsiders: Studies in the Sociology of Deviance* (New York: Free Press).

BROWN, D. and PEDDER, J. (1979) *Introduction to Psychotherapy* (London: Tavistock Publications).

BULLOCK, A. and STALLYBRASS, B. (1977) *The Fontana Dictionary of Modern Thought* (London: Fontana Books).

BURNS, R. (1982) *Self-Concept Development and Education* (London: Holt, Rinehart and Winston).

CHAZAN, M., MOORE, T., WILLIAMS, P. and WRIGHT, J. (1971) *The Practice of Educational Psychology* (London: Longman).

COURT, S. D. M. (1976) *Fit for the future: report of the Committee on child health service* (London: HMSO).

DAVIE, R. (1976) 'Children and families with special needs', *AEP Journal*, 4, 1, 1–8.

DAVIE, R. (1980a) 'Behaviour problems in schools and school-based in-service training', in Upton, G. and Gobell, A. (eds) *Behaviour Problems in the Comprehensive School* (Cardiff: Faculty of Education, University College).

DAVIE, R. (1980b) 'Promoting school adjustment', in Pringle, M. K. (ed.) *A Fairer Future for Children* (London: Macmillan).

DAVIE, R. (1982) 'Child development in context' *BPS Education Section Review* 6, 1–12.

DAVIE, R. (1983) 'Testing and Assessment' in Upton, G. (ed) *Educating Children with Behaviour Problems* (Cardiff: Faculty of Education, University College).

DAVIE, R. (1986) 'Understanding behaviour problems', *Maladjustment and Therapeutic Education*, 4, 1, 7–15.
DAVIE, R., PHILLIPS, D. and CALLELY, E. (1984) *Secondary Schools Research Project: Evaluation of INSET Course on Behaviour Problems* (Cardiff: Welsh Office).
DAVIE, R., PHILLIPS, D. and CALLELY, E. (1985) *Change in Secondary Schools* (Cardiff: Welsh Office).
DES (1978) *Special Educational Needs: the Report of the Committee of Enquiry into the Education of Handicapped Children and Young People* (The Warnock Report) (London: HMSO).
DESSENT, T. (1987) *Making the Ordinary School Special* (London: Falmer Press).
DHSS, SOCIAL WORK SERVICE (1977) *Working Together for Children and Their Families*, Vol. 1. (Cardiff: Welsh Office and South Glamorgan County Council).
DHSS (1981) *Observation and Assessment: Report of a Working Party* (Chairman: Tutt, N.).
FULLER, R. (1985) *Issues in the Assessment of Children in Care* (London: National Children's Bureau).
GALLOWAY, D. and GOODWIN, C. (1987) *The Education of Disturbing Children* (London: Longman).
GILLHAM, B. (1978) *Reconstructing Educational Psychology* (London: Croom Helm).
GILLHAM, B. (1980) *Problem Behaviour in the Secondary School: a Systems Approach* (London: Croom Helm).
GILLHAM, B. (1985) 'School organisation – the control of disruptive incidents', in Frude, N. and Gault, H. (eds) *Disruptive Behaviour in Schools* (Chichester: John Wiley and Sons).
GOBELL, A. (1980) 'Three classroom procedures', in Upton, G. and Gobell, A. (eds) *Behaviour Problems in the Comprehensive School* (Cardiff: Faculty of Education, University College).
HARGREAVES, D. H., HESTER, S. K. and MELLOR, F. J. (1975) *Deviance in Classrooms* (London: Routledge and Kegan Paul).
HERBERT, M. (1987) *Behavioural Treatment of Children with Problems* (London: Academic Press).
HOLLINS, S. (1985) 'The dynamics of team work' in Bicknell, J., Craft, M. and Hollins, S. (eds) *Mental Handicap – a Multidisciplinary Approach*' (Eastbourne: Baillière and Tindall).
HOLMAN, P. and COGHILL, N. (1987) *Disruptive Behaviour in schools* (Bromley: Chartwell-Bratt).
ILEA (1979) *Relationships and Leadership in Child Guidance Units* (London: Medical Department, ILEA).

LEACH, D. and REYBOULD, E. (1977) *Learning and Behaviour Difficulties in School* (London: Open Books).

MASLOW, A. (1968) *Towards a Psychology of Being* (Princeton: Van Nostrand Reinhold).

MIND Working Party (1975) *Assessment of Children and Their Families* (London: MIND/Kings Fund Centre).

MUNCEY, J. and AINSCOW, M. (1986) 'Meeting special educational needs in mainstream schools: a transatlantic perspective', *International Journal of Special Education*, 1, 2, 161–176.

PHILLIPS, D., DAVIE, R. and CALLELY, E. (1985) 'Pathway to institutional developments in secondary schools', in Reynolds, D. (ed.) *Studying School Effectiveness* (London: Falmer Press).

ROGERS, C. R. (1961) *On Becoming a Person* (Boston: Houghton Mifflin).

RUTTER, M., TIZARD, J. and WHITMORE, K. (1970) (eds) *Education, Health and Behaviour* (London: Longman).

RUTTER, M., MAUGHAN, B., MORTIMORE, P. and OUSTON, J. (1979) *Fifteen Thousand Hours: Secondary Schools and their Effects on Pupils* (London: Open Books).

RUTTER, M. (1983) *A Measure of Our Values* (London: Quaker Home Service).

SEEBOHM, F. (1968) *Report of the Committee on Local Authority and Allied Personal Social Services* (London: DHSS).

SPEED, B. (1983) 'Systemic Family Therapy and Disturbing Behaviour', in Upton, G. (ed.) *Educating Children with Behaviour Problems* (Cardiff: Faculty of Education, University College).

UPTON, G. (1980) 'The nature and development of behaviour problems', in Upton, G. and Gobell, A. (eds) *Behaviour Problems in the Comprehensive School* (Cardiff: Faculty of Education, University College).

VISSER, J. (1983) 'The humanistic approach', in Upton, G. and Gobell, A. (eds) *Behaviour Problems in the Comprehensive School* (Cardiff: Faculty of Education, University College).

WELTON, J. (1985) 'Schools and a Multi-professional Approach to Welfare' in Peter Ribbons (ed) *Schooling and Welfare* (London: Falmer Press).

WOODCOCK, M. and FRANCES, D. (1981) 'The nine building blocks of team effectiveness' in Woodcock, M. and Francis, D. (eds) *Organisational Development through Team-Building* (Aldershot: Gower).

WORSTER, A. D. and BIRD, E. G. E. (1980) 'Social skills training in a pastoral care group', in Upton, G. and Gobell, A. (eds) *Behaviour Problems in the Comprehensive School* (Cardiff: Faculty of Education, University College).

PART II
THEORY AND PRACTICE IN CLASSROOMS

An association between learning and behaviour problems has frequently been reported in research studies. In Chapter 3 Hanne Lambley discusses the complex relationship between these two types of problems. She undertakes a review of research in this field, including an examination of educational practices which offer a framework for intervention. With the latter point in mind she argues for a balanced approach for assessment and provision in school. The chapter concludes with an observation plan to provide data for appropriate provision for pupils' needs.

John and Patricia Davies argue in Chapter 4 that while short-term strategies are invaluable for teachers working with children exhibiting behavioural problems, these alone are often not enough. Many of the sound principles of good classroom teaching are based on the assumption that the children will be emotionally mature enough to benefit from them. In practice, most class groups are comprised of children at different stages of emotional development, and many of the overt behaviours expressed by these children will be indicative of the stage of development at which they are functioning. It is futile, the authors suggest, to make unrealistic demands on children – yet, unless we begin to interpret overt behaviour in a meaningful way, this is precisely what we are likely to be doing. The work of both Erikson and Hewett gives clear guidance, it is argued, for a more appropriate approach for teachers' practice when working with children at different stages of emotional development. Additionally, successful practice can be enhanced by the consideration and development of two other factors – deploying these strategies within a whole-school context, and incorporating parental participation in the process throughout. All these are problematic issues, but the authors believe that if difficulties are to be realistically faced, these factors must be addressed.

66 *Managing Misbehaviour*

In the introduction to Chapter 5 John Presland asserts that behavioural approaches are interpreted as arising from a combination of behavioural and humanistic views of behaviour. He describes a sequence of stages during which problem behaviours are defined and measured, and intervention programmes are planned, administered and evaluated. Programmes are described for a primary and secondary school pupil. Towards the end of the chapter the range and scope of behaviour approaches are discussed and methods of training outlined.

Chapter 3

Learning and Behaviour Problems

Hanne Lambley

Towards a definition of concepts

Concern for pupils' learning has by definition always been at the heart of education. As the education system has developed, consideration for those individuals who showed problems with learning increasingly became a priority. Gradually a segregated sector of special education emerged to provide an appropriate education service for a small identified proportion (2 per cent) of handicapped pupils. Recent developments expressed in a government report (DES, 1978) and legislation (Education Act, 1981) have led to a widening of special education by introducing the concept of special educational needs, and abolishing existing categories of handicap. The new concept of special educational needs relates now to all pupils already in special schools (2 per cent) together with those encountering significant difficulty with learning (approximately 18 per cent) in ordinary schools. This new statutory framework removes special education from its former isolation and establishes it as a central concern of *all* teachers and *all* schools. It also presents teachers in mainstream schools with an obligation to plan and implement learning programmes suitable for individual pupils with special educational needs.

The Warnock Committee (DES, 1978) suggested a continuation of the use of certain existing terms of disability to identify particular groups of children who require special educational provision. Additional to descriptions for physical/sensory disabilities and maladjustment, the term 'children with learning difficulties' has been retained, for children who were previously categorised as educationally sub-normal and for those with educational difficulties who are often the concern of remedial services.

There is considerable variation in, and some confusion about, the definition of the concept of 'learning difficulty' as an umbrella term. Over the years children with learning difficulties have been described as educationally retarded, slow learners, remedial, dyslexic, minimally brain-damaged, and perceptually handicapped. The 1981 Education Act has not resolved the confusion by stating that 'a child has "special educational needs" if he has a learning difficulty' (1.1.). A DES circular (8/81) enunciates further that:

> 'learning difficulty' is defined to include not only physical and mental disabilities but any type of learning difficulty experienced by a child provided that it is significantly greater than that of the majority of children of the same age. (4, p. 2).

Amongst professionals the term 'learning difficulty' is used in a descriptive manner, as suggested by the Warnock Committee, and the ensuing discussion is based on the same understanding. It is clear that definitions of educational concepts are very strongly dependent upon provisions; 'Definitions are not truth; they merely set up the conditions under which particular actions are to be taken' (Farnham-Diggory, 1978, p. 16).

Learning difficulties were orginally believed to be organic in origin and interpreted in terms of causes centred *within the child*. Recent thinking has abandoned the theory of internal deficiency by placing learning difficulties *within the context of the environment* in which the child lives and learns.

Bloom (1976) developed a model for school learning which identifies three major influences on pupil performance:

- cognitive entry behaviour (thinking);
- affective entry characteristics (feelings and attitudes);
- quality of instruction (teaching).

He states that the manipulation of these three components can reduce the individual differences which lead to variation in school achievement. In schools it is 'part and parcel' of teachers' responsibilities to help ensure that the above variables are manipulated so as to optimise pupils' learning and behaviour performances. A failure to do so may mean that a pupil encounters learning or/and behaviour problems.

There still exists considerable uncertainty and controversy regarding the causes of learning difficulties but it is now well established that many children with learning difficulties suffer from associated emotional or behavioural problems. Difficulties in the affective area range from severe maladjustment to slight emotional problems (for example minor anxieties or a low self-concept). Their main characteristic, however, is that they *may* constitute an emotional blockage to successful learning.

The concept of 'maladjustment' was introduced in the 1920s and first used in 1945. It was defined in the 'Handicapped Pupils and School Health Service Regulations' as 'emotional instability or psychological disturbance', requiring special educational treatment in order to effect personal, social or educational readjustment. The terms maladjustment, behaviour problems, emotional difficulties, conduct disorder, psychiatric disorder, disturbed behaviour and personality disorders are often used in the literature interchangeably; a practice which often creates some confusion.

As a basis for the following discussion it is therefore helpful to define learning difficulties as an 'academic achievement deficit' and behavioural problems as those 'unhealthy emotional or behavioural conditions which arise from or/and contribute to learning difficulties'.

Learning and behaviour problems – an interrelationship

The recent explosion of literature dealing with learning difficulties, and research into a range of related issues, has been stimulated by the publication of the Warnock Report in 1978 and the ensuing 1981 Education Act.

While attention had previously concentrated on the 2 per cent of the school population within special schools, studies increasingly began to consider a wider spectrum of all pupils with special educational needs in both special and ordinary schools. Swann (1985) identified an increase in children with learning difficulties and those termed maladjusted, and also detected a trend towards the segregation of these children in special schools and special classes in ordinary schools, especially in the younger primary age group. Between 1978 and 1982 he found:

> the proportion of the total population who were in special schools increased in the ESN(M), Maladjusted and ESN(S) categories by 13.5%, 10.0% and 8.5% respectively. In the Physically Handicapped category there was little or no change. (p. 7)

Similarly, 'the number of pupils in special classes rose from 13,803 to 14,502' (p. 9). This increase of numbers in special education is seen as an increase in (or recognition of) the number of children regarded as having special educational needs in ordinary schools. Swann questions whether this is a result of a greater incidence of learning difficulties *and* behaviour problems, or a decline in the tolerance of ordinary schools towards learning difficulties and behaviour problems. It is interesting to note that the major reason for referral to special school was underachievement in reading. Bayliss's (1987) report on Tizard's longitudinal studies of 250 pupils in 33 Inner London Education Authority primary schools concludes that, by the end of the top infant year, 39 per cent were identified by teachers as presenting behaviour problems such as aggression, disobedience and lack of concentration. Along similar lines Webb (1967) reports that of the 500 children who attended an infant school over a trial span of six years, 80 had shown behaviour and learning difficulties. There has been an obvious increase in this group of children with behaviour problems in the 1960s and 1970s and this trend still continues in the 1980s.

This tendency seems also to exist in other European countries. In West Germany, where children must reach a chronological age of ten years to be classed as 'behaviour disturbed', the maladjusted are (after pupils with learning difficulties) the largest group of children in special education (Bildung und Wissenschaft, 1985).

Croll and Moses (1985) in their research in ten local authorities report a 'substantial growth in provision for the maladjusted, which is still continuing' (p. 98). In their enquiry teachers were asked to place pupils in the following three major categories: learning difficulties, behavioural difficulties and health problems. While 18.8 per cent of all pupils were classed as having special educational needs, within those identified as having special educational needs those deemed to have learning difficulties formed the largest group (81.9 per cent) and behaviour problems the second largest (41.1 per cent). There was also a considerable overlap between categories. 28.1 per cent of special educational needs pupils (and 5.3 per cent of all pupils) had learning *and* behaviour problems; two-thirds of pupils with behaviour and/or health problems had learning difficulties.

Although learning difficulties may be present without behaviour problems, and behaviour problems may be shown separately, they often coexist and there may be strong links, in particular, between reading difficulties and behaviour problems. Devereux (1982) interprets learning as an integral part of behaviour within the child's natural development. In discussing the early experiences of young children she explains that they register new information and then respond to it. So, she claims, 'experiences change their behaviour and these more-or-less permanent changes in behaviour are called learning. The rate, the amount and the style of learning vary from child to child' (p. 5).

The association between learning difficulties and behaviour problems was an important element of the Isle of Wight study (Rutter *et al.*, 1975) which established that 40 per cent of pupils with anti-social behaviour also had severe reading problems. Studies in the USA have also recognised the association of behaviour with learning success or failure. Lindsay's (1983) findings were that children with more behavioural problems also tended to be children who used less mature learning strategies, and Epstein (1985) revealed a strong pattern of behaviour difficulties amongst learning-disabled boys and girls aged 6–18. In January 1986, *The Journal of Learning Disabilities* published an analysis of parents' reports which stated that parents of pupils with learning problems observed more behaviour problems in their children than normative samples of parents. Similar results were reported by McConaughy (1986) in her work with parents and learning-disabled boys aged 12–16. Evidence from research clearly suggests that a considerable number of children suffer from *both* behaviour difficulties and an apparent inability to learn successfully. While it is not always clear whether the behaviour problem is a cause of, or a reaction to, the learning difficulties, findings consistently point to a strong relationship between the two variables.

Children's emotional and cognitive performance

Any teacher of children with behaviour and learning difficulties will be able to describe their lack of attention and motivation, as well as their possible anxiety, distractibility and aggressiveness. It is no new observation that these characteristics are concomitants of both behaviour and learning difficulties, and an insight into their existence will help illuminate the principles underlying their influence.

Croll and Moses (1985) analysed pupils' activities in class and suggest a 'slow learner behaviour pattern' (p. 126) which is characterised by children with learning difficulties and behaviour problems spending more time distracted and fidgeting than other pupils. The amount of fidgeting was double that of the control group. Interestingly, the distraction does not always involve interaction with other pupils but can consist of 'solitary distraction'. With less time spent on curriculum tasks, this often leads, understandably, to underachievement. Hunter (1982) suggests a matrix framework for teachers to diagnose inappropriate learning strategies responsible for reading difficulties. Within a hierarchy of pupils' difficulties, attention problems occur more frequently than other difficulties cited (for example memory, sequencing, rhythm and context). She suggests that 'attention relates to apparent concentration difficulties, fluctuation in energy, or interest level characterised by apparent lack of motivation' (p. 148). Rutter and Yule (1972), in a comparison of poor and good readers amongst anti-social boys, state that 'over half the poor readers (52.9%) showed very poor concentration compared with only 13.6% of the good readers' (p. 104).

Other studies report high anxiety levels and very low motivation in low achievers (Cullinam, 1981; Treiber and Lahey, 1983). Why do underachieving pupils with behaviour problems lack attention and motivation? While it is not possible to state with precision what has caused these unfavourable attitudes towards school learning, it is widely accepted by psychologists that behaviour is determined by the world in which we live and that the outcomes of behaviour weaken or strengthen that behaviour. Our behaviour is reinforced by successful actions. The emotional concomitants of learning difficulties, therefore, could be a reaction to school failure and in turn could cause further underachievement. Gulliford (1985) contended that 'A significant feature of learning failure is that rewards may be few compared with those the successful learner obtains' (p. 29).

On the other hand, maladjustment might be caused by factors outside school which then lead to inappropriate learning. Clark (1976), through her investigation of young fluent readers, has emphasised the importance of the adult–child interaction of the young child's school-related affective development and educational success. Wilson (1984) explains the importance of an affectionate relationship with caring adults and the relevance of the caring adult's attitude towards achievement and school success.

The importance of the self-concept, expectancies and locus of control

There is a powerful connection between cognitive and emotional growth. One of the factors in affective development is the child's *self-concept*. This concept of self is fashioned by the individual's interpretation of feedback on his/her performances from significant others such as parents, peers and teachers. Feedback plays a crucial role for the child in defining his/her self-perception of ability. If the performance is satisfactory, future tasks are likely to be approached with confidence. Consequently the development of the self-concept begins with the feedback the very young child receives from parents during pre-school time and develops further from negative and positive school experiences.

It has been found that underachievers tend to have a low self-concept, which often results in lack of motivation for cognitive learning. It is important, however, to note that school achievement is influenced by cognitive ability *and* the pupil's perception of those abilities.

Related to the self-concept are pupils' *expectations* regarding their future performance. Expectations reflect the ways in which pupils predict their own performance level. This in turn depends on previous experience. *Self-expectation* is therefore learned. It is influenced by parents, teachers and others, who signal their expectations through their interaction with individuals. Research has confirmed that patterns of interaction (for example Rosenthal and Jacobsen, 1968) are shaped by adults' expectations of the child.

Children therefore develop a set of expectations regarding their future performance, predicting what they are likely, or unlikely, to be able to achieve. This attitude influences their actual performance. Chapman and Boersma (1980), in their study of 162 children, found that children with learning difficulties had developed a different set of affective characteristics in comparison with normally achieving pupils: they had a low self-concept, and low expectations of themselves for future performance. They also showed a difference in their *locus of control* beliefs.

The locus of control concept, developed from Rotter's (1966) social learning theory, refers to the way individuals feel they can control the outcome of events. A person with an internal locus of control belief perceives success or failure as a consequence of his/her own action. In the case of an external locus of control, outcomes appear unrelated to the individual's action, and beyond his/her control. Success or failure are attributed to, for example, luck, fate, chance, parents or the teacher. Locus of control beliefs are influential in determining pupils' levels of motivation and efforts. These beliefs have been found to be a useful predictor of achievement; underachievers often being externally, and successful pupils internally, orientated. If pupils believe that their own behaviour does not, but external factors do, influence academic outcomes they are likely to be unforthcoming (in terms of effort or persistence) to the point that their apparent laziness might be interpreted as dullness.

Locus of control beliefs are learned. While young children are externally oriented they usually develop towards internality with growing healthy experiences.

It has been shown that the *self-concept, self-expectation* and *locus of control beliefs* often determine pupils' responses to, and achievements in, the learning situation. The investigation of these factors has highlighted the close relationship between affective and cognitive performance.

The nature of the interrelationship – a question of aetiology?

A study of the literature, although emphasising the learning difficulty/behaviour difficulty association, also demonstrates its complexity. Some authors believe the learning difficulties to be the cause of behaviour problems, others suggest emotional problems to be responsible for educational failure. Whichever the cause or effect, once the vicious circle is started it can lead to more severe problems in both areas. The relationship is, in fact, often a reciprocal one. Although there is no consensus on the direction of the cause and effect, the nature and direction of the association are often important to educationalists when making decisions about which intervention programme to use.

Where behavioural problems follow educational failure, a remedial skills' programme may be indicated, while when emotional problems are the primary cause, psychotherapy might be more appropriate. Occasions will also arise when *both* types of intervention will be needed. Recent reports concentrate on the effectiveness of a range of different intervention strategies. Most studies have been carried out in the area of difficulties in reading achievement, this having been established as a major area of learning difficulty. Although a review of the literature presents conflicting findings, research has contributed to a greater understanding which offers a framework for shaping intervention strategies.

Learning failure as a consequence of emotional problems

The existence of emotional problems as a primary cause of academic underachievement seems obvious in Axline's (1964) moving description of the boy 'Dibs', who would neither talk nor play and was, although a highly intelligent child, judged to be mentally defective. Inside Dibs was a child 'very capable of intellectual achievement, whose abilities were dominated by his emotional disturbance' (p. 47), who found eventual help from psycho-therapeutic treatment.

The literature shows a large number of writers who hold the belief that problems in the affective domain precede difficulties in the cognitive area. This created a strong emphasis on therapeutic intervention, often to the detriment of academic programmes. The interpretations of the National Child Development Study (Davie *et al.*, 1972) suggest that emotional problems frequently existed in young children well before school failure developed. In a similar vein both McMichael (1979) and Stott (1981) share the opinion that it is 'the initial maladjustment which produced the poor learning' (p. 163). Stott's results are based upon screening for behaviour problems of 1,292 children. They were assessed for six characteristics (timidity, emotional distance, lethargy, hyperactivity, impulsiveness, hostility) on a 4-point scale; 20 per cent of children were identified as suffering from faulty learning styles. The behaviour problems of the underachievers were not greater after a three-year period of schooling, than they were prior to such instruction. Pre-instructional behaviour problems were therefore found to be predictive of later underachievement in reading. Lethargy and hyperactivity had the greatest association with poor reading performance.

The above research has implications for the early identification and resolving of inadequate learning styles in young children, since it demonstrates that early behaviour problems may interfere with cognitive processes required for successful learning. While early identification procedures have been criticised by some writers for their lack of predictive accuracy (Wedell and Lindsay, 1980) with respect to future learning failure, Pasterniki (1983) draws attention to their predictive validity for pupils who are likely to have maladjustment and learning difficulties. On a small sample of boys from a community home he discusses how the use of a simple social disadvantage index could have been used to identify them earlier. As prevention is often better than cure, the early identification of children at risk of later failure seems a commendable notion. However, as already implied, the predictive validity of many of the screening schedules which purport to do this leaves much to be desired.

Emotional problems as a consequence of learning problems

While emotional problems might be responsible for school underachievement in some pupils, it is a common observation that continuous academic failure can lead to behaviour problems. Pupils who lack success in learning often react to failure by non-involvement strategies. Their withdrawal of effort can show in various forms: total lack of motivation and retreat into dullness and laziness, avoidance strategies (such as distraction, fidgeting, daydreaming) or resistance to the learning task expressed in actions such as antagonistic and aggressive behaviour. Stott (1978) explains these as 'specific anxieties arising from unfortunate learning experiences which block cognitive processes' (p. 148).

While some anxiety can be helpful and motivating in a learning situation, excessive levels can lead to dislike of the particular subject and lowered academic performance. Robinson (1972) contends that 'Social maladjustment and even delinquency and crime have been listed as results of the failure to learn to read' (p. 114).

A number of researchers have found evidence to suggest behaviour problems result from educational failure. One of the conclusions of the Isle of Wight study (Rutter et al., 1970) was that educational underachievement can lead to maladjustment. Herbert (1974), Leach and Raybold (1977) and Carlisle (1983) also stress that maladjusted behaviour is often precipitated by difficulties in learning. Ungerleider (1985) presents a detailed case study of a pupil suffering from dyslexia and describes the growing feeling of contempt, increased school absence and growing behaviour problems. This negative affective outcome of learning failure often becomes the affective entry characteristic in a new learning situation, which makes the question of aetiology within the association difficult to answer.

Third-factor variables

Some writers suggest the concept of correlates, drawing attention to the fact that the initial cause of learning and behaviour problems may lie elsewhere outside the relationship.

One possible third factor is serious otitis media ('glue ear'), a middle ear condition which causes a conductive hearing loss and is said to affect 20 per cent of primary children. In 1974, Berman suggested that glue ear may be the cause of behaviour and learning difficulties in a significant number of children. Masters and Marsh (1978) report a relationship between learning disabilities and middle ear pathology. Developments in speech, language, cognitive and social skills depend on a child's ability to hear. For young children recurring otitis media causes delays in all these areas. Frequently the condition, which is associated with colds or allergies, is recurrent. In many cases it is also undiagnosed, since the child only suffers from the condition intermittently. A report in the *British Medical Journal* (Bax et al., 1983) points out the strong relationship between children with middle ear pathology and problems in speech, language and behaviour. Children with a history of otitis media are known to have lower attainments in reading and do less well on verbal IQ tests. Webster (1986), in a case report, argues that early temporary auditory deprivation results in the child's inability to tolerate competition, stress and frustration and thus has a negative effect upon later behaviour.

Other factors (see Chapter 1 for a more comprehensive list) possibly influencing behaviour and learning difficulties include problems in the home, such as lack of care, parents' illness, economic difficulties, divorce or separation of parents, death in the family, ethnic background, poor teaching, and poor health.

During recent years, allergic conditions, and their effect upon children's behaviour, have attracted considerable attention in medical and educational circles. It has been suggested by some researchers, and it is a widely held belief now, that some common allergens such as dairy products, artificial flavours, colours and salicylates will cause hyperactivity in some children (Crook, 1984; Adamow, 1982) which shows in restlessness, inattentiveness, distractability, low frustration tolerance and aggressiveness, all of which may lead to school failure. Diets have proved effective with some children, but also highly structured learning situations with limited time period for attention have reduced hyperactive behaviour.

Other factors identified as possible causes of behaviour and learning difficulties have been epilepsy (Dreisbach, 1982) and diabetes (Sewell, 1982). The television programme 'Q.E.D.', 'Your Child's Diet on Trial' (BBC1) on 20 January 1988 reported on two research projects where vitamin deficiency had been found to be responsible for learning and behaviour problems.

Intervention

Other research has steered away from the aetiological aspects and concentrated on *intervention strategies* for pupils with behaviour and learning difficulties. The focus is now more on educational needs and less on the causality. The findings of these investigations have much direct relevance for the classroom teacher.

Lawrence (1971, 1972, 1975, 1985) has shown how counselling can be used to improve children's reading attainment *and* personal adjustment. From interviews with poor readers he deduced that many of them had a poor self-image. They had unsatisfied emotional needs (not necessarily showing in overt symptoms of maladjustment) which prevented them from learning. To test this hypothesis, Lawrence set up four groups of twelve junior pupils with reading difficulties to examine the differential effects of three types of intervention upon their reading performance. *Group 1* received traditional remedial help, *group 2* individual counselling, *group 3* a combination of remedial help and counselling: *group 4* was a control group. After twenty weeks' intervention group 2 showed the greatest improvement in reading performance. While remedial teaching had concentrated on reading skills' development, counselling had paid attention to the child's emotional needs, by working on an improved self-image. In his study Lawrence (1978) states:

> Counsellors were asked to establish sincere relationships with each child. The 'emphasis' was on valuing the child . . . changing the child's view of himself and was achieved by giving him self-respect . . . in the company of a person who understood him and enjoyed his company. (p. 14)

He repeated his experiment with non-professional counsellors (mothers) and achieved similar results. While the majority of pupils seemed to benefit from counselling, Lawrence (1975) warns against this approach as a 'panacea for all ills', stressing that children with specific perceptual difficulties and those who are well adjusted are likely to need a different teaching approach.

In a later investigation Lawrence (1985) carried out therapeutic treatments (counselling and drama) with groups of children of different levels of self-esteem and found that the differences between treatment and results depended on the initial level of self-esteem. He emphasised the matching of treatment to each child's needs and therefore the necessity of assessing the child's self-esteem and warns that 'A therapeutic programme should be considered only after the skills approach has failed' (p. 198). One important finding, however, was that skills' teaching supported by therapeutic treatment produced greater improvement in reading, than skills teaching in isolation.

Several studies have since used a counselling approach. Cant and Spackman (1985) describe group counselling carried out by a primary school class teacher. Gains in measured self-esteem were matched by improvements in reading achievement. Counselling also resulted in a change towards pupils' increased internal locus of control beliefs, so that the pupils increasingly accepted responsibility for their success or failure. Charlton and Brown (1982) are of the opinion that the development of such internality should be an educational goal.

A number of other research enquiries have also demonstrated that counselling programmes which enhance pupils' internal locus of control beliefs can also produce gains in their reading performance. Charlton (1986) found that of the two therapeutic interventions (operant conditioning and counselling) counselling produced greater increments in pupils' internal locus of control beliefs. In another project (Charlton and Terrell, 1987), role play was used as a form of counselling. Pupils were presented with a failure setting and asked to identify and discuss behaviours which effected the failure outcomes, and then suggest – and role play – alternative behaviours which might lead to success outcomes. By encouraging pupils to practise strategies leading to success, internal beliefs were enhanced which then appeared to lead to improvements in reading achievement. Jeffreys (1986) describes how school drama improved the self-image, and motivation, of 15- and 16-year-old boys with learning difficulties and behaviour problems. Similarly, Blanton (1983) used role play and problem-solving exercises for the development of social skills and argues that social skills are essential for academic as well as social success. Research results seem to suggest that a breakdown of emotional resistance is a possible way into the vicious circle in the association between behaviour and learning difficulties and that a true remedial approach has to consider the 'whole child' and not just the development of cognitive skills in isolation (Charlton, 1986).

Implications for the teacher

For a long time the concurrent existence of learning difficulties and emotional problems in a substantial proportion of pupils has been ignored. Intervention programmes tended to be geared to one, or the other, of the two areas, usually the one which was most obvious, or disruptive, within a classroom setting for the teacher. Thus children with learning difficulties showing no overt symptoms of emotional maladjustment received remedial education, usually concentrating on skill development (for example phonics) in the area of reading. Pupils with more severe and disruptive behaviour problems would be given therapeutic treatments, often to the neglect of educational programmes.

Mary Wilson (1984) has criticised the lack of emphasis on cognitive growth in the education of maladjusted pupils and comments that 'We generally feel happier talking about aspects of care and treatment than about teaching' (p. 4). She warns that therapeutic treatment should not take precedence over academic work and stresses that 'Motivation and interest can both follow from planned success' (p. 9). Ramasut and Upton (1983) also emphasise that 'attempts to modify behaviour should not be given priority over "good teaching"' (p. 44). Conditions must be created under which successful learning takes place and success is experienced by the pupil. The focus is the teacher's ability and willingness to create a successful learning situation appropriate to the pupil's needs, and the emphasis is on a detailed and carefully structured programme based upon thorough *identification* and *assessment* of the learning difficulty. The initial diagnosis should be carried out for the purpose of teaching and therefore be mainly based upon criterion-referenced and curriculum-based assessment to determine the pupil's present level of performance in the identified area of difficulty. The teaching programme then consists of sufficiently small steps for the pupil to experience success. A behavioural objectives approach (Ainscow and Tweddle, 1979) has proved to be successful for pupils with special educational needs. Continuous assessment is part of the teaching/learning programme, which is best represented in the precision teaching model (Muncey and Williams, 1981).

DATAPAC (Daily Teaching and Assessments in Primary Age Children), developed by a group of psychologists at Birmingham University, offers teachers an example of finely sequenced behavioural objective programmes with built-in assessment in the areas of reading, handwriting, spelling and mathematics. Important for the implementation of such programmes are the choice of resources (for example variety of books at pupils' reading interest level) and allocation of time for tasks (according to identified present attention span). Research projects such as 'Reading Matters' (1986) by the Educational Publishers Council give information of a general kind and have to be complemented by assessment of individual pupils' reading interest (for example Fry's reading interest inventory in Cohen, 1978). Individual learning programmes for skill development, the manipulation of the classroom environment, and the provision of appropriate materials are important considerations which help enhance motivation. Simmons (1987) argues for a focus on appropriate 'materials, resources and teaching methods, rather than on what is wrong with children' for pupils with learning difficulties and disruptive behaviour. She rejects a deficit approach and draws attention to the 'teacher who is failing'.

Access to the mainstream curriculum

Several writers have drawn attention to the organisation of special provision for children with learning difficulties and behaviour problems since this can deny access to a mainstream curriculum (Galloway, 1985; Gipps *et al.*, 1987). Remedial groups or classes can carry the stigma associated with extraction and segregation, and can be questionable especially where it leads to isolation and labelling. Simmons (1986) draws attention to a pupil's comment that 'I hate working in a small group because I feel small and stupid', and pleads for a shift towards the involvement of *all* teachers, and support *within* the classroom. Gray and Noakes (1987) regard segregating pupils as 'taking the easy option'.

The practice of remedial groups and classes is certainly still widely used (Croll and Moses, 1985; Gipps *et al.*, 1987). A close investigation of an on-site unit for secondary pupils (Bailey and Dinham, 1987) revealed a narrow concentration of work in English and Mathematics and a lack of access to all eight areas of experience outlined by HMI (1985) in *The Curriculum from 5–16*. Not only does the organisation of such a limited and unbalanced curriculum hinder cognitive development, it may also create social stigma and lead to associated emotional difficulties. Policies and practices within the school are therefore important factors within the education of pupils with learning and behaviour problems. Numerous studies have demonstrated the strong and reciprocal relationship between behavioural and learning problems and no distinction should therefore be necessary in order to provide a separate form of provision.

Pastoral care

Several writers have drawn attention to pastoral care structures within schools (see Chapter 6) and the importance of the pastoral role in the academic progress of children. Sceeny (1987) analyses the current academic/pastoral relationship in secondary schools and suggests the existence of a territorial divide. He pleads for an integration of the two roles, and regrets that pastoral care is 'to be concerned with the control of pupils but not with their learning' (p. 67). The non-involvement of the pastoral care staff in the academic progress of pupils, which was regarded as entirely the domain of the academic team, is indicative of the situation in many schools, and approaches within classrooms. The academic staff, on the other hand, does not always accept responsibility in providing for emotional problems. A similar situation presents itself in primary schools where teachers, although aware of behavioural difficulties, do not feel they should, or are equipped to, make appropriate provision for these pupils. Croll and Moses (1985) see the reason for this neglect in the teachers' lack of knowledge of intervention techniques and the belief that problems are mainly rooted in the home.

While individual teaching and a good relationship with the special needs teacher often raises the pupil's self-concept, this approach is more incidental than intentional and systematic, and most teachers, in spite of the contrary evidence from research, believe in the sole development of cognitive skills. While special schools for maladjusted pupils have been criticised for their overemphasis on therapeutic treatment, mainstream schools receive criticism for their continued concentration on the cognitive aspects. Elias and Maher (1983) use the notion of 'learning factories' and Askew and Thomas (1987) regard this as the reason for difficulties with the reintegration of children with emotional and behavioural difficulties into ordinary schools.

An unbalanced curriculum

One of the reasons for the unbalanced provision in ordinary schools seems to be that teachers feel their lack of expertise and support in providing appropriately for pupils with learning and behaviour problems (Croll and Moses, op. cit.). In the study by Gipps *et al.* (1987) only 31 per cent of teachers had received any courses on teaching pupils with special educational needs in their initial training.

Some useful suggestions

It has been shown that group counselling, for example, is an effective method, and relatively easily acquired skill, for class teachers to use to enhance the self-esteem and internal locus of control beliefs which often seem to help to promote academic achievement. However, the asessment of the pupils' behaviour patterns is an essential prerequisite to any intervention, and should be part of a comprehensive diagnosis. Observations as suggested in Table 1 can easily be collated and present useful data for the planning of appropriate provision. In addition, a wide range of inventories and checklists for the assessment of the child's emotional state are available including:

Children's Behaviour Questionnaires,
General Self-Concept Scales,
Academic Self-Concept Scales,
Anxiety Scales,
Behaviour Problem Checklists,
Locus of Control Scales.

Assessment lies at the very core of learning and has to consider *all* possible factors, emotional, cognitive and physical, to be embracing and meaningful.

Usually assessment in school, however, is concerned with purely cognitive aspects; and then norm-referenced tests are most used to measure achievement, mainly in literacy and mathematics areas.

Meaningful assessment cannot afford to concentrate on the child's deficiencies but has to evolve from a triangular information on the child, the parents and the teacher. On this information a programme can be based. Most important for the modification of self-concept is the pupil's classroom experience. His relationship with the teacher and peers forms a source of information about the 'self'. The 'feeding' of the pupil's self-concept with positive, neutral or negative reinforcement can enhance, or block, emotional growth and academic performance.

Conclusion

Considering the high incidence of reading difficulties amongst learning difficulties and the recognised association between learning difficulties and behavioural problems, little support is given to teachers, with respect to pupils' emotional development, in the relevant literature. In the past very few books intending to give practical help to teachers have dealt with relevant affective variables, but have concentrated on such areas as perceptual problems, phonic skills and comprehension.

This separation of scholastic performance and emotional development is apparent not only in the content of the literature but also in books and journal titles (for example *Therapeutic Education*). Despite the evidence from research the emphasis is mainly on one variable. This has inherent dangers. The division of the cognitive and affective domain is also reflected in the training of teachers. Programmes for initial and in-service training of courses for 'Children with learning difficulties' and others for 'Children with emotional and behaviour problems' often demonstrate this. It is not surprising that this reinforces present educational malpractice.

One of the few titles campaigning for an integration of the emotional and academic aspects in responding to the needs of children is *Supportive Education* (1986). In this publication Bell and Best argue against 'the pastoral/academic split' and claim that 'The fact that schools can create divided systems of pastoral and academic (remedial) support is an indication of the degree to which such a division is entrenched in conventional thought and practice' (p. 24). They put forward solutions for an integrated support and concentration on assessment and emphasise the need for teacher awareness. Concern for the 'whole child' does not permit compartmentalised thinking but lies in equal consideration of the affective and cognitive domain. Only by integrating therapy and cognitive skill development into one process of education can we hope to be effective in supporting children with learning and behaviour problems and indeed all pupils.

Table 1

```
              pupil
           ↗       ↖
          /         \
         /  success  \
teacher ————→ in ←———— parent
         \  learning  /
          ↘         ↙
```

I For the teacher: Question
1. Have you identified the pupil's exact level of performance in the diagnosed areas of difficulty by assessment on a series of finely graded objectives?
    (Examples in Ainscow and Tweddle, 1979)
2. Have you gained insight into the pupil's learning and problem solving techniques by observing the pupil's strategies, as well as judging end products?
    For example What are the strategies for solving a mathematical problem or dealing with the reading of unfamiliar words (refusal to attempt, ignoring, asking for help, making a wild guess, use of phonic knowledge, guess by using context)?
3. Are you setting tasks at the appropriate level, so that success is achieved, or do you place the pupil under unnecessary pressure by setting tasks too high?
4. Do you give praise and credit for good achievements (even in small and easy tasks)?
5. Do you show a positive attitude in your comments to encourage the pupil?
6. Do you listen to the pupil and guide conversations so that the pupil has an opportunity to talk out any worries and difficulties?
7. Do you know of your pupil's interests and hobbies (choice of reading materials, topics for conversation)?

II About the pupil: Observe
1. Does the pupil have a medical condition?
    (a) vision/hearing been checked
    (b) other physical illness/allergy
    (c) on medication
2. What is the pupil's attitude to school?
3. What is the pupil's attitude to reading/maths/games etc.
    (a) at school?

(b) outside school/at home?
4 Which reading materials is he/she
   (a) reluctant to read?
   (b) willing to read?
   (c) interested to read?
5 Is the pupil:
   (a) lacking motivation
   (b) often inattentive
   (c) very quiet, withdrawn
       (with peers, with adults)
   (d) unsuccessful in most tasks set
   (e) very active, restless
   (f) attempting tasks without interest
   (g) often frustrated – disappointed about lack of success
   (h) wanting a lot of attention from the teacher
   (i) playing the class clown to draw attention.

III Symptoms which indicate possible hearing difficulty
1 Frequent lack of response when addressed in group (often interpreted as laziness or naughtiness).
2 Sudden changes in attention – times of good response change with times of no response; this recurs at frequent intervals. (Possible serious otitis media).
3 Difficulty in following oral instructions.
4 Watching and following actions of other pupils.
5 Defects in speech.
6 Frequent asking for repetition of questions or instructions.
7 Head tilted at an angle.
8 Rushing of words together.

IV About the home: Be aware
1 Are there any problems in the home?
   (a) death of parent or relation
   (b) break of up family home
   (c) financial difficulties
   (d) illness
2 Do parents take a positive and active interest in the pupil?
3 Do parents believe in the child's ability to succeed?
4 Are parental expectations
   (a) too low?
   (b) too high?
5 Are parents prepared to work with the school?

References

ADAMOW, C. L. (1982) 'The nutrition/behaviour link: A review', *Learning Disabilities: An Interdisciplinary Journal*, 1, 7, 79–92.

AINSCOW, M. and TWEDDLE, D. A. (1979) *Preventing Classroom Failure: an objectives approach* (London: John Wiley and Sons).

ASKEW, H. and THOMAS, D. (1987) 'But I wouldn't want to go back', *British Journal of Special Education*, 14, 1, 6–9.

AXLINE, V. (1964) *Dibs – In Search of Self* (London: Penguin).

BAILEY, T. and DINHAM, H. (1987) 'Establishing an on-site unit for secondary pupils who are considered to be disruptive in schools', *Support for Learning*, 2, 1, 41–7.

BAYLISS, S. (1987) 'Black girls flying high in reading and writing', *The Times Educational Supplement*, 3 April 1987, p. 14.

BAX, M., HART, H., JENKINS, S. (1983) 'The behaviour, development, and health of the young child: implications for care', *British Medical Journal*, 286 4 June 1983, pp. 1793–96.

BELL, P. and BEST, R. (1986) *Supportive Education – An integrated response to pastoral care and special needs* (Oxford: Basil Blackwell).

BERMAN, B. A. (1974) 'Hearing loss and allergic management', *Hearing and Speech News*, 72, 14–16.

BILDUNG UND WISSENSCHAFT (1985) *Das Sonderschulwesen in der Bundesrepublik Deutschland* Nr. 9–10 (W-Germany: Inter Nationes).

BLANTON, G. H. (1983) 'Social and emotional development of learningdisabled children', Paper presented at the Annual Convention of the Association for children and adults with learning disabilities (20th, Washington, February 16–19).

BLOOM, B. S. (1976) *Human Characteristics and School Learning* (Maidenhead: McGraw–Hill).

BOWER, E. M. (1981) *Early Identification of Emotionally Handicapped Children in School* (Springfield Illinois: Charles C. Thomas).

CANT, R. and SPACKMAN, P. (1985) 'Self-esteem, counselling and educational achievement', *Educational Research*, 27, 1, 68–70.

CARLISLE, J. (1983) 'Some relationships between behaviour and learning problems', *Links*, 9, 1, 10–12.

CHAPMAN, J. W. and BOERSMA, F. J. (1980) *Affective Correlates of Learning Disabilities* (Lisse Netherlands: Swets and Zeitlinger).

CHARLTON, T and JESSIMAN, J. (1986) 'Reading difficulties: effect of therapeutic interventions', *Links* 12, 1, 23–7.

CHARLTON, T. (1986) 'Differential effects of counselling and operant conditioning interventions upon children's locus of control beliefs', *Psychological Reports*, 59, 137–38.

CHARLTON, T. and BROWN, B. (1982) Locus of control and children's academic behaviours; Implications for the Special Class setting. *Links*, 7, 1, 11–15.

CHARLTON, T. and TERRELL, C. (1987) 'Enhancing internal locus of control beliefs through group counselling; *Psychological Reports*, 60, 928–30.

CLARK, M. M. (1976) *Young Fluent Readers: What Can They Teach Us?* (London: Heinemann Educational).

COHEN, L. (1978) *Educational Research in Classrooms and Schools: A Manual of Materials and Methods* (London: Harper and Row).

CROLL, P. and MOSES, D. (1985) *One In Five: The Assessment And Incidence Of Special Educational Needs* (London: Routledge and Kegan Paul).

CROOK, W. G. (1984) 'Yeast can affect behavior and learning', *Academic Therapy*, 19, 5, 517–26.

CULLINAM, D. (1981) 'School behavior problems of learning disabled and normal girls and boys', *Learning Disability Quarterly*, 4, 2, 163–69.

DAVIE, R., BUTLER, N. and GOLDSTEIN, H. (1972) *From Birth To Seven*, (Harlow: Longman).

DES (1978) *Special Educational Needs* (The Warnock Report) (London: HMSO).

DES (1981) *Education Act* (London: HMSO).

DES (1981) *Circular No 8/81 (London: HMSO)*.

DES (1985) *Curriculum 5–16* (London: HMSO).

DEVEREUX, K. (1982) *Understanding Learning Difficulties* (Milton Keynes: Open University Press).

DREISBACH, M. (1982) 'Educational intervention for children with epilepsy: a challenge for collaborative service delivery', *Journal Of Special Education*, 16, 1, 111–121.

EDUCATIONAL PUBLISHERS COUNCIL (1986) 'Reading for Pleasure: The Case for Voluntary Reading', *Books in the Curriculum*, (London: Educational Publishers Council).

ELIAS, M. J. and MAHER, C. A. (1983) 'Social and affective development of children: A programmatic perspective', *Exceptional Children*, 49, 4, 339–46.

EPSTEIN, M. (1985) 'Patterns of behaviour problems among the learning disabled', *Learning Disability Quarterly*, 8, 2, 123–29.

FARNHAM–DIGGORY, S. (1978) *Learning Disabilities* (London: Fontana/Open Books).

GALLOWAY, D. (1985) *Schools, Pupils and Special Educational Needs* (Beckenham: Croom Helm).

GIPPS, C., GROSS, H. and GOLDSTEIN, H. (1987) *Warnock's Eighteen Per Cent* (London: The Falmer Press).

GRAY, P. and NOAKES, J. (1987) 'Time to stop taking the easy option', *The Times Educational Supplement* 10 April 1987, p. 21.

GULLIFORD, R. (1985) *Teaching Children With Learning Difficulties* (Windsor: NFER–Nelson).

HERBERT, M. (1974) *Emotional Problems of Development in Children* (London: Academic Press).

HUNTER, M. (1982) 'Reading and learning difficulties: relationships and responsibilities', in Hendry, A. (ed.) *Teaching Reading – the Key Issues* (London: Heinemann Educational).

JEFFREYS, J. (1986) 'Lessons from the first world war', *British Journal of Special Education*, 13, 2, 53–5.

Journal of Learning Disabilities (1986) 19, 1, 39–45.

LAWRENCE, D. (1971) 'The effects of counselling on retarded readers', *Educational Research*, 13, 2, 119–24.

LAWRENCE, D. (1972) 'Counselling of retarded readers by non-professionals', *Educational Research*, 15, 1, 48–54.

LAWRENCE, D. (1975) 'Remedial reading and counselling', *Reading*, 9, 1, 12–17.

LAWRENCE, D. (1985) 'Improving self-esteem and reading', *Educational Research*, 27, 3, 194–99.

LEACH, D. J. and RAYBOULD, E. C. (1977) *Learning and Behaviour Difficulties in School* (Wells: Open Books).

LINDSAY, J. D. (1983) 'Paraprofessionals in learning disabilities', *Journal of Learning Disabilities*, 16, 8, 473–77.

MASTERS, L. and MARSH, G. E. (1978) 'Middle ear pathology as a factor in learning disabilities', *Journal of Learning Disabilities*, 11, 103–106.

MCCONAUGHY, S. H. (1986) 'Social competence and behavioural problems of learning disabled boys aged 12–16', *Journal of Learning Disabilities*, 19, 2, 101–106.

MCMICHAEL, P. (1979) 'The hen or the egg? Which comes first – antisocial emotional disorders or reading disability?', *British Journal of Educational Psychology*, 49, 226–38.

MITTLER, P. (1981) *The Psychological Assessment of Mental and Physical Handicaps* (London: Tavistock).

MUNCEY, J. and WILLIAMS, H. (1981) 'Daily evaluation in the classroom', *Special Education: Forward Trend*, 8, 3, 31–4.

PASTERNICKI, J. G. (1983) 'A study of involving use of a social disadvantage index', *Remedial Education*, 18, 3, 137–40.

RAMASUT, A. and UPTON, G. (1983) 'The attainments of maladjusted children', *Remedial Education*, 18, 1, 41–4.

REID, J. F. (1972) *Reading: Problems and Practices* (London: Ward Lock Educational).
ROBINSON, H. (1972) 'Emotional and personality problems of severely retarded readers', in J. F. Reid (ed.) *Reading: Problems and Practices* (London: Ward Lock Educational).
ROSENTHAL, R. and JACOBSEN, L. (1968) *Pygmalion in the Classroom* (London: Holt, Rinehart and Winston).
ROTTER, J. (1966) 'Generalised expectancies for internal versus external control of reinforcement', *Psychological Monograph*, 80, 1 (Whole No 609).
RUTTER, M. (1967) 'A children's behaviour questionnaire for completion by teachers: preliminary findings', *Journal of Child Psychology and Psychiatry* 6, 1–11.
RUTTER, M., TIZARD, J. and WHITMORE, K. (1970) *Education, Health and Behaviour* (Harlow: Longman).
RUTTER, M. and YULE, W. (1972) 'Reading retardation and antisocial behaviour – the nature of the association' in Reid, J. F. (ed) *Reading: Problems and Practices* (London: Ward Lock Educational).
RUTTER, M., COX, A., TUPLING, C., BERGER, M. and YULE, W. (1975) 'Attainment and adjustment in two geographical areas', *British Journal of Psychiatry*, 126, 493–509.
SEWELL, N. J. (1982) 'Project to explore the possibility of a connection between a family history of Diabetes Mellitus and school learning and/or behavior problems in students in Grades 1–8, *Educational Improvement Center – South* (New Jersey, US).
SCEENY, A. (1987) 'Towards the integration of the pastoral and the academic', *Pastoral Care*, February 1987, 62–7.
SIMMONS, K. (1986) 'Painful extractions', *The Times Educational Supplement*, 17 October 1986, p. 19.
SIMMONS, K. (1987) 'Withdrawal Symptoms', *The Times Educational Supplement*, 3 April 1987, p. 25.
STOTT, D. H. (1963) *The British Social Adjustment Guides* (London: University of London Press).
STOTT, D. H. (1978) *Helping Children with Learning Difficulties – A Diagnostic Teaching Approach* (London: Ward Lock Educational).
STOTT, D. H. (1981) 'Behaviour disturbance and failure to learn: A study of cause and effect', *Educational Research*, 23, 3, 163–72.
SWANN, W. (1985) 'Is the integration of children with special needs happening?: an analysis of recent statistics of pupils in special schools', *Oxford Review of Education*, 11, 1, 3–16.
TREIBER, F. A. and LAHEY, B. B. (1983) 'Toward a behavioral model of academic remediation with learning disabled children', *Journal of*

Learning Disabilities, 16, 2, 111–16.

UNGERLEIDER, D. (1985) *Reading, Writing and Rage: The Terrible Price Paid by Victims of School Failure*, (USA Ca.: B. L. Winch/Jalmar Press).

WEBB, L. (1967) *Children with Special Needs in the Infant School* (Gerrards Cross: Colin Smythe).

WEDELL, K. and LINDSAY, G. A. (1980) 'Early identification procedures: What have we learned?', *Remedial Education*, 15, 3, 130–35.

WEBSTER, A. (1986) Facing the hazards of glue ear. *Special Children*, 1, 22–3.

WILSON, M. (1984) 'Why don't they learn?: Some thoughts on the relationship between maladjustment and learning difficulties', *Maladjustment and Therapeutic Education*, 2, 2, 4–11.

Chapter 4

A Dynamic Approach to Understanding and Meeting Emotional and Behaviour Difficulties

John and Patricia Davies

Over recent years the media has echoed the concern shown by academics and teachers regarding the apparent increase in expressions of violence and disruptive behaviour in schools and classrooms. In particular, it has focused on issues relating to the role which schools play in reducing disruptive behaviour, and encouraging it (for example Galloway *et al.*, 1982).

Teacher anxiety about disruptive behaviour has been further heightened as a result of the increasing practice of integrating children who would previously have been placed in special provision for emotional and behaviourally disturbed children. Consequently this has led to a demand by teachers for in-service courses through which they may develop and refine appropriate skills to enable them to modify problematic behaviour exhibited by pupils (Potts, 1983).

Teacher interpretation and understanding of difficulty

Tomlinson (1981) has argued that, as teachers, we frequently create difficulties for ourselves as a result of inappropriate responses to the needs that children are demonstrating; and that professional concerns and vested interest that are directly a result of training, can interfere with what may be best for particular children.

This tendency is nowhere clearer than in consideration of professional responses to overt behaviour exhibited by disturbed children in formal educational settings. Frequently these behaviours are only the manifestation of underlying difficulties which cannot be understood – and from which appropriate action cannot be generated – unless the teacher can relate the behaviour to its meaningful context. By attempting to resolve the learning difficulties experienced by a child, without taking this aspect of his or her development into consideration, we are in danger of creating further difficulties for ourselves and for the child.

Initial teacher training has long been successful in alerting teachers to identify, respond and record stages of a child's development in many areas of functioning at school. What is has generally failed to do, however, is to develop in student teachers the same degree of skill in identifying and managing inappropriate behaviour. Furthermore, the focus in teacher training over recent years has moved significantly away from a deficit 'within child' search for causal factors. This has offered teachers a more positive perspective from which to respond to children exhibiting both learning and behavioural difficulties.

One of the dangers with such a focus however, is that a superficial adherence to such a policy may persuade some to avoid considering the consequences of the way emotionally disturbed children make sense of their reality. This may well distance, in the mind of the teacher, the significance of a child's emotional state from the behaviour exhibited. In practice, however, the two may well be intrinsically linked.

Difficulties in learning and behaviour are rarely entirely focused within the child. It may be more helpful to consider these in terms of the interaction between the child and his environment. In the case of children whose behaviour is perceived as a response to situations that they interpret as threatening, this may reflect emotional difficulties that have also to be taken into consideration in understanding and, thereafter, successfully responding to the problem.

A more helpful view is one that uses information that may help explain difficulties that a child is experiencing and then use this knowledge to direct a more positive, active stance on the part of the teacher in supporting the child within a classroom setting.

At both Initial and In-service sectors of teacher education, there is a need to explore ways of enabling teachers to appreciate that all behaviour is meaningful, and that it is only through appreciating what is being communicated through the behaviour that appropriate action can be taken by the teacher.

This is not to suggest that *all*, or even *most* disruptive behaviour is necessarily a product of emotional conflict. It is accepted that a wide range of factors can, and do, interact to lead to a child or group of children presenting difficulties at various times. Much of the behaviour that some children *persist* in displaying, however, may well reflect their emotional state.

STAGES OF DEVELOPMENT	AGE
Basic Trust v. Mistrust	0–18 months
Autonomy v. Shame and Doubt	18 months–4 years
Initiative v. Guilt	4 years–7 years
Industry v. Inferiority	7 years–11 years

Figure 4.1
Erikson's Model of Development

Conflicting philosophies?

There has long been a tendency for proponents of different schools of thought to expound the virtues and strengths of their own philosophy, while excluding – and often deriding – the virtues of others. Nowhere is this tendency more noticeable than in the conflict between the so-called psychodynamic and behavioural approaches. It is encouraging, therefore, to find a view that attempts to bridge this gap and which ignores the traditional ideological barriers.

Erikson (1965) has offered an explanation of emotional development which is based on psychodynamic principles. It assumes that throughout the process of normally healthy development, presenting emotional needs are appropriately and adequately met. Failure to meet these needs, however, may lead to a degree of imbalance which will subsequently create difficulty for the individual and may become manifest in disturbed, or disturbing, behaviour in the classroom, or elsewhere.

Erikson suggests that young people, who successfully negotiate the stages of development (see Figure 4.1), will reach secondary school having developed a sense of *trust, autonomy, initiative* and *industry*. Inadequate responses to specific needs may result in a child failing to acquire these skills and subsequently exhibiting a sense of *mistrust, shame* and *doubt, guilt* and *inferiority*.

This model suggests that more fortunate children, who have had their needs satisfied, will arrive at primary school competent to meet the demands made upon them by teachers and children alike – eager and able to make use of the range of stimulating opportunities offered them. Such children will be able to manage the challenges of the classroom without undue distress and to interact appropriately with their environment and peers. They will be able to make use of good classroom practice. The child will be ready to assimilate skills that help develop self-esteem and a positive attitude towards work. This, again, is not to suggest that such children will find the process painless and that they will not present various forms of behavioural difficulties at times. It does mean, however, that these problems will generally be transitory and manageable. Their less fortunate peers, on the other hand, may well present a different picture.

Children who are not emotionally integrated as a result of inadequate negotiation of the more fundamental stages of development will find themselves confronted with a wide range of demands – made by teachers in the assumption that most children entering school will have a reasonably sophisticated sense of initiative, a reasonable degree of autonomy and will be able and ready to trust those in authority, as well as having a considerable degree of trust in themselves. This lack of integration will invariably lead to frustration for teacher and child alike and can only culminate in increased problems for both, within the classroom, if the ensuing behaviour is not understood for what it really is.

This model gains added value for teachers if it is considered alongside the work of Frank Hewett (1979) who, while approaching the problem from quite a different philosophical stance, offers a similar picture. The advantage of Hewett's model, however, is that it is presented in language that is immediately relevant to teachers and immediately transferable to a teaching context.

Hewett describes a process, similar to Erikson's, by which children acquire a stable emotional state and suggests that children negotiate stages of *attention, response, order, exploration, social, mastery* and *achievement*. These readily coincide with Erikson's model (see Figure 4.2).

Here again it can be seen that an assumption is made that, for most children, the exploratory stage will have been successfully negotiated by the time they arrive at school. Similarly, that they will arrive having successfully negotiated the attention, response and order stages.

It may, therefore, not be surprising to realise that continued insistence on a child achieving in skills and areas that he has not fully mastered, will inevitably lead to increased frustration on the part of the child,

STAGES OF DEVELOPMENT		AGE
Erikson	Hewett	
Basic Trust v. Mistrust	Attention v. Response	0–18 months
Autonomy v. Shame and Doubt	Order	18 months–4 years
Initiative v. Guilt	Exploratory	4 years–7 years
Industry v. Inferiority	Social Mastery Achievement	7 years–11 years

Figure 4.2
The Erikson/Hewett Model of Development

resulting in the exhibiting of behaviour problems that may well be disturbing to both child and teacher.

By viewing overt behaviour as a cue to areas of difficulty that the child may be experiencing, the teacher can modify the direction of the teaching, and structure the environment so as to enable such children to develop within those areas that have not been successfully negotiated.

Trigger behaviours

Susan Swap (1974) has drawn together these two models and in so doing has identified 'trigger behaviours' that, if persisted in, may indicate that a child is finding difficulty at a particular stage within the hierarchy. She further offers an indication of how these can best be responded to by the teacher. Amongst those behaviours seen as significant at the *attention/response* stages are:

(a) extreme withdrawn behaviour – particularly in unfamiliar situations:
(b) difficulty in maintaining attention – particularly to learning tasks;
(c) inability to form close relationships;
(d) excessive fear of failure; and

(e) often a preoccupation with fantasy.

The value of understanding the behaviour in this light is that the teacher can subsequently take effective action. Additionally it implies that the teacher is not isolated and solely responsible, but can collaborate with parents and other professionals in resolving the difficulty.

Attention/Response: Trust v. Mistrust

Where a child is signalling a serious problem resulting from emotional needs being inadequately met at the Attention/Response or Trust v. Mistrust stage, it is possible to modify the teaching environment to positive ends. Swap argues that such children will require an environment in which safety and predictability can be assured: one in which the child can safely predict the sequence of events and be assured that they will ensue; one in which the child knows that his private area will be permanent and that his precious property will be safely available in the same place hour by hour/day by day.

A CASE IN POINT

Glenn, a nine-year-old boy was exhibiting a high degree of passive dependency. He presented as a helpless individual, unable to take initiative when confronted with a task which involved him taking direct responsibility. He generally conformed when asked to comply and rarely exhibited 'acting-out' behaviour of a disruptive nature which would quickly draw attention to himself.

He, similarly, was reluctant to seek additional guidance or support when he did not understand the task set – but did ask numerous questions when involved in an exercise that he understood and felt comfortable in negotiating.

Glenn competently negotiated work that was based on rote learning, but found difficulty in tackling a problem that required a degree of assertiveness, initiative, problem solving or logical reasoning.

A major problem for Glenn was that of establishing relationships with other children or with adults. He had a tendency to use other children while, at the same time, he was reluctant to contribute much that was positive to the situation in which he was involved. In his play he could be seen to be preoccupied with himself and the gratification that he received from this involvement, rather than being concerned with what his involvement added to the general situation.

This was further complicated by a tendency totally to disregard what might be considered as self-preservation strategies. For Glenn, free time was often a dangerous period, especially when he himself was feeling anxious and unable to share this anxiety with others. At such times he needed to be retrieved, by adults, from perilous situations that he had placed himself in – through climbing high trees or upon rooftops. Added to this he had a reputation of being 'accident prone'.

It is almost self-evident that for children expressing behaviour that shows a low degree of self-esteem competitive situations are singularly inappropriate. Indeed, competition can be seen as being positively harmful. For the teacher, therefore, a major task is to protect the child from situations in which he is expected to compete directly with other children. At the same time, the teacher will need to create situations in which she/he is confident that the child will succeed. Additionally, the teacher must be prepared to accept the effort offered by such a child and avoid criticising his/her work for being incomplete or inadequate. Negative feedback would be detrimental, in the knowledge of the fragility of the child's self-concept.

For some children, the establishment of a firm and meaningful one-to-one relationship between child and adult is fundamental – a relationship in which the child can again express infantile demands and in which he can be confident that these needs will be adequately met. This is perhaps one of the strongest arguments in support of retaining residential environments for a small minority of children, who would otherwise not be able to experience the degree of intense, and demanding, care that may be necessary.

Order: Autonomy v. Shame and Doubt

Children who have experienced difficulty at this stage of development may exhibit trigger behaviours that are particularly frustrating to busy teachers. It is as if the child's un-met need demands that he displays some kind of mastery over his environment, to convince himself (and others) that he *is* in complete control of his destiny. Consequently, he may indulge in a series of trivial rituals. In extreme, these may take the form of disruptive outbursts – often in response to minimal frustration, and may be viewed by the teacher as gross over-reaction to particular situations.

Similarly, such children may frequently show acts of destruction – particularly to their own incomplete or, what they may regard as, inadequate work. This is often used as a defence mechanism to disguise the fact that these children may find considerable difficulty in actually completing a given task. Destroying the incomplete work, while rationalising the act as the response to an inadequate piece of work, can offer the child a respectable solution and help maintain some degree of self-esteem. At the same time, it again demonstrates – in a spurious manner – that the child is in control of his destiny.

A CASE IN POINT

Andrew is an eleven-year-old boy, deceptively powerful, despite his initial frail appearance. He presents as a very charming individual, well versed in the art of deceiving adults by the use of rhetoric. He frequently uses his ability to manipulate others and, in particular, draws on his powerful use of language, together with his charm, to avoid working on tasks that the teacher has set. He is clearly a potentially able child and shows his ability outside the classroom where he frequently uses his ability in incidental problem-solving situations.

Andrew has a tendency to arrive in the classroom wearing an anorak, and finds difficulty in settling to work before drawing the hood of the anorak so that his head is completely covered. He is regarded with considerable caution by many adults, who have previously suffered at the blunt end of his temper tantrum. On such occasions he has 'exploded' in response to minor frustration. He can be observed becoming increasingly tense in a build-up to such an incident, when his face gradually loses colour.

When a task proves threatening, Andrew will often refuse to place pen to paper and revert to a characteristic pouting posture after which he frequently becomes antagonistic when things go wrong.

In response to the overt behaviour, the teacher will need to offer clear expectations to the student: expectations in terms of work to complete and of the form of behaviour expected and accepted. These expectations will need to be realistic; consequently, they must be tempered in the knowledge of what the child is expressing through these patterns of behaviour. To expect the pupil to complete work that is beyond his capability (limited though this may sometimes be), would be destructive. At the same time, a firm – but understanding – insistence on the completion of tasks is desirable. While it may seem logical that such children require clear boundaries set, to be inflexible about their application could again be counter-productive.

Exploration: Initiative v. Guilt

Much sound primary school practice is based on the assumption that children will be able to explore their environment in order to resolve a given task. Most teachers frequently set children tasks which require an investigative and problem-solving approach. Indeed, most primary school children will be able to benefit from such experiential learning.

Children who encounter problems within Hewett's Exploration stage, however, show this through a persistent refusal or inability to use the environment in the expected way. What may appear to be stubbornness on the part of the child, could well be the response to an acute anxiety about exploring the world about him. It may be far safer for such a child to maintain an unhealthy dependence on others – particularly adults – and to limit the exercising of independent initiative to a minimum.

A CASE IN POINT

Mary, an intelligent nine year old, attending a special residential school for maladjusted children, was exhibiting serious difficulty with reading. Despite intensive individual help from remedial specialists, progress was minimal. She lacked motivation in wanting to read and could not be stimulated although she was receiving imaginative and inspired teaching.

Again, despite her innate ability, she would stare aimlessly at materials presented to her, unable to involve herself constructively in using the material to advantage. She would, however, be happy to follow clear instructions as to how these could be used, when prompted by the teacher and would comply when so directed.

On the other occasions, when left alone with small animals in the school's animal house, she often exhibited a callous and cruel side of her personality. On more than one occasion, small hamsters were discovered with their legs broken. Her explanation when confronted was to explain that this *might* have happened accidentally when she was stroking the animal and finding out more about it.

Offering the child more of that which he cannot face – that is, the kind of tasks at which he is already failing, while insisting that he completes it irrespective of his difficulty – will prove futile. Swap suggests that such a child may profit better from experiences that are carefully structured by the teacher. This structure could be so designed as safely to guide the child through the task, rather than to leave him to his own, inadequate resources. This is not to over-protect the child in such a way that he is not exposed to situations that he must resolve through a series of logical stages, but rather to 'buffer' and 'sustain' him in such a way that he is taught how to arrive at satisfactory conclusions.

Social/Mastery/Achievement: Industry v. Inferiority

Again, it is frequently expected that despite initial reluctance, children will be able to interact satisfactorily with their peers shortly after entering school. Consequently, the behaviour of children who find social interaction difficult and are continually involved in aggressive interchanges with their classmates – the child who provokes disruption by teasing and constantly annoying others – often leaves teachers in a state of bewilderment. In the same way, those children who persistently withdraw from contact with others are often perceived as a major problem for teachers.

Other forms of behaviour, that are no more comprehensible when viewed out of context, include those that prompt adults to label a child who finds difficulty in sharing with others, as 'selfish' or 'spoilt'. Yet, all these forms of behaviour may well be indicative of a child who is finding difficulty at the social stage of emotional development.

Again, it is tempting for teachers to insist that children at primary school be involved in group activities – the success of which demands a high degree of social skill. Cooperative enquiry or shared project tasks are common practice in every school in Britain. Yet, many of the children on whom we make these demands are unable to cope. Little wonder that, all too often, the consequence is aggressive outbursts, or similar strategies that will result in withdrawal from the scene which induces inner conflict.

A CASE IN POINT

Mark, an eleven-year-old pupil at a village primary school, found sharing in any form, intolerable. When asked to work on a collaborative exercise, he invariably disrupted the activity to the point whereby it was not possible for the task to be completed by the group.

On other occasions he would provoke his peers by merciless jibing or physical interference. This inevitably resulted in Mark being excluded by the other children from a wide range of activities and his social isolation increased.

In addition to preventing his social development, his behaviour was seen by the teacher to be seriously hampering his progress in academic areas. Tasks which involved cooperation, and in which the children were expected to assume a collective responsibility, seemed beyond his capability.

Clues as to appropriate responses are again to be found in successfully interpreting the behaviour. Children in difficulty at this stage may well be helped by the teacher sensitively exposing the child to group projects in which his role and participation are carefully explained. The importance of the child's part in the collective enquiry may need to be made explicit, and help and support offered in achieving the end result. It may be helpful to solicit the assistance of other children in offering such support – again, in line with practice already found in many of our schools. Here again, what is being suggested is not new. It is the specific focus of the activity and its management that is being stressed.

Hewett argues that it is when a child has achieved the Mastery level of development that he is able to benefit most fully from the experiences that are commonly offered to school-age children. At this point, a major concern for the teacher will be that of encouraging the child to develop and expand his learning, while at the same time involving him in constructive self-evaluation.

Within most classrooms, we will find pupils who are at different stages of this developmental spectrum. For the teacher, the problem that looms large is that of meeting the wide range of needs exhibited and so often expressed in negative ways. There is no easy answer, but through the refinement of existing practice – viewed from this perspective – many of these difficulties can be minimised for both adult and child.

The classroom environment and learning task

The practice of grouping children according to age and/or ability has perhaps increased the assumption that children so grouped are at similar stages of emotional development. This, however, need not be the case. Once we accept that pupils – at any age – are not identical beings, that they will exhibit a wide range of fundamental needs, and individual differences, then it becomes evident that all pupils within one class group will not be able to respond equally to the same stimuli, expectations or set of provisions.

There is often an assumption that alternative provision implies special units or other segregated facilities – into which pupils who do not conform to the accepted norm of behaviour are referred on a short- or long-term basis.

This, however, has many unfortunate and undesirable consequences for pupils and teachers alike. The labelling process with all its consequences is well documented (for example Hargreaves, 1976). Pupils may resent exclusion – however humanely it is presented (Simmons, 1986). Classroom teachers will similarly be affected by the procedure and may ultimately abdicate responsibility for educating 'difficult' children. In so doing, the very structure that has been designed to help the teacher and pupil alike will begin to 'de-skill' the teacher who now sees the resolution of the child's difficulties as the responsibility of an 'expert' who has greater skills and resources than are possessed by the class teacher.

This is not to deny the necessity for special facilities designed to meet the needs of some children. On- and off-site units are successful in helping some children who require close one-to-one teaching in unthreatening situations for some of the time (Tattum, 1982).

The argument, however, is that many more children could be better catered for in the mainstream classroom, if overt behaviour were to be viewed as indicative of underlying difficulties experienced by the child, and so appropriate responses explored to meet individual needs more directly. In order that this can be achieved, close consideration has to be given to the planning of the classroom environment.

Provision has to be made to meet the wide range of emotional and learning needs that may be evident in a group of children. This will require the teacher to examine the trigger behaviours exhibited by individuals and to develop areas within the classroom that are designed specifically to respond to these in a positive and motivating way.

Reference to the range of behavioural differences identified in the Erikson/Hewett model referred to earlier will give some indication as to the kind of provision that may be desirable in mainstream classrooms. For groups of children with a range of behavioural abilities, it is unrealistic to assume a homogenous teaching and learning setting. Nor is it desirable to assume that children with emotional/behaviour difficulties will require 'special' provision at all times. What *is* necessary, is a structure that allows the teacher the flexibility to refer pupils to different areas and activities designed to meet specific needs at different times.

Attention, response and order

In practice, this may necessitate the restructuring of existing provision so that some children can occasionally be directed to areas in which visual and auditory stimuli are minimised. For children who find difficulty in attending to tasks, such an intervention may well prevent disruptive behaviour escalating while, at the same time, enable the pupil to complete work that would otherwise prove impracticable.

Much frustration, as well as resulting disruption, may be prevented if provision is made in which some children can receive closer one-to-one instruction at appropriate times. In the same way, it may be necessary to provide opportunities for others to retreat from the expectations that may be made on the majority of children within a given teaching group.

Some children whose degree of insecurity is such that they find change and unpredictability too threatening, will need to be reminded that their own parameters are constant. For such children, disruption can be minimised if they are presented with a consistent routine, both in terms of the work pattern and working environment.

Exploratory learning

It is misleading to assume that all children are able to make constructive use of an exploratory approach to learning. Children who have successfully negotiated Hewett's Exploratory stage of development, may indeed find such an approach both stimulating and rewarding. Other, less fortunate, children will find that challenge of confronting open-ended tasks absolutely threatening. It is therefore not surprising that such children will evade and retreat and that this may be interpreted as deviant and disruptive. Again, such children may well not be aware of the reason for their wayward behaviour and are dependent upon the skills of the teacher to clarify the meaning of their outbursts. Continued insistence on 'appropriate' behaviour in confronting such tasks is likely to exacerbate the difficulty.

More appropriately, such children will benefit from opportunities to explore their environment – in a way that is structured and safe. For the teacher this may mean structuring activities more finely and relating them to areas of work that are under discussion by the class as a whole. In this way, the pupil can feel reassured by the extra degree of structure and guidelines which help him towards the resolution of the set task. By so doing, the child can be immersed in rich and stimulating experiences in such a way that can prove therapeutic and satisfying.

Social learning

For those children who continue to experience difficulty at the social stage of development, the problem can be further complicated, when they are expected successfully to confront an open learning task – and to achieve this within a group situation, sharing responsibility with others through joint negotiation. Little wonder that the task is often discarded and that the process may well lead to considerable disruption.

These children can benefit from work that teaches them communication skills in small group settings. From this, small group projects can usefully develop, through which these skills can be further practised, in a setting which enables the teacher to be in control. The pupil will need to be supported through this development and appropriately structured tasks will need to be devised.

It is again worth stresssing that pupils will need a variety of responses, and that there is no one setting that can fulfil these many needs throughout the entire school day. It may therefore be necessary to provide a setting that can readily be adapted to meet these changing requirements with ease of transition. The key to achieving this is the appropriate grouping of resources that are likely to be already available in most classrooms.

A whole-school approach and parental involvement

Children with emotional problems are highly adept at manipulating their environment to meet their own demands (Dockar-Drysdale, 1968). Consequently, developing a coordinated and consistent policy within the school is particularly important if the approach outlined above is likely to be successful.

To ensure that this happens, staff will need continued support, guidance and training. The responsibility for arranging that this is made available, rests with the head of the school and his/her senior staff. This stresses the importance of the senior staff commitment to the agreed approach, without which a whole-school policy cannot effectively be achieved.

Effecting a whole-school policy, however, is a highly complex and difficult exercise, one that presently occupies the minds of enlightened headteachers through the country (Thomas and Jackson, 1985).

While the support of senior staff is imperative, this alone is not enough. The major task is how the entire staff of the school can be actively involved in the exercise so that everyone becomes firmly committed to achieving the same ends.

A useful model which offers guidelines as to how this may be achieved is presented by Grunsell (1985) by which the entire staff is involved in prioritising issues for discussion and resolving a policy that is openly democratic and professional.

The importance of close liaison between the home and the school and the way that this affects children's learning is well documented (Halsey, 1972; Tizard and Hughes, 1984; Raven, 1980). For children who also show behavioural difficulties, the development of a partnership between the school and the home is particularly important, as Kevin Jones and colleagues emphasise in Chapter 7. This is not always easy to achieve – not least because the parents who tend to be most accessible and supportive to a school are those whose children are not in difficulty. In adopting an approach which necessitates a search for the underlying meaning to overt behaviours, it becomes increasingly important that sound links are made with the home and that a two-way channel of communication is facilitated.

Over recent years there has been a strong movement gathering momentum in education which has highlighted the primacy of the family as the locus for children's learning. Many teachers have acknowledged the power of this argument and have modified attitudes to encompass this factor within their general approach to working with children in difficulty. Consequently, they have explored ways of giving positive messages to parents which validates their role within this interactive process.

A clear example of this positive outcome resulting from closer collaboration between parents and teachers is to be found in the many projects that have recorded beneficial consequences as a result of paired reading projects. Paul Widlake (1986) suggests that:

> It is probable that good results achieved through these approaches have nothing to do with technique or behaviourism. They are in fact adequately explained by the psychoanalysts Bettelheim and Zelan (1982) during an account of their own non-interventionalist procedures for helping emotionally disturbed children overcome reading difficulties. They suggest that positive attitudes promote reading because it is based on a reciprocal agreement that enhances a child's self respect around reading. Research in Salford and Leicester emphasises this positive attitude which emphasises the parent's role in ignoring the child's errors but immediately to offer a further correct model. In accepting children's misreadings, enthusiasts for this approach may have stumbled upon an important learning principle. (p. 69–71)

This principle will need to become an integral part of a school's philosophy and where staff invest thought and time in exploring a range of ways of facilitating mutual understanding and respect, then deeply rooted attitudes and anxieties can begin to be loosened. Schools which adopt a cooperative, rather than a patronising approach to this task, are likely to be more effective. Tizard and Hughes (1984) emphasise the need for the sensitive implementation of any collaborative policy and claim:

> Almost all parents respond with interest when someone knowledgable shows an individual concern for their child and points out to them aspects of her development which they had been unaware of. We can see a useful role for parent groups and for advice and information centres which respond to these needs, but none for attempts by professionals to alter the way in which parents carry out their education role. (p. 267)

It is the establishment of a policy which involves close interaction between parents and teachers on a regular, informal basis that is more likely to effect a shift in perceptions. Allied to this, is the necessity for the professionals to refine approaches so that parents will see them as helpful, friendly, approachable and available.

When parents become convinced of the value of their own contribution, feelings of helplessness, despair and guilt which may have compounded their child's feeling of failure, can be harnessed, with a profound growth in self-esteem, leading to increased responsibility and motivation. It is the dynamic interaction between parent and teacher, based on an open and professional understanding, that can generate mutual respect and enthuse initiative which can enable a growth of understanding of the child's behaviour. From this will emerge patterns of working with the child that are informed and meaningful, rooted in sound knowledge of individual differences and acknowledging the meaning underpinning the overt behaviour.

References

BETTELHEIM, B. and ZELAN, K. (1982) *On learning to read* (London: Thames and Hudson).
DOCKAR-DRYSDALE, B. (1968) *Therapy in Child Care* (London: Longman).
ERIKSON, E. H. (1965) *Childhood and Society* (Harmondsworth Penguin).
GALLOWAY, D. M., BALL, T., BLOMFIELD, D. and SEYD, R. (1982) *Schools and Disruptive Behaviour* (London: Longman).

GRUNSELL, R. (1985) *Finding Answers to Disruption* (London: Longman).
HALSEY, A. H. (1972) *Educational Priority – EPA Problems and Policies* (London: HMSO).
HARGREAVES, F. H. (1976) *Deviance in Classrooms* (London: Routledge and Kegan Paul).
HEWETT, F. H. (1979) *The Emotionally Disturbed Child in the Classroom* (Boston: Allyn and Bacon).
POTTS, P. (1983) 'Summary and Prospect in Booth, T. and Potts, P. (eds) *Integrating Special Education* (Oxford: Blackwell).
RAVEN, J. (1980) *Parents, Teachers and Children* (Sevenoaks: Hodder and Stoughton).
SIMMONS, K. (1986) 'Painful Extractions' *Times Educational Supplement*, 17 October.
SWAP, S. M. (1974) 'Disturbing Classroom Behaviour: A Developmental and Ecological View', *Exceptional Children* 41, 3.
TATTUM, D. (1982) *Disruptive Pupils in Schools and Units* (Chichester: Wiley).
TIZARD, B. and HUGHES, M. (1984) *Young Children Learning* (London: Fontana).
THOMAS, G. and JACKSON, B. (1985) 'Developing a Whole School Approach', *British Journal of Special Education*, 13, 1, 17–24.
TOMLINSON, S. (1983) 'Professionals and ESN (M) Education', in Swann, W. (ed.) *The Practice of Special Education* (Oxford: Blackwell).
WIDLAKE, P. (1986) *Reducing Educational Disadvantage* (Milton Keynes: Open University Press).

Chapter 5

Behavioural Approaches

John Presland

Behaviouristic, humanistic, behavioural?

Behavioural approaches to problem behaviour can be thought of as arising from a combination of two broad theoretical standpoints, the behaviouristic and the humanistic.

The behaviouristic standpoint

In contrast to the stance which John and Patricia Davies discuss in Chapter 4, the behaviouristic standpoint concentrates on specific observable behaviours, rather than what is going on inside people's heads. These behaviours are seen as being determined largely by the person's environment. The approach to helping overcome problem behaviour accordingly would be:

(i) to describe the problem behaviours as specifically and objectively as possible:
(ii) to draw up a plan to change the behaviours in directions felt to be more desirable.
(iii) To base this plan on knowledge and theories derived from scientific study of behaviour (mainly theories of learning) which are assumed to apply to people in general.

The original experimental work on which these approaches were based was carried out mainly with rats and pigeons, but, from the 1960s onwards, there was much work with human beings. Reviews of the early work of this kind carried out in Education are provided by Altman and Linton (1971), Hanley (1970) and O'Leary and Drabman (1971).

One of the early studies (Madsen et al., 1968) illustrates the kind of intervention with school pupils which came nearest to conforming to the label 'behaviouristic'.

Madsen's study (whose main stages are illustrated in the following chart) was with three young children in a mainstream school, one of whom was called Cliff, a boy of about seven in a class of 29 children. Cliff would sit through entire work periods fiddling with objects in his desk, talking, doing nothing, or misbehaving by bothering others and walking around the room. He had recently started hitting other children for no reason. His teacher said she was unable to motivate him into working on any task during the regular work periods, but that when kept in to do it at playtime, he would complete it quickly and accurately. The specially trained experimental observers who went into the classroom to record his behaviour for three 20-minute periods each week confirmed the teacher's observation and described a whole range of silly behaviour apparently designed to draw attention to himself. The observers had instructions to record a number of very specifically defined inappropriate behaviours, such as getting out of his seat, standing up, tapping his pencil or other object, knocking his neighbours' books off the desk, kicking, talking when not permitted, whistling, turning round or ignoring a question from his teacher.

After six periods of the observations (Figure 5.1), the teacher was asked to make a set of rules about behaviour very clear to the class, so that they knew exactly how she wanted them to behave, and to review them several times a day. Nearly two weeks later, the teacher was asked to continue this use of rules, but also systematically to ignore all misbehaviour (unless a child was being hurt). This was because commenting on misbehaviour, or even punishing it, is a form of attention and, as such, could encourage repetition of the behaviour. After a few days, the teacher was asked to continue with the rules and ignoring, but also to praise or smile at Cliff whenever he engaged in behaviour which followed the rules (such behaviour being made very specific for him by the teacher). The aim was to increase the frequency of this appropriate behaviour and, since it is difficult to behave and misbehave at the same time, also decrease the frequency of the inappropriate behaviour. After two to three weeks of this approach, there was then a return to the handling before the intervention (no rules, ignoring or praise) for a week or so, and then about a month during which rules, ignoring and praise were again systematically used.

Careful measurements were kept of the rates of inappropriate behaviour during the various experimental manipulations and the results are summarised in Figure 5.1. These indicated that:

	Action	Outcome
Week 1	Observers recorded behaviour	Misbehaviour frequent
Week 2		
Week 3	Teacher explained and reviewed rules	Misbehaviour still frequent
Week 4	Rules continued and misbehaviour ignored	Misbehaviour increased
Week 5		
Week 6	Rules and ignoring continued and smiles or praise given for following rules	Misbehaviour decreased greatly – far less than in weeks 1–3
Week 7		
Week 8	Rules, ignoring and praise discontinued	Misbehaviour increased again
Week 9		
Week 10	Rules, ignoring and praise and smiles reinstated	Misbehaviour decreased even more than in weeks 6–7
Week 11		
Week 12		

Figure 5.1

(i) the rules on their own had little effect;
(ii) ignoring the misbehaviour led to its increasing;
(iii) when these measures were accompanied by regular praise and attention for appropriate behaviour there was a striking decrease in the misbehaviour from the original (baseline) level;
(iv) when the baseline conditions were reintroduced, the rate went up again, but fell even more dramatically when the full programme was reintroduced.

Statistical tests indicated reasonable grounds for confidence that the differences were real, rather than due to 'chance'. It seemed fair to conclude that the systematic use of praise and attention as consequences of appropriate behaviours increased the rate of these behaviours, so that they took the place of the inappropriate ones (which were ignored), which thus became less frequent.

The humanistic standpoint

The humanistic standpoint places emphasis on the individual person and his 'self'. Each person has to be understood as a whole – not split into specific behaviours or other elements. He is unique and generalisations about human beings cannot be applied. The person is responsible for his behaviour – not the environment. Where there is problem behaviour, the resulting approach is:

(i) To describe the problem, not as something in itself, but in terms of its meaning to the person.
(ii) To help the individual to come to a better understanding of his 'self' and the overall direction of his life and his potential for growth.
(iii) To help the individual realise his direction and potential by his own decisions and effort, rather than overcome specific behaviours or adapt to particular environments.

The most famous of the approaches which conform most closely to the 'humanistic' pattern is the client-centred therapy of Carl Rogers (Rogers 1951, 1974). Visser (1980) gives a brief account of it, along with a number of other humanistic approaches. Rogers stresses the self and its constant striving to improve or sustain itself by moving towards greater independence or self responsibility and away from control by external forces. A well-adjusted person has a view of himself which relates satisfactorily to his view of the world. It follows that, to help somebody, it is necessary to try to see the world from his point of view. The therapist must try to develop:

(i) *Empathy* – sensitivity to the client's feelings and the ability to communicate these back to the client to show that he is understood.
(ii) *Warmth* – accepting the person and his experience as valuable, without imposing conditions or making judgements.
(iii) *Genuineness* – responding to the client sincerely, in a way that is the therapist's real self, rather than a professional façade.

In describing specific techniques, Rogers makes much of listening techniques. The client is asked to talk rather than have questions fired at him; such questions that are asked need to be open ended so that yes or no answers are not possible, and the therapist has to demonstrate interest and understanding by 'interested noises' and paraphrasing what the client says to show that it is understood. The therapist may need to talk about his own feelings and experiences in a self-revealing way to provide an example for the client. Other specific techniques are described for exploring the client's revelations and resolving problems arising from them.

It has been necessary to illustrate humanistic approaches by an application outside the classroom because there has been little in the way of clear application within it. Bratter (1977) offers an approach with this label for pupils with disciplinary problems, but the humanistic component is minor. Nevertheless, humanistic notions have influenced educational thinking about problem behaviour considerably *from outside*.

It should be realised that both 'behaviouristic' and 'humanistic' are terms standing for a family of approaches, and it is doubtful whether any living member of either family fully satisfies the criteria for either label. Intermediate positions are much more common.

The behavioural standpoint

'Behavioural' is another broad label covering a family of approaches. Recent British accounts include Cheesman and Watts (1985) and Wheldall and Merrett (1984). Behavioural approaches, as recommended by leading authorities, follow the behaviourist line in their emphasis on specific observable behaviour and its objective description, in their strong emphasis on environmental determinants of behaviour and their emphasis on scientific findings. The experimental rigour is, indeed, now commonly stepped up from a means of measuring the effects of the intervention to a part of the intervention itself. There are constant assertions that the behaviours being changed should be measured before, during and after intervention procedures, so that the effects of those procedures can be evaluated and further measures based upon the evaluation.

Behavioural approaches follow the humanistic line in a number of respects. First, there is considerable emphasis on studying each individual and the precise ways in which the individual and environment interact. Second, the specific behaviours involved can be verbal reports of thoughts and feelings, including descriptions of how the person views himself and the world. Third, the individual is encouraged to participate in decisions about the direction of change and the methods to be used and to play an active part in the activities required. His views about his 'self' and how he would like it to change will clearly be relevant here. The major influence in this development has been Bandura's Social Learning Theory (Bandura, 1977) which sees the person, his behaviour and the environment as interacting. The person plays an active role, observing which behaviours of himself and others are followed by desirable, and which by undesirable, consequences; and using this information to formulate generalisations, judges his own behaviour, develops standards of conduct, sets goals, and decides in which situations to use the behaviour concerned.

In practice in schools, behavioural approaches tend to concentrate on changing observable behaviour. This is not inevitable. Such approaches have been used to change thoughts and feelings – but not to any extent in school situations. The bias towards behaviour stems from the nature of schools. The teacher is relating to a group of pupils rather than to individuals. Each member of the group is an individual with his own needs and wishes – and so is the teacher himself. While it is important to consider the needs of an individual who is behaving in unfortunate ways, it is also important to consider other pupils. The teacher also, as an individual human being, may find his own needs and wishes thwarted by the pupil's behaviour and therefore plan to change that behaviour for his own sake.

In this complex situation, behavioural approaches may be 'humanistic' from a number of different perspectives:

(i) The pupil may wish to change. Teacher and pupil may then plan together to decide which behaviours to change, how to go about it and how to evaluate results.
(ii) The behaviour may need to be changed for the sake of other

pupils. There may then be negotiation between teacher and pupil, possibly involving other pupils too and an agreed plan may be formulated. If the negotiation fails, a teacher may feel he needs to impose an intervention.

(iii) The behaviour may need to be changed for the sake of the teacher. Again, the intervention may be either negotiated or imposed.

(iv) A teacher may believe that the behaviour needs to be changed for the individual pupil's sake but the pupil may not agree. Negotiation might still be attempted, but if this fails, an intervention may be imposed.

The basis of a behavioural intervention

Despite the varied perspectives outlined, behavioural interventions have a number of common features, and the same systematic sequence can usually be followed for their implementation. For fuller accounts of the range of possibilities, the reader is referred to Cheesman and Watts (1985) and Wheldall and Merrett (1984).

The sequence to be described is based on the *ABC analysis* or *behavioural analysis*. This starts from the assumption that a behaviour occurs because of the circumstances and events occurring around the same time. Thus, if Philip regularly hits Steven in class, it is because of events that occur shortly before the hitting, shortly after it, or both. It may be that he hits Steven when Steven accidentally knocks his arm. It is also possible that, whenever he hits Steven, other members of the class laugh and he likes this attention and so repeats the hitting either immediately or at another time. The third possibility is that the knocking precipitates the hitting *and* the laughing increases the likelihood of his responding to being poked in the same way in the future. These events are examples of three elements in what has become known as the ABC approach – *antecedents*, which make the behaviour more likely to occur, the *behaviour* itself, and the *consequences* which make it more likely to occur again. The sequence can be represented by the following diagram:

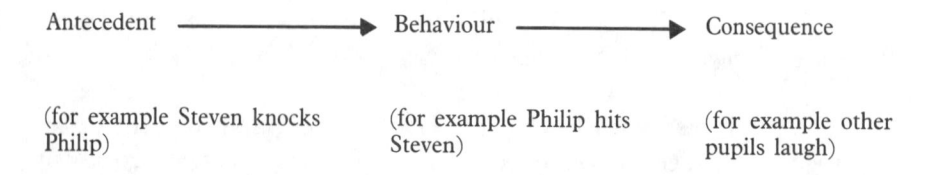

Antecedent ⟶ Behaviour ⟶ Consequence

(for example Steven knocks Philip)   (for example Philip hits Steven)   (for example other pupils laugh)

If these events occur regularly, then hitting Steven becomes an established habit, which may persist even if Philip is punished for doing it.

A behavioural approach assumes that, if a problem behaviour occurs because of particular antecedents and consequences, it can be made to occur less by changing those conditions. In Philip's case, we might change the antecedent by removing Steven to another part of the room, or we might change the consequence by persuading the class to ignore the hitting. Another approach would be to identify some behaviour that we wanted Philip to engage in other than hitting, and set up antecedents and consequences to make that habitual instead. We might, for instance, try to get Philip to continue with his work when knocked, ignoring the knocking totally. We could remind him of this at intervals as an antecedent, and praise him whenever he ignores being knocked as a consequence. If this happens regularly, ignoring being knocked might become the new habit.

The stages in a behavioural intervention

A behavioural intervention can be divided into stages based on the concepts described above. The most common sequence is as follows:

1 *Defining the problem.* A written list is made of behaviours of a particular pupil which need decreasing because they are a problem. Then a further list is written of behaviours that need to be increased. This may be because their low frequency is a problem in itself, as with a child reluctant to speak to anyone. Alternatively, it may be that we wish a particular appropriate behaviour to replace a problem behaviour. When the lists are made, priorities for change need to be established, so that we choose one, or a relatively small number of, behaviours to work on first. Behaviours should normally be described very specifically (for example Philip hits Steven), rather than in generalised terms (for example Philip is aggressive) – so that it is clear exactly what the pupil does that is a problem. Wherever possible, the pupil should be involved in these identification and definition processes. He could be asked to suggest behaviours which need to increase or decrease and contribute to the decision on which behaviours should be changed first.

2 *Measuring the problem.* It is usual to carry out some kind of observation and measuring procedure. First, this can confirm (or deny) that the problem is serious enough to justify the time and effort required to change it. Second, it provides a *baseline* with which similar measures after intervention can be compared to give

an accurate, objective demonstration of how much change has occurred. It is most usual to count the number of instances of a behaviour, but other measures are also possible; for instance, the amount of time a behaviour takes up. There is much to be said for having pupils measure their own behaviour, and this has been shown to be feasible.

3 *Determining existing antecedents and consequences for a problem behaviour.* Steps 1 and 2 have concentrated on identifying the *behaviour* element in the ABC analysis of problem behaviours. It is now necessary to carry out observations to identify the circumstances or events that occur immediately before and immediately after this behaviour. Those that occur regularly could well be antecedents and consequences promoting the behaviour and therefore need changing. Pupils could themselves contribute to identifying these influences.

4 *Deciding what changes to make in antecedents and consequences.* If antecedents and consequences promoting a problem behaviour have been identified it could be helpful to remove or minimise them, as suggested earlier for Philip hitting Steven. Sometimes, in addition or instead, new antecedents and consequences are used to decrease the behaviour – a warning of some form of punishment could be an antecedent and the punishment itself would be a consequence.

A more common practice is to work on the appropriate behaviour that has been identified for increasing. Antecedents and consequences need to be identified that will make that behaviour more likely to occur – as suggested for Philip getting on with his work instead of hitting Steven.

How, though, are these new antecedents and consequences identified? Here, it must be said that the use of antecedents in behavioural approaches is in its infancy. It is rarely described in published studies, and there are no established methods for identifying those most likely to succeed. However, some antecedents are clearly likely to be helpful. Instructions as to how to behave, and regular reminders, are obvious examples. Giving the pupil work he can succeed at, or which he enjoys, are also likely to promote appropriate behaviour. The teacher's knowledge of an individual pupil will obviously help, and the pupil could make suggestions of his own.

The most common device is the use of consequences which make appropriate behaviour more likely to occur. This process is known as *reinforcement*. The consequence which has this effect is called a *reinforcer* and the behaviour which increases is said to be *reinforced*. *Problem* behaviour can be reinforced, as Philip's hitting was by the laughter of other pupils. For a behavioural programme, however, we need to identify reinforcers that will increase *appropriate* behaviour. There are many possibilities. Most children's appropriate behaviour is reinforced by the approval and attention of adults – or, indeed, by their own success at work or in relating to others. Some children, however, are not easily motivated in these ways and, at first, will respond only to more primitive measures. Some may be influenced most by material rewards, such as a sweet, toys, trinkets, or money. Others may react best to being allowed to participate in certain actions, such as a favourite lesson or kind of work, 'free activity', popular group activities or classroom jobs. Pupils of secondary age are most likely to be influenced by prizes, free time and other privileges, good marks (which might be given for behaviour as well as for work), favourable reports and letters home and success for a team or house. Praise also means more at this stage than is commonly supposed, though it can misfire if used with some pupils in front of peers.

Perhaps the most obvious way of discovering effective reinforcers is to ask the pupil what he likes. If this is not particularly revealing, parents, friends and other teachers might be asked to make suggestions. Watching the pupil can be helpful – anything he does at all frequently when left to his own devices might be effective as a reinforcer.

When enough possibilities have been collected, they could be discussed with the pupil and an agreement reached on which could be used as 'rewards' for the behaviour required of him.

5   *Planning and implementing a programme.* From the information gathered so far, an intervention programme can be planned, preferably negotiated with the pupil. Basically, it should be designed to present systematically to the pupil a pattern of antecedents and consequences that will make problem behaviours occur less and appropriate behaviours occur more. To achieve this, it should specify:

(i)   the behaviours to be worked on;
(ii)   the antecedents and consequences selected;
(iii)   the precise ways in which the antecedents and consequences are to be used;
(iv)   when and where the programme will be carried out;
(v)   how the programme is to be introduced to the pupil;

(vi) how the pupil is to be involved in its execution.

Identifying the behaviour and selecting antecedents and consequences have already been described. How should the antecedents and consequences be used? At first, it is probably wise to use the planned antecedent whenever a particular appropriate behaviour is required or a particular problem behaviour anticipated. Similarly, an appropriate behaviour should be reinforced either every time it occurs or every time it has occurred for a pre-determined period of time (say one minute). An alternative is to reinforce the pupil every time he has *not* engaged in a problem behaviour for a pre-determined period – one is, as it were, reinforcing any kind of behaviour *other than* the defined problem behaviour. Philip, for instance, could be reinforced whenever he lasts five minutes without hitting Steven.

A commonly used device for delivering reinforcers is through a *token system*. Here, points, gummed paper stars or other 'tokens' can be the immediate reinforcers. When a pre-determined number of tokens has been won, they can be exchanged for a more meaningful reinforcer, such as being allowed to choose an activity.

Programmes do not necessarily need to be planned to operate full time. Often, they are used for a short period each day to begin with and extended to other times later if necessary.

It is usual to write down the programme planned. Sometimes, this is in the form of a contract signed by teacher and pupil. Whatever the format, the programme should then be implemented exactly as written down. Consistency is most important – even if there is no obvious change in behaviour, the programme should usually be adhered to for two or three weeks before considering changes in design.

Throughout the period of implementation, the measuring procedures carried out before the intervention programme was introduced should continue in exactly the same form, so that valid 'before and after' comparisons can be made.

6 *Further action.* The measuring procedures, combined with the teacher's and pupil's own impressions, will allow a judgement to be made on how successful the programme has been. If the behaviour has improved, the programme may well be phased out. This is best done gradually, since abandoning it suddenly is more likely to lead to the return of the problem behaviour. Antecedents and consequences are, therefore, usually faded out gradually, until eventually only those that can be seen as a part of normal existence

are left – for instance, occasional praise and privileges.

An alternative, particularly where the behaviour tackled by the programme has been the first step towards a larger change or a series of changes, is to transfer the programme to a new behaviour. This, too, can be faded out gradually when improvement has been obtained.

If the programme does not change behaviour sufficiently, then replanning is needed. Each element of the programme needs to be examined in turn and changes made which are thought likely to lead to greater effectiveness. Different antecedents or consequences may be needed, or changes may be required in the precise ways they are used, in the times of day the programme is implemented, and so on.

As with other stages, discussion and negotiation with the pupil are needed, in the hope of reaching agreed decisions.

Throughout the above stages, the pupil's involvement in planning and implementation has been constantly stressed. It is important *that this is more than lip-service*. Serious attempts must be made to discover what the pupil really thinks and wants. This may be difficult if he is reticent or feels he needs to deceive the teacher. The various skills involved in counselling, briefly introduced earlier, should be helpful in establishing the kind of relationship and forms of communication necessary to achieve these objectives. They are more fully described by Munro *et al.* (1983).

To show how the stages of implementation can operate in practice, two examples will now be described, one in a primary and one in a secondary school. Both were carried out by teachers as a result of attending a workshop organised by the author. Teachers were asked to plan and report back on a behavioural programme as part of the workshop activities.

TERRY – A PRIMARY SCHOOL PUPIL

Terry was a nine year old in a primary school class. His teacher, Miss M, reported that he was 'naughty' in so many ways that it was a 'full-time job' to write down all his misdeeds. When asked to list very specifically the behaviours she wanted to decrease, she identified the following: irritating other children by physical interference with them, talking to them and name calling; moving around the classroom at times he is supposed to be working at a desk; fidgeting and playing with things in the classroom; crossing out large amounts of work, and throwing away work; sulking when asked to do things he did not want to do; grinning insolently if reprimanded. The list of appropriate behaviours which Miss M wanted to increase was: actively working on the task given; accepting correction without fuss; remaining quiet while the teacher was addressing the class; sitting in one place for a reasonable period of time. The behaviours selected from these as priorities to work on were interfering with other children and its more appropriate alternative of remaining in his seat and working.

Miss M opted to measure Terry's behaviour during a half-hour period each morning when the class was working at Maths or English. She noted each incident of interfering with other children to find the number of such incidents per period.

No antecedents for the problem behaviour were identified, but it did appear as though consequences maintaining it included attention from other pupils – particularly their telling Miss M about his problem behaviour and retaliating when he interfered with them.

Miss M now began to think about what changes in antecedents and consequences would be helpful. First, it could be helpful to reduce the consequences thought to be reinforcing the problem behaviour. The rest of the class could, for instance, be asked to ignore it rather than reporting it to Miss M or retaliating. Second, new antecedents and consequences could be introduced to make appropriate behaviour more likely to occur. As an antecedent, Terry could be given explanations of the kinds of behaviour required of him. In determining consequences, Miss M first listed possible reinforcers. These were: praise from Miss M; showing the headteacher good work; tokens; playing a specific video game; playing Scrabble; money; and having something from a 'bootie bag'. In drawing up this list, both Terry and his parents were consulted. Terry, for instance, mentioned the video game, Scrabble and the bootie bag, and it was discovered that money was frequently used as a reward at home. Terry also asked if he could have extra Maths or Science or be allowed to read as a reward, but Miss M was doubtful about how effective this would be. From these possibilities, Miss M selected playing the video game, but decided to implement it through use of tokens.

In working out the programme, Miss M consulted both Terry and the rest of the class, and their comments contributed to its design. This was appropriate because Terry's difficult behaviour was a problem for the class as a whole, rather than just for him. Furthermore, Miss M wanted to ensure that the rest of the class understood and were involved in the programme and were keen to help with it. The final form was based on dividing the day into four sessions. During each session, Terry was to be reinforced for every ten-minute period he remained in his seat working without interfering with other children. If he was able to do this, he was to stick a star on a chart. If he gained four stars during a session, he could complete that session by playing with his video TV game with another member of the class. The other pupils were asked, as far as possible, not to retaliate if he did interfere with them, and not to tell Miss M about his behaviour until the end of the ten-minute period. When that period ended, there was a discussion with the class to establish if he had earned the star.

During the operation of the programme, there was further consultation with the class and, even though it was working well, modifications were made in response to their views. They felt that too much was expected of Terry because he was required to behave better than other members of the class. For instance, if one of the other children 'pinched' a friend's pencil for a joke they would not necessarily be punished, but if Terry did it during the programme he probably would not get his star, which they thought was a punishment. They were, therefore, involved in making a more democratic decision about whether he had earned the star or not. This change was introduced after about a week. Another change at this time was to cut down the programme to only the first three of the four daily sessions.

Measuring continued during the programme, but was implemented throughout the whole period of implementation. Strictly speaking, it should have been for half an hour per day as during the baseline, but fortunately the change did not prevent the results being helpful in evaluation. During the eight baseline measuring sessions, the number of incidents of interfering with other children per daily half-hour period ranged from 2 to 6, with an average of 4.1. During the programme, the incidence was measured per one-hour session, but, despite this longer period of opportunity to misbehave, the results over fifteen days ranged from 0 to 3, with an average of fractionally less than 1. Miss M concluded that Terry's behaviour had improved and was somewhat better even at times when the programme was not in operation. She decided to discontinue the programme to see if the improved behaviour was maintained without it. When she did this, she felt that his behaviour did deteriorate slightly, but was still better than before the programme was implemented. She felt that her relationship with Terry had improved as a result of what had happened and that the rest of the class were more understanding towards his problem.

MIKE – A SECONDARY SCHOOL PUPIL

Mike was a thirteen- year-old boy in the second year of a comprehensive school. He was in the 'remedial' band and was generally regarded as a 'pain to everybody'. Miss T taught him French for four half-hour periods per week. She identified the following behaviours to reduce: shouting out comments persistently without raising his hand when the class was working or the teacher was talking; asking silly questions to get attention; moving from his seat without permission; doing minimum work; leaving the classroom when the bell went before being dismissed; delaying the start of lessons by engaging the teacher in conversation usually designed to shock her. Behaviours Miss T wanted to increase were: putting up his hand before talking and waiting for the teacher to ask for his contribution; asking questions relevant to the lessons; staying in his seat until given permission to leave the room or borrow something from a friend; getting on with his work without delay; producing work to the best of his ability; going straight to his seat when he arrived at the lesson.

Misbehaviour in the class was not restricted to Mike, and it looked as though the behaviour of class members generally might provide antecedents which helped set off problem behaviour in others, including Mike. If one pupil talked to another when he was supposed to be working, or threw something at him, this could result in similar behaviour from the recipient. It also seemed very likely that the attention of other pupils to each individual's misbehaviour provided consequences which reinforced it. Possibly, Miss T's attending to the behaviours was also reinforcing.

Miss T began by thinking in terms of an individual programme for Mike, and she measured some of his behaviours and discussed with him the kinds of reinforcers which might be used. However, she eventually concluded that it would be better to institute a programme for the class as a whole. This was done in discussion with the class. In this discussion they made it clear that they preferred to be rewarded for good behaviour and work rather than punished for unsatisfactory work or behaviour. A system was, therefore, worked out by Miss T in consultation with the class.

The system needed to be related in a number of ways to the likely antecedents and consequences maintaining problem behaviour. Means had to be found whereby pupils did not provoke misbehaviour in each other and did not reinforce each other's misbehaviour. It was also important that Miss T did not reinforce problem behaviour with her attention. Ideally, pupils should influence each other to engage in, and reinforce each other for, appropriate behaviours, which also needed to be reinforced by Miss T's attention.

To these ends, the class was divided into two teams subjectively matched for bad and good behaviour and academic performance, trying to keep friends together, but splitting 'nuisances' who might otherwise encourage one another in their misbehaviour between the two teams. For the whole of all four periods, the pupils could win points for their team as follows:

(i) Answering questions correctly during a five-minute quiz time at the end of each period got one team point for each correct answer.
(ii) 8 out of 10 or better for work got one team point. Full marks got two team points.

Team points could also be lost for 'bad' behaviour such as talking without putting a hand up, moving from a seat without permission, distracting others, throwing things across the room and putting feet on chairs and tables. One team point was deducted for each instance. Each team started with 20 points at the beginning of the week. At the end of the week, the team with most points was deemed to have won, unless their total was under 15 points, in which case nobody had won. Each member of the winning team was given a sweet at the end of the week. Any pupil who lost three points for the team during a lesson was excluded from the game for that lesson and sent outside the room into the corridor. This device, agreed by the class as a whole, meant that the pupil was deprived of any reinforcement available within the classroom for his misbehaviour.

To relate the above programme more specifically to changes in antecedents and consequences, the system was explained as a game which would make the pupils work harder and behave better, and get recognition by Miss T and the rest of the class. Miss T tried, also, to ignore bad behaviour and simply take a team point off with the minimum of telling off.

Unfortunately, there were no measuring procedures that were particularly helpful for evaluation of this programme. Measurement of Mike's behaviour was discontinued when the programme began. During the programme Miss T kept records of the points won by each team during the first two weeks, but these were not particularly revealing. In the first week team 1 won $74\frac{1}{2}$ points and team 2 won $83\frac{1}{2}$. In the second week, team 1 won 100 points and team 2 won 60. It looked as though team 1 had improved greatly. However, team 2 gave up towards the end of the second week as they saw their chance of winning disappearing, so it is hard to say, on the basis of these records alone, whether they were improving or not. Miss T's own views, after these first two weeks of the programme, were that the class had been better behaved generally. The most marked change had been in the standard of work, which had improved greatly. Mike, in particular, had taken to the game and had been perfectly behaved and produced pleasing work. The class generally settled more quickly and was more willing to work. Oral lessons were still difficult due to interruptions, but there had been an improvement.

The programme continued for several more weeks, when the end of term came and Miss T left the school. The improved behaviour and higher standard of work was maintained during this period. The pupils modified one another's behaviour as they did not want to lose points.

Range and scope of behavioural approaches

Behavioural approaches have been used helpfully in a wide variety of educational settings. The present author has documented successful applications in primary schools (Presland, 1978a), secondary schools (Presland, 1980) and schools for pupils with adjustment problems (Presland, 1977), moderate learning difficulties (Presland, 1978b) and severe learning difficulties (Presland, 1981). Merrett (1981) has provided a more comprehensive review of the range of applications within the British education system. Access to the much more extensive literature in the United States is provided by Pikoff (1980).

Not only have behavioural approaches been found to be helpful in virtually every kind of educational situation, but they are also applicable to almost any kind of problem – learning problems, behaviour problems, and problems of personal adjustment and happiness have all been tackled by such approaches. Similar techniques have been used to influence how pupils think and feel. For our purposes here, it is safe to conclude that virtually any behaviour problem in school can be interpreted in behavioural terms and tackled by behavioural methods with a good chance of success.

Behavioural approaches are normally offered as 'packages' consisting of a number of intervention activities. The most common package for behaviour problems in schools is some variety of the scheme outlined earlier – identification of specific behaviours, measurement, identifying antecedents and consequences and implementation of a programme based on changes in these applied systematically. It is wisest to use these packages in their entirety, since these are the forms in which they have been validated. There is, however, little evidence to show that deviations lead to disaster. Even in the experimental literature, it is hard to find intervention procedures which do not either leave out, or deal with unsatisfactorily, some aspect of the relevant standard package. It will be noted that the practical illustrations provided in this chapter omit certain parts of the package described – for instance, no antecedents for problem behaviour were identified for Terry and there was no satisfactory measuring for Mike or the class to which he belonged. Despite this, both teachers felt something had been achieved. Falconer-Hall (1982) describes how behavioural principles can be used extensively and apparently successfully within the special needs department of a comprehensive school without devising rigorous individual programmes or measuring systematically. Even detaching individual elements from packages can have its value. For instance, the teacher who, as a policy, replaces constant nagging for misbehaviour with seeking out and praising appropriate behaviour is likely to gain much from it.

There are, of course, many more packages than those described here and the reader should refer to the standard works quoted earlier for relevant information.

Learning to use behavioural techniques

It should not be assumed that teachers can read an account such as is given earlier in this chapter and immediately apply behavioural methods in the classroom. As Merrett and Wheldall (1982) have demonstrated, learning *about* behavioural approaches does not necessarily lead to changes in classroom performance, though it is likely to improve attitudes towards such approaches. Recent reviews of the literature on training teachers in this area (Clayton, 1985; Merrett and Wheldall, 1984) suggest that performance is most likely to improve when teachers actually apply the techniques under some kind of supervision.

What kind of guidance and monitoring, then, do teachers need? First, we must be aware of overgeneralisation – some teachers do *read* how to do it and then apply at least *some* of the principles with apparent success. For the majority needing more than this, there are two main sources of guidance – individual and workshop based.

Individual guidance is most likely to be available from an educational psychologist visiting the school regularly, though there are other possibilities, such as a tutor at an institute of higher education running in-service courses for teachers. The most helpful approach is likely to be some initial reading to absorb the main principles and techniques, then guided observation of a pupil in the classroom along the lines followed earlier in the article, then working out a programme with the help of the adviser, implementing the programme and reporting back regularly. It is also likely to be helpful for the adviser to visit the classroom, observe the teacher in practice and provide supportive and corrective feedback – though his/her presence can make the behaviour of both teacher and pupils different from that in his absence, and this needs to be taken into account.

In a *workshop*, participants would normally engage in some reading and go through the various stages described earlier, implementing each in turn and reporting back to the workshop tutor. In the Wiltshire workshops, more fully described by Clayton (1985), for instance, there were six main sessions, one on each of the following topics: identification of problem behaviours; observation, measurement and recording; selection of reinforcers; construction of programmes; implementation of programmes; and evaluation. Each participant was asked to select a pupil to work on and then implemented the activities introduced at each session and reported back at the following session. There was also a follow-up meeting arranged some weeks after the final main session, when long-term evaluation and future planning were possible. As with the individual supervision approach, classroom visits by the tutor are an additional possibility.

Other workshop models do, however, exist. The work with Mike and Terry, for instance, emanated from a single one and a half-day workshop. Participants were sent, in advance, literature on behavioural approaches and briefing documents for identifying behaviours, measuring behaviour and selecting reinforcers. At the workshop, queries about the approaches were discussed, the data was examined and individual programmes were planned. Further reporting back and guidance were arranged at a later date – by post and through a third party. This 'light supervision' approach was thought possible because the participants all had degrees in psychology and were teaching prior to training as educational psychologists.

Yet another model, recently developed at Birmingham University, is that represented by BATPACK (Wheldall *et al.*, 1985). This is concerned with applying behavioural principles to classroom management generally, rather than to individual problems. Classroom supervision of teachers is an integral part of the approach.

Yet another model could include training in a course for a wider purpose. Chapter 9 describes, for instance, how, in Wiltshire, a full-time three-week course was organised for teachers appointed to work in a support role for schools in dealing with adjustment problems. The course included a two-day workshop on applying behavioural techniques to individual problems, and this included practice in such skills as observation and programme planning.

Behavioural approaches and classroom management

The main emphasis in this chapter has been on dealing with behaviour problems. Techniques which are successful with specific problems of behaviour, however, may well have implications for classroom management in general. These, in turn, may make it possible to prevent behaviour problems from occurring in the first place.

Application of behavioural methods has often moved towards this more general field. The case of Mike described earlier involved their use for influencing behaviour of a whole class, a phenomenon quite common in the behavioural literature. Behavioural psychologists are, moreover, beginning to apply techniques to classroom management generally – as in the BATPACK scheme already referred to, and in a set of proposals for structuring the classroom to prevent problem behaviours provided for teachers in schools for maladjusted children by Bradley and McNamara (1981). However, the evolution of overall classroom managment schemes has not yet become a major aspect of research into and practice of behavioural techniques.

The research on classroom management reported in the literature has not, for the most part, been carried out within a specifically behavioural framework. However, its findings (Emmer, 1987) suggest that many of the elements of behavioural approaches could be extremely relevant. The following are particularly notable:

1 Behavioural approaches define and specifically describe the problem behaviour and the alternative behaviours which should replace it. The classroom management research finds that the effective teacher makes clear to pupils from the start what behaviour is expected from them. Procedures and routines are established for all classroom activities and there are clear rules of conduct.
2 Behavioural approaches attempt to use antecedents and consequences systematically to influence behaviours. The effective teacher makes sure the room is arranged to allow movement without disruption and clear lines of sight for teacher and pupil. Learning tasks are carefully analysed and presented in an appropriate sequence, communication is clear and skills are demonstrated.

Behaviours that interrupt, slow down or deflect the progress of the lesson are avoided. Pupils' problems are anticipated. The consequences of behaviour are also clear. Pupils are given feedback on their work and the work itself is rewarding, as is the teacher's reaction to good work and behaviour. Inappropriate behaviours are noticed, and the teacher either ignores them where this is safe, reminds the pupil of the rules or gives a warning in a way that does not interfere with the lesson. Punishment is reserved for major misbehaviour and is used in a consistent and relevant way.

3   Behavioural approaches measure the occurrence of specific behaviours to assess the effectiveness of intervention. Though effective teachers have not been shown to do this, they do monitor behaviour carefully, moving round the classroom to see what is happening and ensuring that requirements and deadlines for work assignments are adhered to.

Behavioural approaches do, therefore, recommend a number of ways of behaving which have much in common with what effective teachers do. They therefore offer a framework within which knowledge in this area can be conceptualised, investigated and extended.

Where next?

Behavioural approaches lead to many questions being asked and issues raised, practical, philosophical and ethical. They are too numerous to be dealt with in what is basically an introductory account. The basic texts already recommended should resolve some of them and, hopefully, others will be dealt with in some training context. It is hoped that the account of these techniques given here will stimulate readers to seek such further experiences.

References

ALTMAN, K. I. and LINTON, T. E. (1971) 'Operant conditioning in the classroom setting: a review of the research', *Journal of Educational Research*, 6, 277–86.

BANDURA, A. (1977) *Social Learning Theory* (Englewood Cliffs, New Jersey: Prentice Hall).

BRADLEY, G. and MCNAMARA, E. (1981) 'The structured treatment of problem behaviour: prevention is better than cure', *Behavioural Approaches with Children*, 5, 4–12.

BRATTER, E. B. (1977) 'From discipline to responsibility training: a humanistic orientation for the school', *Psychology in the Schools*, 14, 1, 45–54.

CHEESMAN, P. L. and WATTS, P. E. (1985) *Positive Behaviour Management* (London: Croom Helm).

CLAYTON, T. (1985) 'The workshop approach to training behavioural skills', *Educational and Child Psychology*, 2, 1, 69–83.

EMMER, E. T. (1987) 'Classroom management', in Dunkin, M. J. (ed.) *International Encyclopaedia of Teaching and Teacher Education* (Oxford: Pergamon).

FALCONER-HALL, E. (1982) 'Behaviour modification in the special studies department of a comprehensive school', *Remedial Education*, 17, 3, 99–101.

HANLEY, E. M. (1970) 'Review of research involving applied behavior analysis in the classroom', *Review of Educational Research*, 40, 5, 597–625.

MADSEN, C. H., BECKER, W. C. and THOMAS, D. R. (1968) 'Rules, praise and ignoring elements of elementary classroom control', *Journal of Applied Behavior Analysis*, 1, 2, 139–150.

MERRETT, F. E. (1981) 'Studies in behaviour modification in British educational settings', *Educational Psychology*, 1, 1, 13–28.

MERRETT, F. E. and WHELDALL, K. (1982) 'Does teaching teachers about behaviour modification techniques improve their performance in the classroom?', *Journal of Education for Teaching*, 8, 67–75.

MERRETT, F. E. and WHELDALL, K. (1984) 'Training teachers to use the behavioural approach to classroom management: a review', *Educational Psychology*, 4, 3, 213–31.

MUNRO, E., MANTHEI, R. J. and SMALL, J. J. (1983) *Counselling: A Skills Approach*, second edition (Auckland: Methuen).

O'LEARY, K. D. and DRABMAN, R. (1971) 'Token reinforcement programmes in the classroom: a review', *Psychological Bulletin*, 75, 6, 379–98.

PIKOFF, H. (1980) 'Behavior modification with children: an index of reviews', *Journal of Behavior Therapy and Experimental Psychiatry*, 11, 3, 195–201.

PRESLAND, J. L. (1977) 'Behaviour modification in two schools for maladjusted children', *Therapeutic Education*, 5, 1, 26–30.

PRESLAND, J. L. (1978a) 'Behaviour modification – theory and practice', *Education 3–13*, 6, 1, 43–6.

PRESLAND, J. L. (1978b) 'Behaviour modification in Day ESN (M) Schools', *AEP Journal*, 4, 5, 33–7.

PRESLAND, J. L. (1980) 'Behaviour modification and secondary schools', in Upton, G. and Gobell, A. (eds) *Behaviour Problems in the Comprehensive School*, pp. 54–64 (Cardiff: Faculty of Education, University College).

PRESLAND, J. L. (1981) 'Behaviour modification in ESN (S) Schools', *British Psychological Society Division of Educational and Child Psychology Occasional Papers*, 5, 2, 25–32.

ROGERS, C. (1951) *Client Centred Therapy* (Boston: Constable).

ROGERS, C. (1974) *On Becoming a Person* (Boston: Constable).

VISSER, J. (1983) 'The humanistic approach', in Upton, G. (ed.) *Educating Children with Behaviour Problems* (Cardiff: University of Cardiff Press).

WHELDALL, K. and MERRETT, F. (1984) *Positive Teaching* (London: Unwin Hyman).

WHELDALL, K., MERRETT, F. and BORG, M. (1985) 'The behavioural approach to teaching package (BATPACK): an experimental evaluation', *British Journal of Educational Psychology*, 55, 1, 65–75.

PART III
CLASSROOM AND SCHOOL PRACTICES

In reviewing the part that pastoral care systems take in reducing problem behaviour the following main concepts and views are discussed by Kenneth David in Chapter 6. Pastoral care includes a wide-ranging set of arrangements, but pastoral care is also a general educational attitude; all pastoral care depends on the quality of teachers; and teachers require new skills in motivating and relating with young people, as well as academic ability. A series of critical viewpoints of the problems and faults in pastoral care are considered, pupils' needs are reviewed, and developments and changes in pastoral care are considered.

Chapter 7 examines how parents, teachers and other professionals, through a sharing of educational responsibility, can respond more effectively to problem behaviours. Kevin Jones and colleagues illustrate the value of this cooperation by providing examples of recent work with primary and secondary school children.

Kenneth David in Chapter 8 focuses upon the role of outside agencies in working with schools to help resolve or prevent behaviour problems. Consideration is given to the support which voluntary and statutory agencies can give to teachers, particularly where children's problems require time and expertise beyond that which teachers can reasonably make available.

In Chapter 9 Libby Falconer-Hall and Lawrence Harlatt describe an LEA in-service initiative to train support teachers to help secondary school colleagues working with pupils with adjustment difficulties. They describe in some detail the planning, implementation and follow-up stages of the in-service programme. While the in-service programme is biased towards the behavioural approaches it does not ignore others; and aims to inform more widely and to offer a variety of experiences.

The editors in Chapter 10 give a reminder that research enquiries strongly suggest that much of the misbehaviour in school is created, or enhanced, by 'within school' influences. They then reflect back upon the contributions in earlier chapters and, together with additions of their own, offer a checklist of guidelines for good classroom and school management practices for teachers and students to consider.

Chapter 6

Pastoral Care Practice

Kenneth David

Pastoral care

Pastoral care in schools is not new, for teaching roles in this country have traditionally included a pastoral concern. Comprehensive schools, which now contain 90 per cent of our secondary age pupils, have in recent years seen major developments in blending the academic and pastoral roles of teachers.

By pastoral care we mean the primary and secondary school systems planned to care for the personal development and individual support of pupils. In secondary schools this has included the appointment of specialist staff, sometimes including school counsellors. Pastoral care can include welfare, administrative work and pupils' records, assessment and evaluation tasks, coordinated personal and social education schemes and curricula, tutorial work, individual and group counselling, liaison with parents and other agencies concerned with pupils and their families, disciplinary matters, and leisure activities.

In reviewing the pastoral arrangements in schools one might use a checklist such as the following.

(a) What are the quality of relationships between staff, between staff and pupils, and between staff and senior management? What is the style and calibre of leadership in the school?
(b) What pastoral appointments are made and how well and clearly do they operate?
(c) What form of class tutorial arrangements are made and how effective are they? Are they understood by pupils? Are class teachers/tutors trusted? Are they effective in pastoral work? Are problem children dealt with by a team approach?
(d) Do the staff work as a team sharing varied pastoral skills? Is there

staff expertise in counselling and discussion and group work skills; in vocational education, health education and study skills; in administrative skills; and in personal and social education and form tutor or class teacher pastoral arrangements?
(e) Is there effective liaison with other agencies, and useful referral arrangements? Is misbehaviour studied rather than just reacted to?
(f) Is there an effective communication system within the school for staff and pupils?
(g) Are records and profiles of pupils well organised and valued? How involved are parents with the work of the school?
(h) What welfare arrangements are made?
(i) Is attendance of pupils good, and is discipline relaxed and effective? What continuing review is there for discipline problems?
(j) Is there academic achievement and successful learning in the school?
(k) What leisure and social education is there?
(l) Does the timetable and curriculum show a pastoral and social as well as academic attitude? Are teaching methods motivating pupils? Do teaching methods bring problems of behaviour?
(m) Which school rituals are useful and which are without value?
(n) What administrative arrangements are unnecessary?
(o) What regular evaluation of the work of the school is done?

Pastoral care is, of course, in many ways an attitude rather than a list of duties. It can equally carry over into class teaching, as successful motivation through informal teaching approaches can illustrate.

Pastoral care, therefore, permeates all that a school does, and is intended to bring order, increased learning, good diagnosis of problems and reduction of tensions; and it is continuous and preventive in intent.

While pastoral care is aimed at all children in a school, certain arrangements are specifically aimed at reducing problem behaviour. Staff will have planned a set of long-term goals and short-term objectives for problem pupils, will meet regularly to review these, and will have developed the diagnostic skills to review underachievement and to analyse problem behaviour as reviewed in this book. The morning tutorial time must be planned and positive, and illustrate the fact that every child must be very well known to at least one member of staff. So much depends, of course, on the quality of the teachers – the basic question in the effectiveness of any school's pastoral care.

The quality of teachers

The majority of teachers, in my experience of meeting many thousands over the years, are reasonable people, often anxiously committed to their work. Many can be pedestrian in their aims and imagination at times, and have the normal failings of lack of patience and fear of being seen to fail; urban living can also produce many who are under pressure, cynical and militant. A percentage of these, as with doctors and plumbers, are of low quality and are too safeguarded; every headteacher and adviser knows teachers who should not be teaching, and who succeed in producing bored and difficult pupils. Nevertheless, the majority are responsible, reasonably competent, and hurt by their reduced public esteem, and professional quality is outstanding among a large minority of teachers, often senior in position. The basic training of teachers is better, except markedly in preparation for their pastoral responsibilities; a graduate profession is evolving, and headteachers' and deputies' leadership skills are being emphasised and improved through training and better selection procedures. These leadership skills are increasingly required in a restive and beleaguered profession.

The work is demanding, for families in our society are producing pupils who are lively, less disciplined, more questioning of authority, and more difficult to motivate. The effect of school leadership of high quality cannot be overemphasised; good headteachers eventually produce good schools, and the converse is all too clear as well. Headteachers can be isolated and vulnerable, and sometimes serve too long, but when they are of strong personality and intellect then commitment in teaching, rigour in achievement, and contentment in human relationships tend to increase in their schools.

Relations with young people

New relationships are necessary with the youngsters of today, as they test their teachers' authority, humour and abilities. Confrontation seldom succeeds, a fact misunderstood by the public, and too relaxed an approach is also mistaken; Hargreaves (1975) writes of lion tamers and entertainers. Woods (1978) suggests that pupils of 'working class' background value relationships more than the intrinsic value of work, and the newer skills of teaching lie partly in making work more interesting, and partly in improving our methods and ability in facilitating relationships. These skills are the foundation of good pastoral care practice, implying not a 'soft' approach, but one which seeks enthusiastic and friendly motivation of children, a perfectly feasible aim with the majority of pupils. We want them to want their schooling. We can do this partly by good humoured, committed and interesting teaching, and partly by a planned and progressive form tutor or class teacher programme of personal and social education, which then demonstrates the school's caring ethos: this is how much problem behaviour can be reduced.

Young people are now emerging from a society which has had forty years of confused decline, and they see a confused and apparently threatening future, have shorter and different family traditions and memories, and belong totally to their demanding present and their strengthened peer groups. They see a traditional and ageing society around them, and have no knowledge of anything other than a welfare state. To educate them for their future we need now to change many educational approaches, and good pastoral care practice underlies the changes which preparation for the third millenium appears to require. 'Human capital is the most important resource of post-industrial societies' Stonier (1983) reminds us, and, 'A massively expanded education system to provide not only training and information on how to make a living, but *also on how to live*' is suggested.

Selected critical viewpoints

(a) A fault of pastoral care practice is that it is still seen in some schools as being concerned only with control and mundane welfare, rather than being seen as a developmental system in its own right, a system and an attitude which is concerned with the all-round education of a child. Twenty years of comprehensive education, of pastoral care developments, of extensive in-service training, and a plethora of literature should have clarified this point, but there are still failures. Such failures can be caused by unimaginative or cynical leadership in schools, and partly by a continuing well-intentioned view of pastoral care as 'doing some good'. Hamblin (1981) writes of hard working, but ineffective, teachers providing 'emotional first aid . . . as the equivalent of a social worker or welfare officer' (p. 3).

To be of any real value pastoral care should be demanding, practical and positive. It demands objectives, clear forward planning, rigorous evaluation, and the best teachers; then academic achievement and better standards can build on the right foundations. Hamblin (1983) comments, 'Guidance . . . becomes self defeating or ineffective unless we scan continuously and monitor the implications of what is offered' (p. 4), and, '... poor pastoral care reflects a malaise in other aspects of teaching' (p. 3). The need for school based in-service training is clear, with priority of emphasis on the relationship between pastoral and academic aims.

(b) Disruptive pupils exist in schools and appear to have increased in numbers. Galloway (1982) points out that there can be a question as to whether more suspensions have been identified officially or more have actually occurred. There is, he says, less fear of the system by pupils, more are willing to risk disruption, and violence and dissent are more legitimised. Not all schools are affected: *Aspects of Secondary Education in England* (1979) states, 'The majority of schools reported they had no disruptive pupils ... 36% said they had some ...' (11.3.7). HMI continue, '... poor behaviour and discourtesy being more frequently associated with schools serving inner city areas' (9.3.26).

Disruption can, of course, be caused by poor teachers, dull teaching, ugly settings and urban pressures. Sadly, a report on a survey of science teaching in London Schools (*The Times*, 21 March 1987) notes that inspectors reported that 15 per cent of 200 science lessons were good, 30 per cent satisfactory, 40 per cent unsatisfactory, and the rest unrelievedly bad. This makes disruption likely, and almost reasonable.

In some desperation schools turn to suspension and attempt expulsion, but these are ineffective measures of disapproval rather than any cure for disruptive behaviour. Other schools use withdrawal units. While putting disruptive or difficult pupils aside in such units is often an admission of failure, in that class teachers are stating they cannot interest, motivate and control their pupils, such units can be necessary and helpful. With good teachers in charge (one of the best units I have seen was run by a very patient and very large teacher!), withdrawal units can be useful for arranging appropriate work, fresh motivation, and useful cooling-off periods. It would be better still if such units, imaginatively staffed, could be part of a 'development unit'. A variety of special educational needs teaching could be done, counselling and group work developed, coaching carried out with pupils returning after absence, difficult pupils given a different setting and approach, sometimes with 'personal tutor' attachments from among the staff, and even extra tutoring of gifted children developed.

Ill discipline has always existed and can best be controlled by in-school methods, providing there is adequate and efficient staffing, local authority support, adequate liaison with other agencies and parents and occasional exclusion for a very limited number of violent, perhaps mentally and emotionally distressed pupils. There is a case also for occasional early leaving, before the statutory leaving age, for a few exceptional cases, with certain obvious safeguards, and with the potential for education continuing later.

(c) Pastoral care can be condescending at times in underestimating pupils' potential for sensitivity and maturity. Childishness is common, but children live in families in their communities and can be old beyond their years. Teachers need to be aware of the continuum from innocence to sophistication, from naivety to an intimate knowledge of family life and adult behaviour, in every class. Peter Lange (1983) discusses pupils' comments on pastoral care procedures, and says, 'Some pupils possessed a very high level of understanding, in some cases as good or maybe better than that of many teachers' (p. 167). Pupils can have accurate perceptions, and a resentment at being 'talked down to'.

In classroom teaching and in pastoral arrangements we can thus underestimate pupils' potential for cooperation. Planned and thoughtful informal teaching methods can change the motivation of pupils, and reduce the proportion of bored and difficult children. An element of insecurity and even occasional fear can underlie teachers' attitudes to their pupils, and the young can be labelled as immature, unresponsive and difficult, to conceal our nervousness at being challenged. Teaching can be about risk taking in teaching methods, and once pupils glimpse relaxed sincerity in their teachers, as well as strength, then ill discipline lessens. The problem remains for many headteachers as to how best to manage the work of weaker teachers.

(d) Part of that belief in pupils can be used in teaching them how to use the school's systems. We need to explain exactly what the tutorial and other pastoral arrangements are planned to do, and should discuss the school's successes and failures as much as possible, instead of distancing ourselves and presuming it is 'our' school rather than 'theirs'. We can also teach pupils how best to use the welfare state, teaching responsibilities as well as rights, of course, for considerable and continuing ignorance exists.

Liaison with other agencies concerned with children can be better developed by schools. Schools could be a central point for the family work of such agencies, which are also the referral points for the school when teachers reach the limits of their competence in counselling cases. There should be a constantly renewed network between schools and the agencies discussed in Chapter 8 and elsewhere (BAC, 1984), and such contacts can be shared with pupils to some degree, particularly in their 'interviewing' visitors to the school. We have to avoid an overkill in the use of the welfare state, such as the generous Danish state welfare perhaps involves, but better knowledge of the support the state offers could reduce many problems.

Wetton (1982) writes of the school having a central position in inter-service attachments and multi-professional in-service training. Too much inter-agency cooperation is developed accidentally and incrementally, sometimes with a political background, instead of an emphasis on children's needs rather than the safeguarding of the system itself.

(e) One view of the way pastoral work is developing in secondary schools could depress us, and is expressed in an article about the opinions of French visiting teachers (Mille, 1987).

> Lessons start very punctually in France, whereas here . . . . .

> The tutorial period is bedlam for the form teachers. It is a ridiculous opportunity of theoretically seeing the pupils differently, but more often than not it is the opportunity of starting the day in noisy, idle gossip.

> . . . my English colleagues conceive it as a 'playtime in the classroom'.

> Pastoral staff are only there to make excuses for their pupils.

Children's needs

We can presume on some needs, based on the evidence of counselling and child care agencies, though we can never fully explore a child's involved world of thoughts, fears, hopes and family feelings. These needs can sometimes be met through teaching, through personal or group counselling, or by class or tutorial group discussion sessions.

(a) In primary schools we shall be concerned with children's understanding of physical growth and development, with family life and emotional growth, with the expansion of relationships and friendship, and with intellectual development and the problems of learning. These needs will underlie some of our planning in pastoral care. Razzell (1969) writes of 'children at the flood' between the ages of 7 and 12, 'delightful people to live and work with . . . full of zest'. Not all are always delightful, we might think. There can, of course, be many worries and pressures on these young children, occasionally crippling in their effect, which schools ought to be able to discern and lessen, partly by school means and partly by better liaison systems with the helping agencies.

(b) Secondary pupils have similar and additional needs, which can affect learning and make teaching a burden if our pastoral concern does not bring observation, support and counselling of individuals and groups. One list of the normal problems of adolescents which has been used in in-service training with teachers, is as follows:

Puberty and adolescent status
Independence
Emotions, moods and self-control
Sexuality
Intelligence level and learning skills
Physical development, clumsiness and body image
Temporary worries and self-consciousness
Family relationships and feeling of security
Social competence and coping skills
Relationships with contemporaries
Relationships with authority
Money, jobs and career prospects

It is interesting to compare the needs and problems of early teenagers with those of the 16–19 age group. Hamblin (1983) comments, 'What is essential (with the 16–19 age group) is the process of negotiation with students and their involvement in the selection and construction of (guidance) materials' (p. 164). The same can apply with varying emphasis with younger pupils. Hamblin emphasises, 'Colleagues should be helped to see that a system of guidance has to be developed over four to six years, and that development will reflect the professional skills of staff. They may anticipate having to battle with students . . . instead of seeing that pupils can be involved as participants in designing and operating a guidance module' (p. 164). Differing methods of teaching, including more open discussion work in groups, for example, may take some years to develop fully through the school after being introduced with lower school classes to begin with.

(c) Adams (1986) reviewing Warnock (1978) reminds us that special education is about meeting individual needs, and commends as much integration of pupils with special educational needs as possible. The

Report, he points out, was criticised on certain points, the most serious being that the youth employment problem now brings the near impossibility of providing meaningful and satisfying work for such young people. Rather there should perhaps be education directed to preparing such youngsters for long-term (often lifetime) unemployment and 'leisure'.

In considering this view there are several implications for debate by the staffs of all kinds of schools. Has integration of handicapped pupils in mainstream schools worked in practice, with the resources and staffing available? Are schools, in fact, successfully dealing with the needs of the 20 per cent of children who will at some point during their school lives experience learning difficulties, and are teachers attempting new approaches? Does pastoral care simply patch and support, or does it permeate a school's approach to all pupils, particularly those with special educational needs? How far do our curriculum and assessment procedures take account of the changed concept and expectations of work in the future?

(d) In considering needs we should also reflect on the weakening of family structures in our society. There were 160 000 divorces in 1985 in England and Wales (145 000 in 1984); 23 per cent of couples divorced in 1985 had at least one partner who had been divorced before (9 per cent in 1971, 21 per cent in 1984); 19 per cent of all births are now illegitimate; about one million one-parent families in Great Britain care for some 1.6 million children (Social Trends, 1987, Family Policy Studies Centre Fact Sheet 3, NMGC Annual Report, 1986).

Teachers, whether they wish it or not, are faced with a major social and family dimension in their pupils' ability to learn, and pastoral attitudes, more professional and less intuitive and incidental, are essential if we are to educate successfully now and in the future. Linked with this is the need for coordination between academic and pastoral work in curriculum matters, to reinforce understanding of our society, of life and work in the future, and of human relationships, family life and personal values. Talking together, reading stories, knowing poetry, glimpsing the lessons of history, comprehending something of religion and music, learning the feelings of others through activities and discussions in tutorial time – the opportunities are there for teachers to influence children's attitudes, and if there is coordination and planning the influence is stronger.

Family life sets most of a primary child's perceptions of life and attitudes to relationships, to work, to imagination and feelings; but teachers are a more than marginal influence, and in some cases are a child's sole reference point in preparing for a satisfying adult life. We cannot solve all family and society problems, but we can clarify them for children, individually or in classwork, and we are capable of developing more positive attitudes instead of what is sometimes apathy or defeatism.

(e) In considering the needs of children and the resulting aims of pastoral systems, the following from *The Practical Curriculum* (Schools Council, 1981) seems useful.

> Schools have the capacity and the will to help their pupils in at least six ways:
> (i) to acquire knowledge, skills and practical abilities, and the will to use them;
> (ii) to develop qualities of mind, body, spirit, feeling and imagination;
> (iii) to appreciate human achievements in art, music, science, technology and literature:
> (iv) to acquire understanding of the social, economic and political order, and a reasoned set of attitudes, values and beliefs;
> (v) to prepare for their adult lives at home, at work, at leisure, and at large, as consumers and citizens;
> and most important of all:
> (vi) to develop a sense of self-respect, the capacity to live as independent, self-motivated adults and the ability to function as contributing members of co-operative groups.'
> (p. 15)

Later, the same paper suggests that the teaching and learning process should lead pupils towards, 'an ability to be sensitive to the needs of others in order to develop satisfactory personal relationships' (p. 16).

Osman (1973) usefully reminds us, '. . . educators must remember that their goal is to produce well adjusted, rational people who can relate and feel, not just non-linear calculating computers'. The latest debate on the core curriculum and more centralised control causes us great concern.

Developments and changes

(a) While so much of what is done in primary schools can be a lesson to some of their secondary colleagues, it has to be said that much is unplanned and intuitive in curriculum planning and in assessing children's present and future needs. 'Formal pastoral systems in primary schools are underdeveloped' was the opinion in Best et al. (1983), and David and Charlton (1987) suggest, 'The generalist primary teachers seem to have negligible initial training preparation, few in-service courses provided, little educational literature, and very little advisory interest in a more professional approach to their pastoral roles and to the Health/Personal and Social Education curriculum'.

The effects of social change on the pupils in primary schools are well known to teachers, and their hard work and care can be admirable; their resources and support are insufficient, and they deserve better initial and in-service training. Headteachers need training, advisory support, and some pressure to give more shape and purpose to pastoral care structures and liaison, and some firmer guidance in the way the curriculum can better prepare primary pupils for their personal and community lives.

There are good examples. An interesting and successful counselling and group work scheme in Devon is described here by Gillian Feest.

We start from the viewpoint that it is not enough to assume that personal and social education (PSE) with primary children just happens in the course of normal school life, and that a regular weekly slot for PSE, with a clear structure and language, better enables children to develop skills to cope with the world as they find it, and to make choices about possible change. This is a brief account of how some schools in Devon developed a way of training teachers and of working with children to provide such skills.

Teachers and then children were given encouragement and skills to:

- practise a language to express their feelings;
- express how they feel about the world as they are experiencing it, and to listen to others doing the same;
- gain insights through games and exercises into how groups work, and to become more effective group members;
- offer physical, verbal and emotional support to one another;
- engage more effectively with the world of other people outside their immediate group.

The training model for teachers was based on the work of Leslie Button (1981). The County provided funds for teachers to attend an initial ten day residential course. In this time they personally practised the work they later used with children. They engaged in experiential learning at an individual level in small groups, and in a larger training group, as well as taking the work out into their schools. They were provided with an outline programme for the following term and offered five further training days during the following academic year. They were encouraged to design their own programme as they learned new skills and methods. They were also encouraged to support each other, and if possible to visit group work sessions in each other's schools. We found, of course, that the work is most likely to succeed where the Head Teacher is supportive or actively involved, and where at least two teachers come together on the initial training and then jointly introduce the work into their school.

The children work in class groups, and they and the adults present sit in a circle, preferably in their own classroom with furniture moved aside. Instructions for activities are given as briefly as possible and children are encouraged to participate in a way appropriate for them at that time. Respect is given to all expressed views, including the view that the task might be too hard because the adult instruction was unclear or inappropriate. Attention is gained by waiting for the children to be ready to move on to another task, rather than by imposing an adult decision. All activities are carefully debriefed, both the content and the process. Children are encouraged to say how they feel and felt about the activity, and to focus on what was helpful or unhelpful for them in their own and other's behaviour.

At the beginning of the school year attention is paid to themes like 'Getting to know each other', 'What do we need to be able to work together?', 'Our environment', 'Learning to trust each other', and 'Coping with being nervous in a new class or position in the school'. As the year progresses topics might include: friendship patterns; caring for ourselves and others; authority; ourselves as seven, eight, nine year olds; how we behave as individuals, as members of a family, and as members of other groups; bullying; coping with loneliness and stress.

When group work is working well the teacher can use the session to develop what is happening in the class group as well as dealing with particular issues or problems that arise, such as accepting new members into the group, disruptive behaviour, non cooperation, action needed for change in playground behaviour, and changing patterns of family life, such as the birth of a child or the death of a grandparent.

In the schools where most of all of the children and staff have the opportunity to work in this way it appears to us that the level of trust and support is clearly heightened. This allows more efficient functioning of the school as a learning community. The schools have experienced excellent liaison with parents and the community, and out of these things a service is now developing which offers group work and counselling to children and adults.

There have been other excellent developments in such approaches as 'interviewing' visitors to primary classrooms, in the use of computers to ensure better pupil records and assessment and development in learning, and in cooperation between parents and teachers. More needs to be done, for the importance of the primary school as the foundation for the improved diagnosis of problems, as the beginning of understanding in relationships, and as the start of good health and other habits and attitudes is obvious. The commitment of the primary school world needs both a more effective pastoral approach, and improved welfare resources in skilled ancillary help.

(b) In secondary schools there have been considerable improvements in tutorial work in recent years, the sound basis of pastoral care. Blackburn (1975), Baldwin and Wells (1979–83), and Button (1981) and others have argued the case well, and much in-service work has been done in well-led schools. A daily period of contact between tutor and pupils who have progressed through the school together means that every child is well known to at least one or two of the staff, a benefit in a large school. Two or three longer periods of contact in the week, or a full weekly period, can bring planned and purposeful discussion work – the 'pastoral curriculum' of preparation for the future. Brilliant, difficult and backward pupils are passably well known to secondary staffs; good tutoring ensures that the middle group, sadly anonymous at times, are known well also. So improved tutoring systems have had many advantages: planned programmes of health education, study skills and personal development issues have had more thought; the start of the day has been more purposeful; and teachers report that they have developed better 'survival' tactics for their own enjoyment of teaching through the discovery of informal methods, and in better motivation of poorly motivated and difficult pupils.

Knowledge of the dynamics of groups and of the skills of counselling are useful to all teachers but are seldom introduced well in initial training. There is a need to further strengthen school-based in-service work in these areas, as progressive schools have often done. Such work helps to enliven and enthuse classroom teaching, increases teachers' awareness and observation of children, and makes more likely the care and attention for children with special personal or education needs. Sensitivity can be strengthened with training.

Pastoral structures are not changing much, though there are decreasing numbers of pastoral responsibility posts, often with a corresponding increase in the authority and value of the form tutors, a change that is probably inevitable with reducing school rolls and improved pastoral methods. Staff tutorial team developments, sharing colleagues' skills in group work, counselling, study skills, careers work and personal and social education, are of great value, and improved record keeping and profiling have added to the way children are valued. There have been improvements in the community use of schools in some areas, which can reduce the gulf between parents and teachers.

(c) Personal and social education includes the teaching and informal activities which are planned to enhance the development of knowledge, understanding, attitudes and behaviour, concerned with: oneself and others; social institutions, structures and organisation; and social and moral issues (David, 1982). Put more simply personal and social education includes the elements of school pastoral care and academic work that help pupils to develop as individuals and citizens. As a balance to the media presentation of today's society such coordinated curriculum work is a modest effort to combat powerful influences on pupils, and offers the only major support for families trying to help their children with moral and other attitudes. It can help also in illustrating for children disenchanted by school life, that school relevance in their personal lives is possible.

Many schools have a senior member of staff responsible for coordinating what departments do in normal academic classwork with tutorial work, developing an agenda of topics considered to be essential in preparing for adult life and work. Such an agenda can vary from school to school, and should be constructed with the cooperation of parents and pupils. All pupils, to take a random selection, need to know what others think of work, marriage, authority, childhood, morality in relationships, AIDS, and old age, perhaps? There is at last a growing realisation of the value of such whole-school curriculum approaches, and from earlier condemnation of anything other than 'get their heads down to basic subjects' authorities seem to be encouraging the development of such work. One hopes that a centralised core curriculum will not negate these developments.

(d) Hamblin (1981) reminds us, 'Schools are not only for pupils: they are for teachers who have a right to satisfaction in an arduous task' (p.

20). It is useful to remind ourselves that problems and stress are not limited to pupils. Stress affects teachers also, and an article by Freeman (1987) suggests that the group of teachers found to be most stressed was the pastoral year heads. Breakdown and stress among teachers are familiar to most headteachers and advisers, and pastoral care has an extension into counselling for teachers, as well as career and personal development advice and support. This may be of increasing importance in future, and some authorities are encouraging and training staff tutors in schools.

(e) If asked to summarise the precise ways in which pastoral care can be improved, to demonstrate its effectiveness in dealing with children's problems and problem children, the following questions might be considered by headteachers and their staffs.

(i) Does the management of the school remain remote from children and parents?
(ii) Are there progressive in-service training opportunities for all the staff, particularly in group discussion skills, in tutorial time preparation and programmes, in counselling skills, in understanding of welfare provision for pupils, and in diagnosis of and action with problem behaviour? Are problem pupils bored pupils?
(iii) Are parents welcomed and at ease in dealing with and trusting the school staff?
(iv) Is there developing and continuous liaison with other agencies caring for children and families?
(v) Is there a coordinated approach to personal and social education through both academic and pastoral work?
(vi) Is the teaching good?

We can extend these questions by noting that HMI (1979) report that the majority of secondary schools in their survey, and we might add primary schools as well, were evidently concerned that their pastoral care should:

attempt to co-ordinate consideration of the pupils' personal, social and academic development;

facilitate the development of good relationships between teachers and pupils;

try to ensure that each pupil knows and is known by a particular adult;

make available relevant information through the development of effective communication and record systems;

involve parents and outside agencies in the work of the school, where appropriate;

enable someone to respond quickly and appropriately to pupils' problems or indeed to anticipate a problem which might arise;

by these means improve the learning of pupils. (p. 219)

Improved pastoral practice

The reasons underlying the improvements in pastoral care in recent years are both idealistic and pragmatic. Idealism lies in a belief that education can be improved, and is not only about knowledge and qualifications; it is about being valued as an individual, being prepared for a changing future in which personal competencies will be demanding, and having education made more personal, purposeful and meaningful. Pragmatism requires better support and less stress for teachers with more motivated pupils, more effective control, more humanising of large institutions, and with gaining the cooperation of the disenchanted.

This chapter has attempted a personal and critical reflection on the purpose of pastoral care and on a few of its failings and values, with some attention on meeting the needs of pupils with behaviour problems. Carl Rogers (1969) wrote, 'It is the perception, not the reality, which is crucial in determining behaviour'. Introducing children to knowledge is a traditional teaching reality, but in the future we need increasingly to help them to clarify their perceptions of what life today is, and what it can be in future.

References

ADAMS, F. (1986) *Special Education* (Harlow: Longman, Council and Education Press).

ARGYLE, M. and TROWER, P. (1979) *Person to Person* (London: Harper and Row).

BALDWIN, J. and WELLS, H. (1979–83) *Active Tutorial Work* (Oxford: Blackwell).

BEST, R., RIBBINS, P., JARVIS, C. and ODDY, D. (1983) *Education and Care* (London: Heinemann).
BLACKBURN, K. (1975) *The Tutor* (London: Heinemann).
BRITISH ASSOCIATION FOR COUNSELLING (1984) *Counselling Agencies and Organisations* (Rugby: BAC).
BUTTON, L. (1981) *Group Tutoring for the Form Teacher* (London: Hodder and Stoughton).
DAVID, K. and COWLEY, J. (1980) *Pastoral Care in Schools and Colleges* (London: Edward Arnold).
DAVID, K. (1982) *Personal and Social Education in Secondary Schools* (London: Longman).
DAVID, K. and CHARLTON, T. (1987) *The Caring Role of the Primary School* (Basingstoke: Macmillan Education).
FREEMAN, A. (1987) 'Pastoral Care and Teacher Stress', *Pastoral Care in Education* 5(1).
GALLOWAY, D. (1982) *Schools and Disruptive Pupils* (New York: Longman).
HAMBLIN, D. (1981) *Problems and Practice of Pastoral Care* (Oxford: Blackwell).
HAMBLIN, D. (1983) *Guidance 16–19* (Oxford: Blackwell).
HAMBLIN, D. (1986) *A Pastoral Programme* (Oxford: Blackwell).
HANDY, C. B. (1981) *Understanding Organisations* (Harmondsworth: Penguin).
HARGREAVES, D. (1975) *Interpersonal Relationships and Education* (London: Routledge and Kegan Paul).
HMI (1979) *Aspects of Secondary Education in England* (London: HMSO).
HOPSON, B. and SCALLY, M. (1979) *Life Skills Teaching Programmes* (Leeds: Life Skills Associates).
JENKINS, C. and SHERMAN, B. (1979) *Collapse of Work* (London: Eyre Methuen).
LANG, P. (1983) 'How Pupils See It', *Pastoral Care in Education* 1(3).
MCGUINESS, J. (1982) *Planned Pastoral Care* (London: McGraw-Hill).
MILLE, R. (1987) 'French Teachers' Reactions', *Pastoral Care in Education* 5(1).
OSMAN, J (1973) 'A Rationale for using value clarification in health education', *Journal of School Health* XLIII No. 10.
RAZZELL, A. (1969) *Juniors: A Postscript to Plowden* (Harmondsworth: Penguin).
ROGERS, C. R. (1969) *Freedom to Learn* (New York: Merrill).
SCHOOLS COUNCIL (1981) *The Practical Curriculum* (London: Methuen Educational).

STONIER, T. (1983) *The Wealth of Information – A Profile of the Post-Industrial Society* (London: Thames/Methuen).

WARNOCK REPORT (1978) *Report of the Committee of Enquiry into the Education of Handicapped Children and Young People* (London: HMSO).

WETTON, J. (1982) 'Schools in the Welfare Network', *Child Care: Health and Development* 8, 271–282.

WOODS, P. (1978) 'Relating to Schoolwork: Some Pupils' Perceptions', *Educational Review* 30 (2), 167–75.

Chapter 7

Working With Parents

Kevin Jones
Mick Lock
Martin and Terri Webb

Introduction

Despite considerable advances in the development of effective working relationships between parents and professionals, particularly within the area of reading (Widlake and Macleod, 1984; Wolfendale, 1986), there have been comparatively few reported accounts of successful liaison which focuses upon behaviour problems (McConkey, 1985). Recent research suggests that practice is, indeed, often counter productive, in that when confronted with behaviour problems some teachers and parents have been ready to 'blame the other side' (Galloway, 1985, p. 60). Croll and Moses (1985, p. 47), show, for example, that teachers see behaviour problems as . . . 'in the main deriving from the home and parental circumstances of the child'.

It is our intention, within this chapter, to illustrate how teachers, parents, and other professionals have moved towards more positive procedures whereby they share responsibilities in order to respond in more appropriate ways to problem behaviours.

The benefits of such an educational partnership are discussed, together with examples of particular approaches, used at both primary and secondary stages, which show how the sharing of information, advice and practical support can be of benefit to the pupil concerned.

The chapter also considers the practical steps which need to be taken in the development of effective working relationships and examines factors which appear to affect the degree to which behaviour problems can be ameliorated in this way.

The concept of a shared educational responsibility

There is now a considerable body of advice which suggests that teachers and parents can usefully work together in active partnership (Warnock Report (DES, 1978), Para 4.29, Fish Report (ILEA, 1985), Ch. 14). This advice is based upon the belief that through the sharing of information, advice and practical support, the resultant assessment of, and subsequent provision for, special educational needs, will reach a level which neither the teacher nor the parent would have been able to achieve on their own.

In response to the above statement, we propose that the development of a shared educational responsibility towards behaviour problems, will allow for a deeper understanding of the whole range of factors which are relevant to a particular behaviour and subsequent responses to it. This will require a positive form of joint action which seeks to describe accurately the behaviour, factors which contribute towards it, and the consequences which follow.

The results of various parent-professional initiatives, described throughout the text, present evidence to support the above view that joint responses can, and often do, lead to more effective responses to behaviour problems.

The potential value of joint action is clearly illustrated in the following description of how a mother, working with an educational psychologist, was able to assess and respond appropriately to the behaviour problems which were being exhibited by her daughter.

HEATHER

Heather's mother describes the background to the problem:

> Heather has been a very difficult child to cope with for some years now. She suddenly has very bad outbursts of temper tantrums, usually over some minor incident; having a bath, or being told to get dressed, brush her hair, her teeth, or being told to come into the house after she has been out playing. Over the years the tantrums have gradually decreased but she still has occasional outbursts. If she got really bad and was badly behaved for a few days, I would talk with her headmaster at school and he would have a word with Heather. After this she would calm down again for a few months.
>
> When Heather reached the age of eleven years, she obviously had to change schools. I expected a certain amount of trouble over this, as Heather shows great resistance to change, and since she was going to a special school she not only had to accept the change of school

and teachers, she also had to make new friends, as all her other friends were going to the local comprehensive school.

At first, all went surprisingly well. For the first couple of weeks she was quite happy and seemed to have settled in her new surroundings very well. Then suddenly the tantrums started again. Usually they were about coming in at night when she was told, but eventually things got so bad that life seemed to be one constant argument with Heather. At this time I decided to have a word with her headmaster, as I felt that I had completely lost control over her. No matter what I asked Heather to do the answer was always NO. When I insisted that she did as she was told she would start to swear, kick, scream and throw things and I really felt that I was at the end of my tether, and that if things went on as they were, I would be in danger of cracking up under the strain. I have an older daughter who is 21 and at work all day and she also felt that things could not go on as they were. I would like to say, at this point, that my friends and family were very helpful, in that they would fetch her for an hour or so until she had calmed down. I would also like to point out that Heather only behaved in this way with me or her sisters and with no one else. When the tantrum was over she would behave as if nothing had happened.

The response which the parent makes in this situation suggests that there are a very limited number of ways in which she can respond to the problem behaviour. Seeking to get over this commonly held illusion, the psychologist tried to help Heather's mother to solve the problem for herself.

In this case Heather's mother was asked to cassette record a typical argument with her child. Such a request forces the parent consciously to consider the factors which appear to lead up to and support the problem behaviour. This procedure is often, within itself, a successful form of intervention.

When the parent and psychologist listened to the tape recording together, it soon became apparent to Heather's mother that, through the very solutions she was using to solve the problem behaviour, she was helping to maintain it. She explains the insights she obtained:

After discussing the matter at some length it became apparent that on the occasions that I had not argued back with Heather, or by switching off and ignoring her, she calmed down much more quickly. Heather does not like to be ignored, and we decided that what she was doing, and in fact succeeding, was getting my *total* attention.

When I was arguing with her, I was not reading, watching television, or talking to anyone else. She had my total attention, to the exclusion of everything else.

We decided that what I had to do was to be completely consistent in my approach to Heather. From now on I would not argue with her at all. I would ask her to do something and if she refused, then I would say 'then I am not going to speak to you for five minutes'. During the five minutes that I was not going to speak to her, I did not have to react in any way at all to show that she was getting to me, no matter what she said or did.

The resultant action, which was jointly planned by psychologist and parent, was based very heavily upon a change in the mother's behaviour. This required her to adopt a consistent approach, through sometimes difficult circumstances. The following account demonstrates, quite clearly, the resources which parents can, themselves, offer in dealing with problem behaviours.

The first time I tried this out on Heather, she was stunned. Although I had ignored her before, I had never stated that I was doing it and never set a time limit on it, so she obviously thought that if she was outrageous enough I would react, but this time I had to be careful not to react at all. The first time I did it she calmed down, almost immediately, but as days went by she got gradually worse. At the end of the first week I was ignoring her, about five times a night. At this stage I saw the psychologist again; after discussing it with him I realised that she was getting really desperate to get my attention. She had always succeeded before by throwing a tantrum and she could not understand why she was failing now. Anyway we decided to carry on. By the end of the fourth week, things were almost unbearable. I was hardly speaking to Heather at all. I must stress, at this point, how extremely difficult it is not to react when a child is screaming and swearing at you. I never realised how difficult it would be, until I actually tried it. Sometimes I had to walk out of the room, because I felt that if I stayed there another minute I would have to smack her. I usually consoled myself by thinking that I had stood it for four weeks and that if I reacted now I would have undone all the good I had done. If I had broken down just once, Heather would have kept on and on until I did it again.

By the time the fourth week was over Heather was really getting desperate to get my attention and she was trying every way she knew to get me to react. She decided to change her tactic, shouting and swearing was not working, so she decided to start pushing me. Again I must point out how difficult it was not to start arguing with her. When she started to punch and smack I thought, this is the end. I can't stand any more, but carried on.

I found that when the pushing started I had to go out of the room, and she followed me from room to room, trying desperately to get me to speak or react in some way. In the end I had to lock myself in the bathroom because I really felt that I couldn't stand it any longer. I didn't want to break down, but I felt that if I didn't get away from her, I would. On the final day, I spent almost the whole day locked in the bathroom, out of her way, and again I must stress that it was very difficult not to just give in to my feelings to smack her.

After this really bad day, Heather seemed finally to realise that there was no way, no matter how badly she behaved, that I was going to argue with her and she simply gave up. For the next nineteen days we did not have one day when I had to ignore her. The difference was absolutely unbelievable. When I asked her to do something, although she had a little moan and groan about not wanting to do it, while she was complaining she was doing as I asked and never refusing to do anything. I must also say that Heather was much happier in herself and much more cheerful than she had been before. I also felt much better. I felt for the first time that I was in control and that I didn't have to turn to other people all the time for help.

Occasionally, Heather will still test me out and try and argue, but when she does, it is only occasionally, and as soon as I say I am not going to speak to her, she is the one who walks away. She just goes to her bedroom for a while and when she comes down again, she is quite calm, and although there are minor disagreements occasionally, as there are with all children, there have been no more major upsets or arguments as I refuse to argue.

I must also say that it is very important, that when Heather is being good, I go to great pains not just to ignore her, but to talk to her all the time, so that she realises that to gain my attention she has got to be good and not naughty.

Heather's mother wrote the above account over twelve months ago and at a recent follow up meeting she confirmed that she is still able to respond to the behavioural needs appropriately.

We are left with very little doubt, in the above example, that parents and professionals, when working together, can, even under difficult circumstances, assess and make appropriate responses to problem behaviours.

The success of the above case did, however, depend upon the high level of *cooperation* which was achieved between parent and professional. The mother's eventual response was clearly dependent upon the guidance of the psychologist, who in turn relied heavily upon the responses of the mother. We can also appreciate the high level of *trust* which was required when the mother was required to examine, in detail, the effects which her own responses had upon Heather's behaviour. This process would have been very difficult if suitable levels of cooperation and respect had not been built up.

When behaviour problems occur in school the probing of the circumstances leading up to and sustaining the behaviour will need to be based on a similar level of respect and trust between teacher and parent, both of whom will need to examine the effects which they are having upon the behaviour. This level of cooperative activity will demand a very open and frank exchange, which will be very difficult to achieve if parents and teachers are intent upon blaming each other for the problem behaviour.

The first task, then, in developing positive joint responses to behaviour problems in school, must be to create conditions whereby suitably cooperative relationships can emerge. This issue is now examined, in some detail, in the following section, where it is suggested that this might best be achieved through four stages.

Stages in the development of a shared educational responsibility

Misunderstanding between teachers and parents, and the apportioning of 'blame' for certain behaviours, may come about because of:

(a) a lack of understanding of the role and intentions of each other.
(b) a failure to appreciate the constraints under which the other person is working.
(c) an insufficient awareness that certain behaviours may be specific to particular situations, occurring, for example, in school, but not in the home and vice versa (Rutter *et al.*, 1971; Hanko, 1986, p. 96).

If the above misconceptions are to be avoided, it would appear to be necessary as Smith (1980, p. 176) suggests, to establish a procedure whereby parents and teachers, in the course of their own duties towards a pupil, are given the time and opportunities to develop an understanding of, and appreciation for, each other's role and how they might usefully complement each other. This change in perception is least likely to occur if teachers and parents only liaise when something appears to be 'going wrong'. It is more likely to develop if they can meet, initially, under positive conditions which are part of a normal and integral part of the education of all pupils.

Experience suggests that a useful way to avoid potential conflict and to build up the above levels of understanding and shared responsibility towards behaviour problems, is through the following stages of parent–teacher involvement, which we have called:

1   The introductory stage.
2   The informative stage.
3   The joint provision stage.
4   The shared responsibilities stage.

Throughout each of the stages, which are described in more detail below, schools will signal the extent to which a sharing of educational responsibilities is supported.

If the school wishes to promote an active partnership with parents this message will need to be made clear from the earliest stages, since this is likely to influence not only the extent to which parents feel welcome in the school, but also future patterns of working. The clearest message will be carried by the extent to which the school values contributions from parents, compared with teachers. If both sets of contributions are considered to be equally valuable, this is likely to be interpreted as a positive sign for joint involvement.

When schools present teachers as 'experts' to guide parents this is likely to be seen as a suggestion that their contribution is not as valuable as the teacher's and that they, therefore, should adopt a more 'passive' role. The result of this process, as will become clear in later sections of this chapter, is likely to have a marked effect upon the eventual pattern of working which is adopted in response to problem behaviours, with consequent effects upon the degree to which the difficulties are ameliorated.

Cunningham and Davis (1985) describe three ways of working, each of which is likely to give parents a good indication of the degree to which a school wishes to incorporate them into the educational process. The first model presents the teacher as the *expert* and is very similar to the example given above. A more active form of participation is implied in the *transplant* model, within which certain aspects of the teacher's expertise are transferred (transplanted) to parents, who might then be able to utilise this to effect certain changes in their own and the pupil's behaviour. This model, while involving parents in certain ways, retains a high level of dependency upon the teacher and does not recognise that parents may be able to participate in a reciprocal pattern of working, whereby they can offer useful guidance and support to the teacher. The acceptance of this 'equivalent expertise' is more evident in the *consumer* model, where parents, as consumers of a service, are considered to have important contributions to make regarding the educational provision which is made.

Schools will need, therefore, throughout the various stages of parent–teacher involvement, to be wary of the messages they transmit. If an active partnership, which is potentially more valuable to pupils experiencing behaviour problems is to be achieved, this will require clear indications, throughout the four stages, that both participants have equally relevant parts to play. Those stages are now described in more detail, with practical illustrations to demonstrate how various schools have moved towards a sharing of educational responsibility.

1 The introductory stage

In the beginning stages of any new working relationship neither parents nor teachers may be aware of the expectations which are being made of them, or of the benefits which may accrue if they develop certain methods of working together. Their own views about liaison might well be out of date. Parents' impressions of the degree to which they should get involved with the school might, for example, reflect views which existed during their own school days, during which their parents might not have been welcomed 'across the threshold'. Likewise, teachers new to particular schools, or experiencing a change in school policy, might also need to change their attitudes towards parental involvement to accommodate new ways of working. It is important, therefore, that adequate opportunities are provided within an introductory stage, during which new levels of understanding can emerge.

Activities, at this stage, if they are to enhance educational provision, should seek to introduce parents and teachers to each other in such a way that they can feel comfortable together, develop a mutual understanding and respect for each other's intentions towards a particular pupil, and begin to realise the benefits of working together more closely. The relevance of this process will not be limited to the early years of schooling and should, therefore, be a recurrent feature which takes place at any significant time in a pupil's education (for example change in class, curriculum etc).

There are many ways in which schools can introduce parents and teachers to positive ways of working together. Educationally and/or socially biased activities can be designed to allow teachers and parents to meet in non-threatening situations. Helpful examples of activities which fulfil this introductory function have been described by Bailey *et al.* (1982) and include invitations to assemblies, displays and concerts, coffee mornings, introductory talks about selected aspects of the curriculum, and discussions about ways in which teachers and parents can join together in the sharing of educational interests. If a school wishes to demonstrate that it places a high value on a sharing of responsibility, it may convey this message, quite clearly, to 'new' parents by involving 'experienced' parents in the planning and running of some of these introductory functions.

The school will also introduce its views on the value of partnership by certain hidden messages. These include various hints and may suggest, for example, whether all parents are equally welcome, whether success in pupils is only ascribed via academic excellence, and whether pupils experiencing behaviour problems are considered to be a 'nuisance' or to have needs which are seen to be proportionate to any other educational need (for example reading needs). The way in which the school, unwittingly, broadcasts these messages is likely to have an effect upon the eventual success of joint ventures which aim to respond in the most relevant and effective way to problem behaviours.

The introductory stage, so far described, has focused attention on the development of working relationships *within* the school. Not all parents, however, become involved in this way, often leading teachers to complain that certain parents, who they would most like to see, never turn up. Some parents, due to various constraints (for example shyness, transport problems, single-parent households) have genuine reasons for not being able to attend the introductory sessions, while others will need their interest aroused. Successful schemes, such as the Oerlinghausen Project, described later, have overcome this problem by arranging for teachers to work through the home base, rather than attempting to bring all parents into the school. This change of venue often helps to erode barriers and introduce parents to useful ways of working with teachers.

At the culmination of this stage, parents and teachers will have received certain messages, either consciously or unwittingly transmitted, about the degree to which they are encouraged to work together. If these messages have sought to welcome their joint involvement this may have a considerable effect upon their readiness to work together, rather than against each other, if behaviour problems occur. The next stage of activity is designed to build upon these introductory activities by involving teachers and parents in the process of information sharing.

2 The informative stage

Having started to build suitable relationships, through the above activities, the informative stage offers opportunities for consolidation and the beginnings of a more active involvement between teachers and parents which focuses, more directly, upon the development, needs and interests of *a particular child* in whom they have a mutual interest. Activities within this stage are directed towards the practice of giving and receiving information.

By keeping each other informed about educational progress, needs and interests, parents and teachers may be able to adjust particular aspects of educational provision at school, or within the home, to match those general needs. Parents may, for example, highlight a specific feature of the curriculum which their child has shown particular interest in, or conversely, may bring to the attention of the teacher the pupil's negative reaction to certain experiences within the school which may, if they are not given suitable attention, lead to the occurrence of certain undesirable behaviours.

Teachers, in a similar way, can also use the informative process to relate progress to parents who may, in cases of strengths (for example desirable behaviours), consolidate success by appropriate forms of praise (for example verbal praise, special treats). Where difficulties occur information should still be passed on, but should not stop short at merely conveying that something is amiss. This could, as will be discussed later, lead to inappropriate responses being made in a retaliatory manner. The most appropriate response, in this situation, would be to stress the importance of working together through the following two stages which emphasise the need to respond to the behaviour in a carefully considered way which is based upon an adequate analysis of the difficulties which are being experienced. Without this move towards carefully considered action, information giving will be an empty and, at worst, dangerous process.

Informative liaison most often occurs through consultation evenings. A typical pattern is for parents to have a specified ten minute 'slot' with the class or subject teacher. Despite the time limitations which are imposed at these events, a useful, confidential, exchange of information, as suggested above, can still occur. Some schools, because of the time constraints, choose to supplement this activity by developing home–school diary systems. These can be used in a number of ways to allow parents and teachers to inform each other about daily progress in selected areas of interest (for example reading development, specified behaviours). Enhanced opportunities for discussion might also be afforded through involvement in the next stage (joint provision) where parents and teachers work closely together within the school or on a joint scheme of provision for a particular child.

3 The joint provision stage

A transition to the joint provision stage should occur, fairly naturally, from the previous stage of information sharing, which as discussed above, will be somewhat of an empty process unless it is seen to lead to the planning and implementation of suitable provision.

Joint provision can be made at two levels:

(a) for whole classes/groups/individuals within the school, and
(b) for a particular child in whom both teacher and parents have a mutual interest.

At the level of general help within the school, parents may be involved in activities such as workshop sessions (for example redesigning and building a resource area), classroom support (for example helping pupils on individually structured programmes) or by working with particular groups within a particular area of their own interest (for example a hobby). Through these activities parents and teachers can begin to develop much closer working links which will help them to understand and appreciate each other's role and the constraints acting upon them.

Joint provision for particular pupils may take a number of forms. There are now well-documented accounts of the various benefits which accrue from the joint involvement in the teaching of reading (for example Webb *et al.*, 1985). At a more individualised level parents, class/subject teachers and special educational needs support teachers might be involved in providing, in a coordinated way, for specific pupil needs. An account of this method of involvement has been given by Jones *et al.* (1986).

The advantages of joint provision through these structured forms of involvement can be measured in terms of the provision of additional support to the school and individual children, and in affording opportunities for teachers and parents to work alongside each other and consequently to have opportunities to understand and appreciate each other's roles. The next stage moves beyond this level of 'guided' involvement, towards a situation where both participants accept a greater sharing of responsibility.

4 The sharing of responsibilities stage

The aim, throughout the above three stages, has been to develop a working relationship, based upon mutual respect and trust, which will promote a sharing of responsibilities. By the time the fourth stage is reached various forms of joint action at the informative and sharing of provision stages will already have given indications of ways in which educational responsibilities can be shared.

The sharing of responsibilities stage attempts to utilise and build upon the success of previous forms of collaboration in order to merge roles even further. This is particularly important when behaviour problems are encountered since, as will be argued later, an *adequate* assessment of, and provision for behavioural needs, is dependent upon the contributions of both teachers and parents.

Before considering the actual form which those contributions should take, let us first consider a scheme which clearly demonstrates how the behavioural needs of pupils, in secondary schools, have been met by a sharing of responsibility between parents, teachers and other professionals. We have, for convenience, entitled the scheme 'The King's Lynn initiative'.

THE KING'S LYNN INITIATIVE

The aim of this project, which has been described by Melton and Long (1986), was to attempt to modify the behaviour of secondary aged pupils, by linking their performance in school to specific consequences in the home. It was hoped, through this form of joint action, to provide for pupils' behavioural needs within the mainstream school, thereby avoiding the need for transfer to off-site units.

Members of the schools psychological service joined with pastoral staff in the school to set up behaviour contracts with pupils and their parents. The particular needs of pupils were discussed and parents were asked to provide rewards and sanctions, within the home, according to their child's behaviour in school.

The first move, following referral from the school, was to set up a meeting at which parents, teachers and psychologists could set out to define the problem and to recommend relevant solutions. It was considered important, within these meetings, to consider carefully factors which led up to, and maintained particular behaviours. Disagreements between home and school were explored so that any conflicts could be ironed out during the early stages. Once the relevant facts had been adequately established a procedure for meeting the needs was discussed.

The next stage involved the development of a contract which used the control of highly valued activities and privileges within the home (for example pocket money, TV viewing, being allowed out), to attempt to modify behaviour within the classroom. Parents were asked to issue rewards and sanctions according to daily performance, which was recorded within the school. Pastoral heads kept a daily check on performance within each lesson of the day by asking subject teachers to give a clearly defined grade, from nought to five.

Once the programme had been finalised the scheme was put into operation, with frequent contact being maintained to ensure that it was being operated appropriately. When the scheme was running successfully, the reporting period was gradually lengthened from one day, to one week, and then subsequently faded to monthly checks.

In the first term of working, staff reported a considerable improvement in the behaviour of 18 out of 20 pupils, who were continuing their education, profitably, in the mainstream school. It was suggested that the relative failure of the other two cases was due to inconsistency in the management of rewards and sanctions by parents.

The above initiative demonstrates the degree to which problem behaviours can be responded to, more effectively, when parents, teachers and other professionals enter into a sharing of responsibility.

We do not, however, wish to suggest that *all* forms of shared activity would necessarily result in the above level of success. There appear, as suggested earlier, to be certain factors which determine the outcome of these initiatives. One variable, which has already been discussed, concerns the degree of cooperation which can be achieved. The following section of this chapter examines other factors.

Factors affecting the successful outcome of educational partnerships

An analysis of cases where parents and professionals have jointly, and successfully, responded to behavioural needs leads us to suggest that the outcome of various forms of involvement will be dependent upon the quality of shared:

1 Information
2 Advice
3 Practical support.

Various ways in which teachers and parents could work together under each of these headings will now be examined in order to assess their relative worth in meeting behavioural needs.

1 Information

Information sharing will only be of maximum use if it helps to determine relevant responses to problem behaviours. Two kinds of activity can be distinguished, the first of which 'keeping each other informed' is potentially less influential than the process of 'shared information gathering'.

(i) Keeping each other informed

We have already seen, at the informative stage, that the sharing of information about particular needs, interests and levels of motivation, might be useful in helping to match the curriculum to general needs. It was also suggested that this action might help to prevent the occurrence of problem behaviours. We now go on to consider the usefulness of this procedure once difficulties have been encountered.

Parents and teachers, through a sense of commitment, or legal duty towards each other, may wish to 'keep each other informed' about a certain problem behaviour, passing on impressions or facts about which the other person may, or may not, be aware. The very act of 'passing on' information in this way suggests that both parents and professionals are intent to take their own forms of action upon the basis of the information which they are given. When action becomes separated in this way, it is possible for parents and professionals to make quite different response to a behaviour which, due to the resultant inconsistency and confusion to the pupil concerned, may have only a limited impact.

Information which is 'passed on' in this way also runs the risk of being too shallow to guide relevant action. Vague descriptions such as:

> Jill doesn't pay much attention, she is always gazing out of the window, or chatting to others,

and

> Paul drives us mad in the evenings, always arguing with us and never doing what he is told,

tell us very little about the behaviour itself or what is *needed* in a particular situation. Indeed, armed with information, which at worst may be impressionistic, some parents and teachers might take action which, because it is not founded on an adequate analysis of needs, could lead to a worsening of the situation. If, for example, parents were to punish their child for undesirable behaviour at school, this could, feasibly, lead to a worsening of the situation, resulting, for example, in school refusal.

There is also the danger that certain levels of anxiety might interfere with the process. The need to 'tell' another person about certain behaviour problems is often accompanied by the desire to 'offer an explanation'. This process, at worst, could lead to the 'naming' of a particular behaviour, a process which, we suggest, is often entered into to make the listener more comfortable about the occurrence of the difficulties, almost as if it is acceptable because other people have 'got it'. Labelling a particular behaviour in this way, will not, however, clarify exactly what the *needs of the situation* are, and will not 'lead to a plan of action about how to change it' (Westmacott and Cameron, 1981, p. 9).

The process of 'keeping each other informed' about problem behaviours, if it is limited to the above levels of activity, is not then sufficient to lead to the planning of appropriate provision. If, however, the procedure goes further in an attempt to guide some form of consistent, joint activity, it could result in a much more positive outcome whereby parents and teachers are able to develop joint plans of shared action. If information sharing reaches this level, however, we would suggest that something more than 'keeping each other informed' is taking place, and that participants are now entering into the process of shared information gathering.

(ii) Shared information gathering

The process of shared information gathering is a much more positive procedure, whereby teachers and parents accept a joint responsibility for getting adequately informed.

It is all too easy, as we have intimated previously, to describe problem behaviours in vague, or general terms, which are not based on a sufficient account of the difficulties which are being experienced. Describing a pupil as disruptive, lazy, withdrawn or maladjusted is a labelling process which suggests that the 'problem' lies entirely within the child. Information which is couched in these generalised terms cannot help parents and teachers to plan appropriate joint responses because it fails to give any indications of precisely what is required. Attempting to plan action from these vague descriptions can only lead to hazardous guesses about the responses that should be made, which might, at worst, include reactions such as 'she needs a good spanking' or 'he'll grow out of it'.

If information sharing is to lead beyond uncalculated, or negative reactions to problem behaviours, it will need to move towards a much more precise gathering of information which describes, precisely, the difficulties which are being encountered. This implies a process which goes beyond the lighting up of problems within the child to a wider beamed search which comprises an analysis of *all* the factors which promote a particular behaviour.

Within the process of shared information gathering teachers and parents will need, therefore, to collect adequate and appropriate data which will allow them to act in a much more positive way. To do this effectively they will need, first, to arrive at a precise description of:

(a) the behaviour itself
(b) factors leading up to and surrounding it
(c) the consequences which follow
(d) expectations about future behaviour.

The rationale behind this detailed form of analysis is discussed by Presland (Chapter 5) who also describes a relevant procedure which can be followed to arrive at an adequate understanding of behavioural needs. When this kind of procedure has been followed (for example as in the case of Heather) this has often led to appropriate pointers for action which, because they have led to a consistent approach, have often resulted in success.

If parents and professionals enter into the above process *together* the resultant outcome is likely to lead to a gathering of information which neither party would have been likely to achieve on their own. This enhanced level of needs analysis is likely to occur because of the high level of objectivity which is implied in the above process. In attempting to assess, in a carefully calculated way, *all* of the factors which contribute to and sustain a particular behaviour, parents and professionals, by working together may:

(a) highlight significant aspects about a behaviour which might otherwise have been overlooked, perhaps because either party 'didn't want to see them' (McConkey, 1985, p. 97), and
(b) promote a more accurate account of the behaviour which is not distorted by the 'strong emotional attachment between the child and the parent (Cunningham and Davies, 1985).

When an adequate assessment of needs has been achieved, through the above form of joint action, it is then possible, through the next stage of advice giving, to begin to plan action to meet those needs.

2 Advice

The outcome of this form of joint activity can be evaluated in a similar way to that of information sharing. Two different kinds of sharing of advice are suggested, the first of which, 'Advising another person', is considered to be potentially less influential than the practice of 'Advising each other' about the most relevant form of action to take.

(i) Advising another person

At the most basic level, a person could seek to give 'advice' to someone else by adopting the role of *expert*, which was described earlier. This level of activity, while suggesting various ways in which it might be advisable to respond to a particular behavioural need, may have only limited success, due to the fact that it is often only based upon a general recipe for action, which seems to work 'in most cases'. This level of advice may or may not work, depending upon how closely the particular case fits the general pattern.

The second level of advice giving adheres to the *transplant* model, whereby various skills are transferred to the parent, who then attempts to assess needs and to modify a particular behaviour through their own resources. This process could again be based upon very generalised responses to behaviours, which might not, necessarily, lead to successful intervention. If, however, the model involves the parent heavily in the process of needs identification (as in the case of Heather) this can have a considerable effect upon the behaviour.

In cases where both parents and professionals are directly involved with the behaviour, as in the case of problem behaviours in school, there is a need to enter into another level of advice sharing, whereby they attempt to 'advise each other' about the most relevant form of action to take, with the ultimate aim of agreeing upon a response which they can both make, with some consistency.

(ii) Advising each other

When parents and professionals advise each other about the most relevant response to a problem behaviour (for example changing the consequences, or promoting a different behaviour) they may be able to guide each other about specific factors, relevant to the plan of action, with which the other person might not be familiar.

It has been suggested, for example, that parents have a particular knowledge of their children . . . 'their needs and strengths and how they feel those needs might best be met' (Hanko, 1985). This aspect of a parent's knowledge was used to guide the action which was taken in the King's Lynn initiative, described earlier. In that particular case the parents' knowledge of particular rewards and sanctions which their children valued were used to modify that pupil's behaviour in school.

Professionals themselves may be in possession of another form of knowledge, which we might term 'technical knowledge', which could be useful in guiding both participants through tried and tested procedures which help to determine behavioural needs and provision. This form of guidance was brought into operation in the case of Heather, which was described in the early part of this chapter.

Advising each other about particular forms of intervention which may work in particular situations is also vital to their successful outcome. Teachers may, for example, be able to offer general advice about what forms of action might 'work' within the home, but it is the parents own intimate knowledge of that situation which is required in fine tuning the plan to ensure success.

When an agreed form of action has been agreed, it is then possible to consider what action might take place in the final stage of practical support.

3 Practical support

A sharing of responsibility, through the final stage of practical support, can, if it takes advantage of the resources which each of the partners have to offer, lead to a change in behaviour, which might otherwise have been difficult to achieve.

At school some teachers may be at a loss for rewards and sanctions which are as powerful as those which are available to parents in the home. Where parents can become involved in the control of the various treats which a child enjoys these can, as we have already seen, lead to a modification of a pupil's behaviour. Further evidence to support this view can be found from an analysis of the results of the Oerlinghausen project, which follows.

THE OERLINGHAUSEN PROJECT

The Oerlinghausen Project was coordinated by two of the authors (Webb and Webb) and Geoff Eccles, in a school for children of service families in West Germany. The aim of the project was to involve parents of primary aged pupils in a greater sharing of responsibility towards the behavioural needs of their children. The parents had already been involved with the teachers through consultation evenings and other activities within the school (for example shared reading projects) but the school now sought to extend this involvement. The scheme was directed at children who were experiencing behaviour problems in school.

The project was based upon a behaviour modification approach. The first move was to arrange a meeting with parents in their own home, stressing that the teachers would be visiting to talk about the child in a helpful way and not to make complaints. This was to be an evening meeting with no time constraints imposed upon the length of the visits.

The parents, who, as mentioned above had already built up relationships with the staff, were all cooperative about meeting in their homes and were generally more relaxed than parents often appear on consultation evenings.

After an introductory chat the most significant points about the children's behaviour at school were discussed (both strengths and areas of need) and parents were invited to discuss any problems at home. A combined list was produced and selected behaviours were chosen where parents and teacher thought that some modification of the behaviour was desirable.

The next stage was to define the behaviours precisely and to attempt to identify those factors which appeared to lead up to and sustain them. Once the facts had been established as clearly as possible, parents and teachers then agreed upon the most relevant forms of action to take in attempting to modify the behaviours. This involved a discussion of the forms of action which might be taken in both school and home, and very often involved a change in the consequences of the behaviour. Methods of recording the occurrence of the behaviours were also discussed.

A certain number of points were to be awarded for each target behaviour on the list, when improvement was shown. The award of points was to be given on an agreed basis between school and home. Once the points were gained they were recorded on a chart which consisted of a picture of a snake with various sections for the child to colour in, thus inviting him/her to record progress. Each child had a maximum number of points he/she could receive daily. Points could only be gained and not lost, hence the modification programme was totally positive and not negative.

The children had to present their chart to their teacher at the end of the day for marking and discussion, and to their parents at home. This means that both parents and teachers could see at a glance how successful the child's behaviour was, on a daily basis. The child's ultimate goal was to complete the chart, and once this task had been achieved, he or she would be rewarded by a small reward at school, and a special reward from the parents. Also on each chart after every ten points there was a small bump, and here the child could receive a small intermediate reward from their parents. The parents suggested the following kinds of rewards:

(a) Allowing the child a session playing on father's computer.
(b) Buying the child a book.
(c) Allowing the child to select a video at the weekend.
(d) A special outing for the child.

After the children had been on a modification programme for about a month, the parents were revisited. Most parents, at the two month stage reported that they were very pleased with the way the scheme was progressing. In some cases the charts were amended, concentrating more on the points where the children were failing. In fact, out of the ten children who were involved, there was only one case where the teacher saw no improvement. This chart was amended to two target objectives with subsequent improvements.

After two months of the scheme both parents and teachers agreed that there had been an improvement in behaviour. In several cases this was reported to be a very significant improvement.

Conclusion

Various parent–professional initiatives, which have been outlined in this chapter, lead us to suggest that a sharing of educational responsibility towards behaviour problems can result in a change in the total environment in which the child finds her/himself, thereby leading to more desirable behaviours.

Joint responses towards problem behaviours rely, however, on a high level of cooperation between parents and professionals, which is not likely to occur if they seek to blame each other for the behaviour. We have recommended, therefore, that four stages of collaboration are necessary if appropriate relationships and understandings are to be developed.

Where good relationships have been built up through the above stages, the effectiveness of the resultant joint activity appears to be dependent upon the quality of the shared information gathering, advice giving and practical support which takes place. Various factors which appear to affect the quality of these three factors have been discussed.

References

BAILEY, G., BULL, T., FEELEY, G. and WILSON, I. (1982) *Parents in the Classroom* (Coventry LEA Community Education Development Centre).

CROLL, P. and MOSES, D. (1985) *One in Five* (London: Routledge and Kegan Paul).

CUNNINGHAM, C. and DAVIS, H. (1985) *Working with Parents: Frameworks for Collaboration* (Milton Keynes: Open University Press).

DES (1978) *Special Educational Needs* (The Warnock Report) (London: HMSO).

GALLOWAY, D. (1985) *Schools, Pupils and Special Educational Needs* (London: Croom Helm).

HANKO, G. (1985) *Special Needs in Ordinary Classrooms* (Oxford: Blackwell).

ILEA (1985) *Educational Opportunities for All* (London: ILEA).

JONES, K., COX, R. and WEBB, T. (1986) 'Support for Learning in Service Children's Schools (North-West Europe)' *Support for Learning* Vol 1 (4) 39–43.

MCCONKEY, R. (1985) *Working with Parents. A Practical Guide for Teachers and Therapists* (London: Croom Helm).

MELTON, K. and LONG, M. (1986) Alias Smith and Jones, *Times Educational Supplement*, 11 April.

RUTTER, M., TIZARD, J. and WHITMORE, K. (1971) *Education, Health and Behaviour* (London: Longman).

SMITH, T. (1980) *Parents and Preschools* (London: Grant McIntyre).

WEBB, M., WEBB, T., and ECCLES, G. (1985) 'Parental participation in the teaching of reading', *Remedial Education* Vol. 20 (2).

WESTMACOTT, E. V. S. and CAMERON, R. J. (1981) *Behaviour can change* (London: Macmillan).

WIDLAKE, P. and MCLEOD, F. (1984) *Raising Standards. Parental Involvement*, Programmes and the Language Performance of children (Coventry: LEA Community Education Development Centre).

WOLFENDALE, S. (1986) 'Involving parents in behavioural management, a whole-school approach', *Support for Learning* Vol 1(4) 32–8.

Chapter 8

The Involvement of Outside Agencies

Kenneth David

In Gloucestershire some years ago one troubled family was found to have some twenty agencies and voluntary bodies in contact with them providing varied support, control and criticism. Our welfare state does make great efforts to provide services to help children and families in need, whether they are deviant, improvident, aggressive, inadequate or unfortunate.

There can be difficulties for the teacher who may be seeking support or advice in dealing with the problems of a pupil: not only may there be a local absence or inadequacy of particular support, but also there can be difficulty in managing liaison with, and understanding the characteristics of, various aid agencies who do not necessarily work well together, and who may even give the appearance of being mutually antagonistic at times. Many headteachers and their staffs long for a more standardised and efficient liaison system with the outside agencies with which they seek to deal. The school appears increasingly to be the institution at the centre of the web of aid which is best suited to manage liaison about children with the various professional and voluntary workers, but there may be occasional professional jealousies, differing qualities of staff, differing standards of training, contrasting professional values, and sometimes even a dislike or distrust of a teacher or school, to bedevil the smooth coordination of aid for problem pupils that is available.

Bureaucracies always produce liaison problems. The fundamental good will and caring nature of most professional agency workers does produce a great deal of support for teachers, pupils and families, but it clearly could be better. The occasional well-publicised cases of children who come to harm through failures of the school and welfare services illustrate this. A team leader needs to be clearly identified in all care groups linked with a school, and an occasional public rap on the knuckles of professional workers who do not cooperate with each other, or who do not give loyalty to such a group or team leader, can be necessary. Sometimes a headteacher could be the leader for such referral and liaison; more often it will be someone from the psychological services, from health or social services, or from senior education welfare staff. Experience and seniority should count most, rather than professional status ranking. Such an improved team approach has often been used in child abuse and drug education matters, and local 'committees of concern', 'Professional liaison groups' and 'care committees' do exist and function usefully in many areas.

A more structured approach to such liaison is increasingly necessary, with agreed regular meetings, appropriate leadership and secretarial and communication arrangements. Most agencies have their eyes on the ground dealing with pressing everyday matters, which can be a limited viewpoint when we are trying to chart future plans for a child with a problem. In our society the managing of a system of dealing with problems is as important as the expertise of various agencies.

Secondary schools have usually now developed strong pastoral systems. Such systems may attempt to deal with varying objectives which could be as follows.

> Dealing with learning difficulties and developing study skills.
> Supporting the various welfare needs of pupils.
> Watching for and attempting to cope with physical, emotional and behavioural problems.
> Assessing and recording achievement.
> Liaising with parents and outside agencies.
> Ensuring order, and enforcing discipline in company with all staff.
> Managing a coordinated programme of tutorial work and personal and social education.
> Organising and dealing with administrative matters of the school.
> Concern with sports, leisure and community affairs.

It would be interesting to discuss with a group of colleagues from outside agencies which of these objectives involves liaison with other professions, and where there are mutual interests and concerns.

Larger secondary schools have a teenage population which inevitably will have normal adolescent problems, and the larger numbers involved produce a greater number of pupils with problems of learning or behaviour, compared with primary schools. Secondary schools have the advantage of more senior staff members concerned with managing such problems, often with considerable expertise; there are very many excellent secondary pastoral care schemes, including good referral and liaison arrangements with other agencies. Experienced and senior teachers with obvious management skills are usually acceptable as equal colleagues and perhaps as leaders in inter-professional liaison, and good tutorial arrangements and pastoral care teamwork in a school produce a reasonable screening of pupil problems, though no school ever avoids its share of failures. The strength of the National Association for Pastoral Care in Education illustrates the growth of pastoral care professionalism in recent years.

Some schools have 'extra care' lists for staff, noting particularly vulnerable children – families involved in divorce or separation, bereavement or recent unemployment, for example. Other schools have regular 'concern groups' of pastoral and academic staff who meet at intervals to review the development of all the children in a year or house cohort. Most schools must have attempted to gain personal knowledge of, and easy communication with, their colleagues in outside agencies, with occasional termly meetings to exchange knowledge of pupils and their families and knowledge of each other's work. The discussion of how best to deal with problem pupils belongs easily to such meetings. There are two clear priorities: easier communication between professional workers, and better knowledge to help pupils.

In primary schools there may be a greater depth of knowledge of the children and better contact with their families than in a secondary school, but there is less specialisation of staff, less available time for managing pastoral matters and contact with other agencies, great reliance on the educational welfare officer (EWO) and his abilities, and less inclination by outside agencies to liaise with small educational units. Sometimes primary schools can group themselves to arrange larger gatherings of primary teachers with their agency colleagues, for mutual increase of trust and exchange of information. Advisory staff can often take the initiative with such gatherings. With economies bringing less training in pastoral care and personal and social education, and with limited opportunities for in-service training in the school, such meetings are essential.

With a population of fifty five million this country inevitably has a proportion of families which are inadequate, or with a variety of handicaps which prevent them functioning well with their children. Because we can never see inside any family other than superficially we have to be sensitive in judgement, but evidence of immaturity, inadequacy and violence is common. Much problem behaviour is the fault of schools themselves, but clearly poor family life creates children who are more vulnerable to problem behaviour. We have a clear duty, therefore, to the children of such families, as well as the normal care for all children, whose families may or may not be well known to us.

We act on behalf of parents, and pastoral care and close cooperation with the other caring professions is part of our task, however much we find it stressful, and however much we attempt at times to retreat into the purveying of knowledge as our sole task.

It is wrong to be too idealistic. We cannot change society only through education, and we cannot cure ills and problems which are rooted in political and economic decisions, but we can do a lot better than we are doing at present. With prison populations rising, mental illness and stress so common, and materialistic and selfish attitudes commonplace, we have a social role in schools. The diagnosis of and action on child abuse is one example; schools may sometimes provide the opportunity to break the circle of abuse which can repeat itself in families. Social class is likely to be a poor measure of the potential for behaviour and other problems, which can appear in varied forms in every type of school and area.

Teachers resist the gibe of 'amateur psychiatrists' for their main role is to ensure learning opportunities for their pupils. To manage learning, however, requires a dual academic/pastoral role for teachers – they cannot educate without it in fact, for society and its pressures permeates every classroom, and care is an inter-professional matter.

In the following list we provide a reminder of the agencies with whom schools need to liaise at times, in providing inter-professional care, for there are limits to teachers' time and expertise in dealing with more serious behaviour problems.

School Psychological Service

Teachers with qualifications in psychology provide schools with advisory support as *educational psychologists*. A principal educational psychologist coordinates the service, and each educational psychologist normally serves a group of schools. They are concerned with the development of all children, and may work in the community with pre-school children and their parents and with medical and social service colleagues, usually with handicapped children. In schools they may work with individual children or with their teachers, working on assessment of intellectual, psychological and emotional development and behaviour problems, on recommendations for transfer of children to special schooling, and on a wide variety of other educational advice mutually negotiated with teachers.

When working with the Child Guidance Service the educational psychologist will consult with the *child psychiatrist* and attached *social workers*, as well as with medical and other professionals such as EWOs, in dealing with individual children's problems, and with home situations. Other professional staff located in the *Child Guidance Clinic* may include the *child psychologist*, the *clinical psychologist*, the *psychiatric social worker*, the *child psychotherapist*, and perhaps *special needs support teachers*. The consultant child psychiatrist is in charge, with the senior psychiatric social worker often acting as deputy.

Chapters in this book illustrate the wide variety of helpful liaison which can develop between schools and their educational psychologist and child guidance clinic. Educational psychologists are seen nowadays as valued members of school care teams, and the whole psychological service is concerned with the reduction or solving of children's normal and abnormal problems.

The Education Welfare Service

The Education Welfare Service employs *education welfare officers* who have statutory responsibilities relating to compulsory education, the general welfare of children at school, and their part-time employment. They are involved in court work in school attendance cases, and prepare reports for juvenile courts. The basic duty of the service is to provide a social work service within the educational setting, ensuring that every child receives and benefits from the opportunity of a suitable education. Experienced EWOs often have a deep knowledge of their communities and of the families of school children, and can help in establishing close links between teachers and parents. They regularly deal with problems of school lateness, truancy, and non-accidental injury, and help with cases of badly clothed, unclean or under-nourished children. They deal with free school meals, travel and clothing grants, and employment permits. They can be the major contact with the Health and Social Services departments, Police, Probation and the NSPCC, as well as the WRVS clothing scheme and other voluntary agencies.

The School Health Service

The National Health Service is responsible for school health services with a *specialist in community medicine (child health)* responsible, assisted by *clinical medical officers* who are concerned with emotional and behaviour problems as well as physical examinations. The *school nurse* (who may be qualified as a *health visitor*) does routine hygiene and physical examinations and immunisations and liaises with parents. An *area nurse (child health)* supervises school nurses.

178 *Managing Misbehaviour*

Health visitors are experienced in the normal development of children and can give valuable advice in this field. Their duties are to visit all young children to promote their welfare and proper development, and to advise and assist parents in this. Health visitors are helpful in their links with local medical practitioners (with whose practices they are often closely linked), and they also contribute to teaching and advising in health education.

General medical practitioners have much knowledge of patients which is additional to medical history and current ailments. Together with their attached health visitors they are in a good position in many instances to diagnose situations of risk for children. Doctors place a high value on confidentiality as part of medical ethics, and this can cause conflict in some situations when liaising with other professionals.

Area dental officers supervise *dental officers'* inspections. *Audiology clinics* and *speech therapy clinics* and their staffs deal with specific disability problems. *Paediatricians* are consultants on child health based in hospitals or clinics, and are specialists in the medical care and treatment of children. They can arrange exhaustive examinations of a child and its parents when child abuse is suspected, and can give expert advice concerning the significance of injuries. *Psychiatrists* in child guidance clinics are also administered by the NHS.

Nurses and midwives may often gain information or impressions of children and their parents which may be of significance in the context of other circumstances.

Teachers normally deal with their school nurse or health visitor, and their clinical medical officer (school medical officer) who are likely to have considerable knowledge of local homes and families. It should be noted that no one has the legal power of entry to visit a child, and no power to examine a child without parental consent.

Social Services Department

Social workers employed by local Social Service Departments can institute civil proceedings in respect of a child thought to be in need of care and protection or control, and can obtain through a justice of the peace a place of safety order for the removal of a child for a period. A juvenile court may effect a Supervision Order where a child may be supervised by a social worker, EWO or probation officer. A court may also effect a Care Order committing a child to the care of the local authority.

Social workers have a statutory duty to investigate all complaints relating to the neglect or ill-treatment of a child, and have a general duty to promote or safeguard the welfare of children for whom the department of social services has a responsibility. The Children's Act of 1948 and the Children and Young Persons' Act of 1963, 1969, 1975 and 1980 form the basis of their work with children.

Other professional social workers are employed in hospitals, voluntary agencies, child guidance clinics, residential establishments, nurseries and day centres, and some schools. Social workers are trained in group work, counselling and community casework, and an important part of their work is attempting to make professional relationships with their clients. Their role places them in a good position to recognise the signs of family and personal problems as potential risks to a child. Good relationships cannot be achieved without trust, involving confidentiality, resulting sometimes in inter-professional conflicts.

Social Services register and supervise child minders, foster parents, private nurseries, play groups, and adoption arrangements, and provide intermediate treatment facilities for young offenders.

Other helping agencies

Police officers have powers to institute proceedings against an adult alleged to have ill-treated or neglected a child, and can institute civil proceedings in respect of a child thought to be in need of care or protection. Senior officers have discretion as to whether or not to institute proceedings of either sort. A police officer can remove a child under a place of safety order on his own initiative. Officers often have information which might suggest a situation of risk, directly through a complaint about a child, or indirectly perhaps by being called to a domestic disturbance or a neighbours' quarrel. Investigation of an alleged offence is not necessarily followed by a prosecution, and may begin and end at a case conference.

Police community relations officers can be useful allies of teachers and *Schools liaison officers* are appointed in some areas to work closely with schools.

Probation officers have the task of advising, assisting and befriending probationers, reporting breaches of probation orders to magistrates. They are usually experienced in counselling skills, as well as marital counselling, and can be helpful with individual problem children from families known to them. They would normally expect to take on Supervisory Orders made in the Juvenile Court on offenders over 14 years of age.

NSPCC inspectors are required to take action 'to prevent the public and private wrongs of children and the corruption of their morals' and to take action 'for the enforcement of laws for their protection' (quoted from the Royal Charter of the NSPCC). They can institute civil proceedings in respect of a child thought to be in need of care and protection, and can obtain through a justice of the peace a place of safety order for the removal of a child. They offer teachers experienced support and local knowledge.

The Samaritans, Marriage Guidance Councils and Citizens' Advice Bureaux. Young people are increasingly using these agencies for help with their problems, and close liaison by schools can be useful. The CABs are a treasure house of information on our welfare society, and are increasingly helping families with debt counselling as well as other advice.

Youth Workers often have considerable knowledge of young people of a locality, frequently having a very different view of pupils in informal and out-of-school settings. They are trained in groupwork and counselling, and form good members of liaison teams.

Local clergy can be helpful with their knowledge of the community and local families. Some are experienced in counselling skills, making them helpful in referral work, when this is acceptable to them. Some churches have organised youth counselling schemes.

Local authority housing officers know local community affairs well, and often have a deep knowledge of disadvantaged and problem families.

School ancillary staff are local people who know pupils and their families. They can sometimes be the trusted confidants of children. Some schools have co-opted ancillary staff to their pastoral care team meetings, when they are known to be particularly popular with pupils.

Local people such as shopkeepers and neighbours of a school can be helpful in advising on potential or actual behaviour problems of pupils, and even in commending good behaviour.

Specialised national support services exist in great numbers and can be contacted through social and health workers, through EWOs and advisory and teachers' centre staffs, and through public reference library facilities.

Examples of agencies concerned with various aspects of family life and pupil problem behaviour could include the following:

Advisory Centre for Education (parents, and child-centred education)
Alcoholics Anonymous (families)
Children's Legal Centre (children and the law)
Child Poverty Action Group
Commission for Racial Equality
Council for Children's Welfare (pre-school children)
Cruse (widowed parents and their families)
Dr Barnardo's (children in need, fostering and adoption)
Depression Anonymous
Family Conciliation Councils, in some areas
Family Planning Association
Family Rights Group (advisory and publications)
Family Welfare Association (families in need)
Friends of the Children's Society (needy and deprived children)
Gingerbread (single parents and their families)
Institute for the Study of Drug Dependence (help for parents)
Law Centres (legal action groups)
Minority Rights Groups
Narcotics Anonymous
National Association for Maternal and Child Welfare
National Association for Remedial Education
National Association for Gifted Children
National Association for Special Education
National Children's Bureau (needs of children)
National Childbirth Trust (childbirth and child care)
National Council for Civil Liberties
National Advisory Centre on the Battered Child
National Council for the Divorced and Separated
National Council for One Parent Families
National Federation of Solo Clubs (loneliness)
Shelter (housing pressure group)

A useful list is contained in the *Macmillan TIPS Teacher Information Pack – Support Services Guide* by Tricia and Ron Dawson (Macmillan Education, 1988) and by reference to Citizens' Advice Bureaux or reference libraries.

This chapter concludes by listing some actual case studies, with altered identities, to illustrate the nature of liaison in problem behaviour, and perhaps to form the basis of discussion in college or in-service training groups.

The first two case studies are from the infant reception class of a primary school in a large housing estate of a medium sized town. The teacher is a young woman of some six or seven years experience, committed and capable.

KEVIN

Kevin started school with very aggressive behaviour. He kicked, scratched, bit and swore if asked to do anything he didn't want to do, and my main worry was that he would seriously harm other children in the class. I had to spend most of my time sitting with him as one minute he would be stringing some beads and the next attempting to throttle another child. A major problem was that he didn't like any physical contact, and was big for his age so he was hard to handle in a tantrum. I wrote about his problems in my record book each week and the headmaster asked Kevin's mother to come to school after the first half term. Kevin was the eldest of four boys, mother in her twenties. She wouldn't admit to having any problems with Kevin at home, although it was local knowledge that he had set fire to his bedroom when he was three, and neighbours reported that he was tied to the garden fence during the summer holidays. The mother eventually agreed for the educational psychologist to see Kevin in the classroom situation and at home. The educational psychologist kept reviewing Kevin's case every six months and finally after three years in the infant department he was transferred to a special school. The Head there said Kevin should have been sent to him when he was four. In my opinion it was unfair on the children in the class and the class teachers to have to contend with the child as he required so much individual attention.

WENDY

Wendy was a very unhappy little girl and when she entered school she had a very low opinion of herself. Her father had mistreated her and her mother. I was able to form a relationship with both Wendy and her mother, and the child responded to affection and praise, but it was impossible to give her all the attention she needed with twenty-four children in the class. Wendy never used to let me out of her sight or touch. She held my hand in assembly, sat on my lap in the classroom, and was very agressive to other children who needed my attention. I told the Head of my concern over Wendy and he asked her mother to come to school. The mother admitted she couldn't cope with Wendy's tantrums and stubbornness at home and she was quite willing for the educational psychologist to see her. The educational psychologist suggested that as Wendy was so attached to me would I be prepared to keep her in my class for an extra year? I didn't feel this was the answer for either of us. I felt under a strain all the time trying to meet Wendy's needs and at the same time to strike the right balance with the rest of the class. I was always worried that Wendy wasn't integrated with the rest of the class or forming friendships with other children. The educational psychologist reviewed Wendy's case every six months but it wasn't until she was nine years old that she was sent to a special school. As Wendy progressed through the school she had personality clashes with some of her class teachers and grew more unhappy and alone, hence more anti-social behaviour. She suffered increased feelings of failure and isolation through her time in a mainstream school.

There are times when pressure from within the community is far more effective than even the strongest combination of other services!

MEG

Meg was a large woman, with a voice to match, and language that was chosen to express her feelings immediately and clearly. One day the doors of the Family Centre burst open to admit Meg, with her two youngest trailing somewhat unwillingly in her wake. She stood for a moment, arms akimbo and teeth out; then, with a motherly clip round each ear, sent her offspring to play. She sat for the rest of the session sternly surveying the scene. She accepted a cup of tea with a loud sniff and moved only once – to administer a sound cuff to her youngest, who was about to cover his sister in paint. At the end of the session, she gathered the two children up roughly and swept out.

The next week Meg came back – this time with teeth in and her knitting. We noted that the expression had softened just a little. It was only a couple of weeks later that Meg was to be found at the dough table with her own children and sundry others too – the teeth remained firmly in, but the knitting never appeared again. Furthermore her sister's child was added to her two and, on occasions, her sister was unceremoniously bundled into the Centre to 'do her bloody bit as well!'

Meg became a strong supporter of the Family Centre – she always expressed her views strongly and loudly, but was always there when help was needed. There were two families on her estate who all the local services and the Family Centre were trying their best to help and to get to regular sessions. One day in came Meg with the number three from one of those families, one hit hard by unemployment, illness, very bad living conditions and inconsistent parenting. This meant that she had two of hers, one of her sister's, and now another under her ample wing.

The story did not end there. Meg managed to get the single mother of the other family to let her bring the youngest in. In this case there were suspicions of both drug and sexual abuse. The mother was extremely introverted and unwilling to come to the Centre herself. Meg now had five to collect, bring and get involved in Centre sessions, but the parents were not forgotten. Meg's sister put in appearances periodically, grumbling and swearing, but occasionally admitting to some degree of enjoyment. The father of the first family was seen joining in a music session with one child, while mother looked on and bounced the latest on her knee in time to the music. As for the single mother, she began coming just inside the door to pick up her child at the end of the session, but she accepted a cup of tea the other day! It was Meg's strong and caring personality, coupled with her approval of the Centre, that got first the children, then the parents, involved – other services had tried but failed!

TRACEY AND GARTH

Tracey and Garth were in the top class of an urban primary school, and caused concern to the staff because of wildly fluctuating behaviour, from being engaging and cooperative youngsters full of life, to a mood of sullen awkwardness. They were not twins, but behaved in similar ways. It was through the parents of other children in the class that the headteacher eventually found that the children were terrified of their father, who had legal access to them periodically. The mother was dead, and they were living contentedly with good foster parents.

Both had been treated badly by the father in their earlier years, when their mother was alive, and before the family was broken up. The mother had been of low mentality, and the father was often violent, and possibly abused the children sexually, though this was not certain.

There had been no contact between the school and Social Services over the children for some years, but contact was soon made after the discovery of the children's terror of their father, which was not known by Social Services, and had not been reported by the foster parents, who had merely thought the children moody at times.

The father was eventually denied access to the children, and the Education Welfare Officer and the foster parents kept closer liaison. Regular discussions with Social Services, the Education Welfare Officer and the staff were arranged.

JEAN

A Social Services office received an anonymous telephone call one afternoon from a girl threatening suicide and complaining of sexual interference by her stepfather. She refused to give her name and eventually rang off. A social worker reported on this call at a regular case liaison meeting at the local comprehensive school, asking staff to try to identify the child.

The Deputy Head invited class tutors to have 'an ear to the ground' on the matter, and eventually a third year tutor reported hearing from girls in the class that a girl, Jean, had been complaining to her friends about her stepfather.

After staff discusions it was decided to invite the parents in, with a pretext of discussion on a school medical examination. The parents were a quiet couple, clearly wishing to be cooperative with the school, though they had had little contact with the school before. They soon talked of the behaviour of Jean, the stepfather claiming he was 'at his wit's end' in knowing how to deal with tempers and moods. After one example of teenage rebellion he had lost his temper and hit the girl, and had pulled her off balance by his hand catching in her loose jersey. The mother and he had then watched the girl storm out of the house, and clearly this was the girl's excuse for telephoning Social Services.

This story was volunteered by the mother and stepfather, who clearly had been worried by the girl's general behaviour, and further discussions with parents, with the Educational Welfare Officer and the school doctor, and with Jean, indicated that the fault was the girl's.

The parents welcomed the possibility of help from the staff in coping with Jean, and a useful and helpful liaison was established with the class tutor and the Educational Welfare Officer.

RUTH

The form tutor of a lower secondary school class found Ruth to be often irritable and sleepy in class, falling behind in lessons, and defensive when questioned.

The mother was invited in to school, and came eventually. It transpired that she was separated from her husband, and refused to have any dealing with him, refusing also to take any money from him.

This wish to be independent from the husband meant that her daytime job did not provide sufficient money for her to provide for herself and Ruth. She worked every evening, therefore, in a bar. Ruth was put to sleep in their car outside the pub, being woken when the mother came off duty. They then returned home and went to bed very late.

The story came out gradually, with further discussion between the Deputy Head, the tutor and the mother.

Social Services were asked to advise the mother, and eventually the father contributed money which was used for Ruth's clothes and holidays. A job was found for the mother much nearer her home, and a neighbour cooperated in sitting in with Ruth on some evenings.

Chapter 9

In-Service Training for Support Teachers

*Libby Falconer-Hall
and Lawrence Harlatt*

Introduction

In Education Observed 5 (1987) HMI reported:

> The general picture of behaviour within schools which emerges from these publications (HMI reports) is that the overwhelming majority of schools are orderly communities in which there are good standards of behaviour and discipline; poor behaviour is unusual, and serious indiscipline a rare occurrence. (p. 3)

Nevertheless, if teachers *perceive* they are having to deal with more problem behaviour (Merrett and Wheldall, 1987) then teachers' perceptions have to be acknowledged and appropriate help offered. But how – especially as research cited by Galloway and Goodwin (1987) indicates schools may be generating, or exacerbating, that very behaviour they despair about? Galloway and Goodwin (op. cit.) review evidence which suggests consistently that:

1 Schools exert an enormous influence on their pupils. Whether a pupil is considered disruptive or maladjusted depends at least as much on factors within the school as on factors within the pupil or the family.
2 In general, schools which cater successfully for their most disturbing pupils *also* cater successfully for the rest of their pupils.
(p. 132)

Similar findings are reported upon in Chapter 1 by Tony Charlton and John George.

This research, and the good practice observed by HMI, suggests the need for a whole-school approach (that is, to include everybody involved) which provides a positive climate offering a well-balanced and appropriate curriculum for *all* pupils. However, while many teachers appreciate these facts, they still have to deal with problem behaviours in their classroom, some of which are 'relatively minor repetitious incidents of misbehaviour that may be perceived as seriously disruptive by teachers' (McNamara, 1985, p. 35). These incidents include such things as inappropriate talking, turning round in seats and non-attending which, although trivial in themselves, help to erode teachers' confidence and sap their energy when it might be used to tackle larger issues.

It appears, therefore, that while the problem of pupils with adjustment difficulties should be tackled by a whole-school approach, an essential part is by giving support to, and so helping to generate success for teachers who often perceive the number of pupils with adjustment problems as growing. Moreover, this supported success cannot happen by transferring the problems. As Galloway (1985) points out:

> One of the characteristics of the four schools with exceptionally low rates of disruptive behaviour in Sheffield and New Zealand was a tendency to discourage referral to senior members of staff. Teachers were generally expected to deal with problems themselves (but) . . .:
>
> The tendency . . . to discourage referral to senior staff did not imply that teachers lacked support. On the contrary, senior staff saw their job as helping colleagues to deal effectively with children's learning or behavioural problems. . . . Psychologists use the term locus of control to refer to an individual's sense of control over his own environment. In the successful schools we studied, locus of control seemed to be centred firmly on the teacher. . . . This sense of professional responsibility could not, however, have been achieved without a highly effective network of professional support.
>
> (pp. 150,151).

Furthermore, as McNamara (1985) suggests, if behaviour problems, as perceived by teachers, are most often those of a relatively minor repetitious nature, they are 'the very problems most amenable to amelioration using classroom contingency management procedures . . .' (p. 42). But, Presland (1980) warns that:

> The major problem in trying to encourage the use of behaviour modification in secondary schools seems to be the reluctance of secondary school teachers to accept and implement these approaches.
>
> (p. 53)

Presland recommends that schools seek help from their local educational psychologist to maximise the chance of successful applications.

However, this help is more likely to take root if it is sustained by a specially trained support teacher who not only can work with individual teachers in order to help them to see themselves as successfully managing the behaviour of difficult pupils, but can also work alongside colleagues in order to be part of Galloway's highly effective network of professional support. Moreover, this 'in school' support appears to offer the most cost-effective type of provision as described by Topping (1983) who, while acknowledging that pupils may need to be withdrawn even to an off-site unit, considers that:

> resource continua, offering a flexible range of services from total withdrawal of the child through to advisory support and training work with ordinary teachers, can prove very effective, and they are certainly organisationally well placed to ensure generalisation and duration of gains, and maximise cost-effectiveness. Again, the behaviourally oriented operations demonstrate highest effectiveness.
> (p. 158)

Thus for a number of reasons – humane, practical and economic – it appears that on-site behaviourally orientated support for pupils with adjustment problems is most likely to help schools and individual teachers to make the appropriate provision if these pupils are to have their needs met.

Background to making the additional provision in Wiltshire

A re-think of some of the provision for supporting pupils with adjustment problems was undertaken for a variety of reasons. First, the retirement of a teacher who ran what was perceived as a highly successful unit in one of the rural comprehensives raised the issue of how she could be replaced. Second, three other comprehensives requested similar provision. These four rural schools brought pressure to bear on the LEA and a working party was set up which included representatives from all the schools and two officers from the LEA.

The working party met on several occasions, discussed at some length various types of provision, looked at research (for example Rutter *et al.*, 1979; Galloway, 1983), visited provision in a nearby authority and finally decided that on-site provision would best meet the needs of the four rural schools. The Education Committee agreed that four scale 2 teachers should be seconded for two years to run a pilot scheme in the four rural schools, the aim being 'To help schools support pupils experiencing emotional and behavioural difficulties'. These support teachers were to be appointed by the LEA in consultation with the four headteachers concerned who would organise and manage their on-site arrangements.

Preparation

At this stage it might be useful to raise the question: If an LEA project is to be successfully carried through what aspects have to be carefully considered?

First, as successful implementation depends on the commitment of the schools concerned, it is essential they be involved from the start so they feel *their* perceptions have been taken into account and that the project is being planned to meet *their* needs. If schools feel they have something to gain, that the plans indicate an understanding of their current needs and will support and build on good practice (their own and others), then proposals are more likely to be well received and implemented.

Second, the project should be planned taking into account current research and good practice so that it has sound theoretical and practical underpinning.

Third, clear aims and objectives incorporated into a model of practice should be agreed by all involved.

Fourth, relevant provision should be made to carry out the project – in this case a teacher appropriately trained to support on-site work for pupils with adjustment problems, their teachers and the school as a whole.

Fifth, monitoring and evaluation should be built in to provide feedback both during the life of the project and as a summative overview.

In Wiltshire's case, a working party had been formed as a response to requests from some schools, had considered relevant research and practice and asked for financial support for a pilot project to be conducted in four schools in order to fulfil the aim of helping pupils with emotional and behavioural difficulties. More details were then needed in order to understand the schools' needs and state of development. To this end, the four schools were consulted by a special needs adviser about how *they* saw the newly appointed teachers' function. The central question was: *How do you see your school using this scale 2 support teacher for pupils with adjustment problems?* In the event, the four different schools saw things in four very different ways! However, as a result of these discussions, and others with the educational psychologists, the following main points emerged as a basis for a model for the newly appointed support teachers:

1   A whole-school approach has to be built in from the first so that the support teachers could be seen as a support not only for pupils, but also for their teachers for the most important aim was eventually to help *all* teachers to cope successfully with difficult pupils. As there may be a variety of factors within the school environment which might contribute to pupils' poor adjustment, these factors needed to be investigated and dealt with.
2   The support teacher has to be directly responsible either to pastoral care heads, or deputy heads, or heads of special needs, in short, to be part of a support network contributing to the whole-school approach.
3   Pupils needing support have to be channelled to the support teachers by an agreed procedure linked to the County First Aid Procedures (these procedures are part of the County's implementation of the 1981 Education Act and aim to streamline liaison work between all concerned – classroom teachers, schools, parents and all outside agencies).
4   A continuum of provision has to be offered from within class support to temporary and short-term withdrawal.
5   Flexible use has to be made of the support teachers' time in order to deal with problems which might arise in lunch hours and breaks.
6   Support teachers have to be trained for their new roles.
7   Monitoring and evaluation of the project has to be built in.

Bearing in mind these organisation and management points a general job specification was drawn up which defined the responsibilities of the proposed support teachers who should be able to:

1   assess the needs of pupils experiencing adjustment problems;
2   plan appropriate, negotiated programmes based on pupils' and staff needs;
3   teach pupils by supporting pupils in mainstream classes or by withdrawal work;
4   monitor progress to ensure effective feedback to all staff concerned (this to entail the setting up and keeping of appropriate records);
5   evaluate the work in conjunction with relevant staff, both within the school/the Authority.

Each school had to supply information about how the support teacher would relate to their management structure, and a description of what duties the support teacher would be expected to undertake in their school. Applicants were appointed in the summer term by a joint panel which consisted of the four head teachers, the Area Education Officer and the Adviser for Special Needs. The field work done, the next step was to proceed with the in-service training. Naturally, all the head teachers wanted the candidates to be trained in the latter part of the summer term so they would be ready to begin when schools started in September. However, it was too difficult to release candidates from present posts and it was finally agreed that three weeks' intensive in-service training would be carried out at the beginning of the autumn term following guided reading to be undertaken during the Summer holidays.

The in-service training

The course aimed to prepare teachers for their support roles in helping mainstream schools to make appropriate provision for pupils with adjustment difficulties. It was envisaged that this support role would *not be* a *crisis service* but would aim to 'nip problems in the bud' by early identification and appropriate, continuing supportive action. However, it was recognised that crisis services would probably have to be offered if the new teachers' competence was to be viewed positively.

The in-service training planning team of four comprised two educational psychologists and the two Advisers for Special Needs. Considerable discussion and planning time was given to this in-service training and it is hoped the following description will give some idea of the intensity and extent of the course and the demands which it made on the newly appointed teachers.

Planning training

If in-service training is to be relevant and appropriate, it should match the needs of those being trained, hence the necessity for careful fieldwork at the planning stage. At the same time, in-service training should clearly state what it aims to achieve and how it proposes to do this. While it was appreciated that school organisation and management would differ between schools, the support teachers had to have certain essential skills, knowledge, experiences and attitudes if they were to be able to help schools in the ways intended and to fulfil their four main responsibilities:

1 To work as part of a team in order to develop a whole-school approach to pupils with adjustment problems.
2 As part of this process, to support individual teachers in order to develop their loci of control and to help them to perceive themselves as being successful with working with difficult pupils.
3 To work with these same pupils in order to help to resolve their adjustment difficulties.
4 To work with appropriate outside agencies.

To this end, it was important that the new teachers should have knowledge of relevant theory and provision and basic competence in:

1 assessing pupils' needs;
2 planning programmes to meet needs;
3 teaching these pupils, either by withdrawal or in mainstream classes;
4 monitoring and evaluating progress;
5 knowing how to support teachers;
6 liaising with parents and outside agencies;
7 understanding the organisation of the systems in which they were to operate;
8 self-management (for example time management, programme planning, organisation of administrative tasks and recognising job specific signs of stress).

As a result of long discussion three different stages of in-service training were planned:

1 *Stage 1* – The pre-placement course consisting of twelve units.
   Unit 1 – Pre-course work (to include a visit to their schools and directed reading on which three written assignments were based).

Unit 2 – The problem.
Unit 3 – Theoretical approaches to adjustment problems.
Unit 4 – Patterns of provision.
Assignment based on Topping handed in.
Unit 5 – Identification, referral and assessment.
Unit 6 – Assessment and intervention by behavioural methods.
Assignment based on Cheesman and Watts handed in.
Unit 7 – Assessment and intervention for learning.
Unit 8 – Other approaches to intervention.
Assignment based on Munro handed in.
Unit 9 – Organisation and politics of schools.
Unit 10 – Bringing things together.
Unit 11 – Stress and self-management.
Unit 12 – Evaluation of the pre-placement course and identification of further needs for in-service training.

2 *Stage 2* – Training to meet needs which would arise after placement and might differ considerably.
3 *Stage 3* – A distance learning package which would have to be developed for subsequent appointments.

If teachers are to be in a position to assess needs, they must know about the range of needs with which they might be faced, as well as various assessment processes. Once an assessment has been made of pupils' needs, ways of meeting those needs should be made practicable by planning relevant, negotiated support programmes based both on pupils' and teachers' needs. Although the course focused on pupils with adjustment problems, the close link between learning and positive teacher expectations for academic progress has been clearly recognised (Rutter *et al.*, 1979) and, in turn, the possible links with health – sensory loss, physical handicap etc. – so the support teachers had to have knowledge of learning and allied health problems. When assessing pupils' needs and planning their programmes, it was considered important that the support teachers take into account the attitudes of all concerned – pupils, parents, teachers and other professionals – and learn how to cope successfully with these attitudes. It was also felt that the support teachers would enhance their credibility by substantiating their practice with knowledge of relevant theory and provision. The fieldwork (that is, the working party's investigations and the Special Needs Advisers' discussions with schools) had demonstrated a range of organisation and management in which the support teachers might find themselves, and raised the issue of systems analysis. Indeed, while the importance of this was considered at the planning stage, it was difficult to know how much to include which would be of relevance in the pre-placement course to the support teachers. With hindsight, far more emphasis might have been given to the understanding of how systems work so that the support teachers could have analysed the organisation problems which subsequently arose and, in one case, proved to be too much.

Apart from school systems, the support teachers had to be familiar with the various support agencies. Liaison work with parents and outside agencies can often be a delicate business (as is shown in Chapters 7 and 8) and for support teachers intent on working *within* and *through* extant systems (a whole-school approach) it could (and indeed did) prove to be even more delicate.

Finally, self-managmeent had to be considered. Although the support teachers would be working to the school management on a day-to-day basis, their open timetables would mean they would take far more responsibility for planning their own programmes than is normally the case for scale 2 teachers. Time management, programme planning and organisation of administrative tasks all had to be tackled. Since this work might prove to be isolated and frustrating, the support teachers had to be trained to recognise and deal with any stress which might arise.

This knowledge, these responsibilities and competences were turned into course objectives which appeared on the certificate awarded to each support teacher who completed the course (p. 196).

This certificate was signed by the Chief Education Officer. Perhaps it was just as well that the formidable list of objectives was given to the support teachers after they had accepted their appointments!

Stage 1 Implementation of pre-placement training

Much care had been given at the planning stage to ensure the smooth running of the pre-placement training. First, head teachers had to be kept fully informed about the aims, objectives, content and timing of the course as well as the proposed second stage follow-up dates. Second, the support teachers had to have all this information and, additionally, had to arrange their advance work which consisted of a visit to their schools, and the pre-course reading and assignments. These made up Unit 1 of the course. The other eleven units were worked on during the three weeks' training time.

> ### In-Service Training for Support Role for Adjustment Problems
>
> This is to confirm that .... attended a three-week full-time course of training to prepare him/her for a role in supporting secondary schools in helping pupils with adjustment problems. He/she satisfied the course organisers that he/she had achieved the course objectives, and
>
> (i) Has a knowledge of the range of adjustment problems encountered in schools and of the attitudes to them among teachers, other professionals and parents.
>
> (ii) Has a knowledge of the range of theoretical approaches to adjustment problems.
>
> (iii) Has a knowledge of the range of provision made both nationally and locally.
>
> (iv) Has a knowledge and a good idea of how to use a range of assessment techniques for adjustment problems and associated learning problems.
>
> (v) Has a knowledge and a good idea of how to use, a range of intervention and recording techniques for adjustment problems and associated learning problems.
>
> (vi) Has an understanding of the organisation and politics of schools
>
> (vii) Can plan the organisation of his/her own work within a school.
>
> (viii) Has a knowledge of the work of a range of support services and can liaise effectively inside and outside the school, including with parents.
>
> (ix) Has an understanding of himself/herself in relation to the demands of the job and has devices for coping with stress and knowledge of how to obtain support.
>
> (x) Has undertaken reading assignments on topics fundamental to the work.

Unit 1   Pre-course work

This work included two main elements. The first was a visit to their schools by the support teachers in order to study the organisation and communication patterns. To help with this visit, a short questionnaire was sent to the support teachers who had to send their written answers to the Senior Adviser for Special Needs before the end of the term preceding the actual course. The second was a requirement to read three key books in order to write assignments in response to specific questions posed by the course team. These books were:

CHEESMAN, P. L. and WATTS, P. E. (1985) *Positive Behaviour Management* (London: Croom Helm).
MUNRO, E. A. et al. (1983) *Counselling. A Skills Approach*, second edition (Auckland: Methuen).
TOPPING, K. (1983) *Educational Systems for Disruptive Adolescents* (London: Croom Helm).

Together these three books provided a systematic account of behavioural approaches (Cheesman and Watts, 1985); a description of counselling skills (Munro et al., 1983); and a survey of research pertaining to educational systems for disruptive adolescents (Topping, 1983).

Unit 2 The problem

It was hoped the support teachers would start by looking at the mainstream teachers' perceptions of problems in the four schools and, to this end, the headteachers had been asked to provide a list of behaviour and adjustment problems that had caused concern in their school during the previous twelve months. As this information was not forthcoming (due, presumably, to lack of time), the article by McNamara (1985) was used instead. The support teachers' perceptions of pupils with adjustment problems were probed and their answers compared with those offered by McNamara. Rob Grunsell's (1985) work was drawn on to help focus on personal definitions of disruption in order to explore the support teachers' own attitudes in an attempt to sensitise them to possible feelings they might meet amongst colleagues. This unit also gave time to study an overview of the course, to emphasise the problem-solving approach to difficulties, to discuss any immediate anxieties and to exchange information.

Unit 3 Theoretical approaches to adjustment problems

This unit looked at various approaches which were discussed under three headings which were paired opposites – humanistic v. behaviouristic; medical v. psychological; and systems v. individual client. A range of approaches was thus considered, including behavioural techniques; non-directive counselling as practised by Carl Rogers;

various other techniques described as humanistic; social learning; behavioural counselling; social skills training; and discussion groups.

Unit 4   Patterns of provision

Here focus was on the range of national and local provision which had been introduced by the Topping assignment which was handed in and discussed. It was important for the support teachers to understand in more detail why on-site provision could be so effective and how it fitted into a within-school continuum of provision (in class support or withdrawal work), while appreciating the whole range that was available right through to residential special schools.

Unit 5   Identification, referral and assessment

This unit dealt with the purposes of assessment, the kinds of information required and suggested various techniques including Coulby and Harper's (1985) 15-step Procedure for Individual Cases. The techniques included a range of referral forms and assessment instruments which included record forms of behaviour to be filled in by individual teachers; behaviour questionnaires; devices for rating behaviour (for example Bristol Social Adjustment guides); pupils' self-report forms (including the use of repertory grids); and techniques for identifying social structures of the classroom (sociometry). Support teachers were thus given the opportunity to consider what information they might want to collect, and to explore a range of assessment techniques which could contribute to referral forms which they planned to design for use in their future placements.

Unit 6   Assessment and intervention by behavioural methods

The Cheesman and Watts assignment was handed in. This had covered the background and assessment of behaviour problems, and intervention and positive behaviour management in practice. The core of the behavioural approach was outlined:

(a) identification and clear description of the carefully observed, measured and recorded behaviour to be changed – the targeted behaviour;

(b) any possible antecedents – causes that might precede or contribute to the targeted behaviour;
(c) consequences arising from the behaviour – effects of the behaviour which might be worked on in order to change the targeted behaviour.

Consideration was given to the problems of applying behavioural approaches in secondary schools and the possible use of contracts to influence behaviour as well as systems in which the home and school might cooperate. A range of recording forms was considered and practice activities undertaken with the help of a video film.

Unit 7   Assessment and intervention for learning

The link between learning and adjustment problems was re-emphasised in this unit. A range of assessment techniques, based mostly on the observation of what pupils *do* rather than assessment by standardised tests, was suggested in order to help teachers to clarify what the learning problems might be. Possible health problems were discussed. On the basis of this information, activities were suggested to be negotiated with the learner. Careful monitoring and recording were also emphasised. Consideration of the learning environment was taken into account (for example timetabling, sets and the ecology of the classroom – seating arrangements, availability of resources etc.). These activities reflected Child's (1985) six major features which any theory of instruction must specify. These six specifications are:

1   the cognitive predisposition of the learner – that is, the knowledge, skills and abilities which a learner brings to a task and which would influence performance;
2   the affective pre-disposition of the learner – that is, the interests, attitudes and self-concept brought to a task;
3   how a body of knowledge needs to be structured in order for efficient and effective learning by individuals to take place;
4   the sequencing and best methods of presenting that body of knowledge;
5   the reinforcement mechanisms necessary to ensure continued interest such as rewards, incentives, feedback; and
6   evaluation of pupils' performance in the system used (p. 17).

Unit 8 Other approaches to intervention

While the core of the training was behaviourally orientated, it was felt support teachers should have some understanding of other techniques. These included counselling; handling, and relating with groups; an approach to social skills training, drama therapy and roleplay. There were practical sessions which included roleplay and feedback for course participants by video film. In some instances, behavioural techniques were included in the approaches presented. The assignment on Munro was handed in at this stage of the course.

Unit 9 Organisation and politics of schools

In order to provide as objective a view as possible, a headteacher outlined organisation, communication patterns and politics within schools and the support teachers compared these with their perceptions of their own schools. This consideration of the context – a brief systems analysis – only just touched on an issue which proved to be a central concern for support teachers involved with the whole-school approach.

Unit 10 Bringing things together

Before this unit, the support teachers had opportunities to visit other educational establishments for pupils with adjustment difficulties and were now able to report back and discuss the implications of their findings. At this stage, the County First Aid Procedures were discussed and the importance of working within their framework emphasised. Various support services were considered, their availability discussed and how the support teachers might best liaise with them and also with parents. The support teachers had begun to plan their work, based on their visits to schools and preliminary liaison work, and including consideration of referral systems and how they were going to 'play themselves in' once they joined their schools permanently.

Unit 11 Stress and self-management

Coping with stress – their own and others – and self-management were considered in this unit. As with the rest of the pre-placement course, the group was encouraged to work as a self-help group.

Unit 12   Evaluation of the pre-placement course and identification of further needs for in-service training

Evaluation was by feedback discussion and questionnaire. The questionnaire asked a standard set of questions about content, utility, presentation and sufficiency of each unit and sought feedback on the general administration and running of the course. Space does not allow for full details but generally speaking the content was considered relevant and the course arrangements satisfactory. Suggested improvements included:

1   More possibilities to be allowed for group-forming activities, especially at the beginning through such events as communal, social lunches and possibly a residential element.
2   The handouts to be included in a booklet.
3   Aspects of topics to be grouped more closely together and timetabled sessions to match better with the stages of referral, assessment, intervention and evaluation.
4   'Heavier' theoretical sessions to be timetabled for the mornings and for more practical elements to be included.
5   The need for some sessions to be presented in a less difficult way because the support teachers had problems when theories of some complexity were introduced (Unit 7, Learning) or because too much pre-existing knowledge was assumed (Unit 5, the published checklists; and Unit 10, the 1981 Act and County procedures).
6   Various school visits were not always seen as particularly relevant to the support teachers' work (for example residential special schools). Better briefing was needed for visitors and visited.

Stage 2   Training to meet needs after placement

The pre-placement course might be considered as the primary stage of the in-service training and the monthly meetings that followed as the secondary. Although the first official meeting was scheduled for a month after the support teachers took up their new posts, it was decided by the whole group that they wanted an informal meeting far sooner to share their experiences and to help each other.

Much of the discussion at this unscheduled meeting focused on how they were organising themselves in their new roles and how schools were making use of their time. As they had given considerable thought to the organisation of their work, all four were in a position to produce impressive documents which demonstrated how they had started to streamline referral, identification and support processes. These documents were exchanged and discussed. All had had to negotiate their new roles. They felt (in some instances) that, whereas their training had emphasised the preventive and support roles, they were in practice often being asked to provide crisis help for teachers who found a few pupils too difficult to handle.

The support teachers were reminded of the need to log what they were doing in order to monitor progress. In addition, the schools were asked to note what problems (for example pupils truanting, being abusive, disruptive or manifesting other behaviour likely to cause concern) arose during the following weeks so the work of the new teachers could be seen in that context.

At this stage, in-service training might be seen as the sharing of problems. Indeed the careful analysis applied, and practical suggestions made, demonstrated the support teachers had, indeed, absorbed the problem-solving approach emphasised on the pre-placement course. Moreover, the sensitivity which they demonstrated in dealing with various problems highlighted the difficulty of their new roles. At the time, all this put them under considerable strain which, a year later, has lightened as the work has taken on new perspectives. For example:

The teacher in *School A* had initial problems with role boundaries (for example how directly she should approach parents as this was really the year heads' job) but quickly appreciated the advantages accruing, and the status to be gained, by working with the support team led by a Deputy Head. The Headteacher has written to praise the work done by the support teacher.

School B was unfortunate to lose their new teacher before the appointment was ever taken up! She left to get married. A new teacher has had to be appointed and trained. He has settled in quickly and the headteacher has written his appreciation.

School C had an uneasy start, partly because of the undoubted perceived success of the previous structure, and this probably made it more difficult for the school to re-perceive the role of new teacher. Unfortunately, the support teacher decided to move on and a new appointment will have to be made and trained.

School D has responded in a most positive way to the suggestions put forward by the support teacher and the headteacher's overview of the support teacher's work has been extremely complimentary.

The monthly meetings continue to act as in-service training. On some occasions team members brought case studies to which all present contributed and this further developed the problem-solving process. The drama therapist returned to give more training and one of the team members offered a session on Personal Construct Theory (Kelly, 1955). The groups also asked that senior management teams should be offered in-service training to support their work (this has been arranged).

Stage 3   The distance learning package

As school B lost its teacher before pre-placement training course, stage 3 – the distance learning package – had to be put together more quickly than anticipated. This will be written up elsewhere. Essentially it has the same format, but includes a book by Coulby and Harper (1985), *Preventing Classroom Disruption – Policy, Practice and Evaluation in Urban Schools* (the first course was lucky enough to have Tim Harper to talk to them). As the first course was expensive in terms of the time given by Educational Psychologists and Special Needs Advisers, much more had to be offered as self-teaching packs rather than by direct teaching.

Other courses

The in-service training described has not been carried out in isolation as it is only a part of a County approach to in-service training for supporting teachers of pupils with adjustment problems. Two other courses have been or will be offered which, it is hoped, will support the work of the newly placed teachers. First, a two day course was offered to any teachers who were interested in dealing with 'Challenging Children'. The two days were a month apart to allow follow-up work from day one to be completed before the second meeting. The opportunity for follow-up feedback was offered to course participants during the next term. Second, a course is to be offered to senior management (either Head or Deputy Head plus one other, who should be a head of year or a faculty head). The team who planned these two courses included a psychologist and the Special Needs Adviser from the original team, with three other psychologists and two Deputy Heads for the second course.

Future plans

The two year project is half-way through, but the in-service training continues. School C has been given permission to replace their original appointment and to start their two year project afresh and so the distance learning package will have to be reactivated. Meantime, those in post will continue with their in-service training by discussing case studies, helping each other with problem solving, by offering their own 'specialities' and with the help of outside agencies. Funding has been built in through the new GRIST bids.

Although school B's teacher was appointed after his colleagues, already he is running his own in-service training for his school using the PAD materials. He is also helping the Science and Special Needs working party with these same materials.

As has been said, plans are afoot to provide training for senior management. At this stage, hard evaluation of the in-service training is difficult as some of the teachers had relevant experience before they came into post. Perhaps the next stage should be handed over to them to redesign the entire process! Indeed, the results of the questionnaire and evidence from these teachers' work in school will help the planners to make any necessary adjustments.

Summary

A good deal of this chapter was taken up with describing the background work to the in-service training. If in-service training is to meet the needs of those involved, it should arise from their needs – in this case an initiative taken by schools.

The working party's decision to provide on-site support for pupils with adjustment difficulties arose from various investigations which indicated segregated provision did not necessarily offer better opportunities for the effective education of those pupils. Although segregation might have protected their peers and offered relief for hard-pressed teachers, it did not get to the heart of the matter – the need for schools to look at how their academic and pastoral work (the formal and the hidden curriculum) affects the lives of all pupils for better or worse.

The in-service training was planned bearing in mind the support teachers' responsibility 'to help schools support pupils with emotional and behavioural difficulties'. The on-site provision of an appropriately trained teacher allows for this continuous support for pupils and their teachers as it should model useful and usable practice and thus provide ongoing support and in-service training for the whole-school approach. The objectives for the training arose from research which indicated that schools and their teachers make a difference (clearly overviewed in Galloway and Goodwin, 1987) and that the overall school climate is central to this difference. Galloway and Goodwin define the school climate as '. . . the network of relationships between pupils, between teachers and between pupils and teachers that determines what they expect of each other and what kinds of work or behaviour they regard as acceptable' (op. cit., p. 135). There are a large number of variables which contribute to this school climate and the ten objectives defined for the in-service training attempted to incorporate many of these (even if only at the awareness level on the pre-placement course). Necessarily some knowledge and understanding requires deepening and some experiences enlarging according to the support teachers' previous levels of development. The regular meetings provide for monitoring these continuing in-service needs, and the problem-solving approach helps to give the planners some idea of the support teachers' perceptions of and competence gained from the pre-placement course and to monitor the support teachers' development.

Meantime early feedback appears encouraging. An unpublished M.Ed. dissertation based on research into two of the schools concludes:

> The results show that there has been significant reduction in the adjustment difficulties of the pupils in the study. This can be seen from the perceptions of the pupils, support teachers and other teachers who deal with the pupils.
>
> (Moore, 1987)

The summative evaluation for the whole project will, among other things, look at the schools' perceptions of the work of their support teachers. It will also attempt to probe staff attitudes to pupils with adjustment problems and to see whether any changes, and if so what, have taken place in practical approaches, for example that teachers acknowledge their responsibility for *all* pupils, are willing and *able* to accept this and to act appropriately. Indeed, the planners see the in-service training as a central and integrated part of this process as in-service training should not only respond to needs and extend horizons, it should also show results.

References

CHEESMAN, P. L. and WATTS, P. E. (1985) *Positive Behaviour Management* (London: Croom Helm).

CHILD, D. (1985) 'Educational Psychology: Past, Present and Future' in Entwistle, N. (ed.) *New Directions in Educational Psychology 1. Learning and Teaching* (London and Philadelphia: The Falmer Press).

CHISHOLM, B. K., KEARNEY, D., KNIGHT, G., LITTLE, H., MORRIS, S. and TWEDDLE, D. (1984) *Preventive Approaches to Disruption* (London: Macmillan).

COULBY, D. and HARPER, T. (1985) *Preventing Classroom Disruption – Policy, Practice and Evaluation in Urban Schools* (London: Croom Helm).

DES (1987) *Education Observed 5. Good Behaviour and Discipline in Schools. A report by HM Inspectors* (London: DES).

GALLOWAY, D. (1983) 'Disruptive Pupils and Effective Pastoral Care', *School Organisation* 3, 245–54.

GALLOWAY, D. (1985) *Schools, Pupils and Special Educational Needs* (London: Croom Helm).

GALLOWAY, D. and GOODWIN, C. (1987) *The Education of Disturbing Children* (London: Longman).

GRUNSELL, R. (1985) *Finding Answers to Disruption. Discussion Exercises for Secondary Teachers* (London: Longman).

KELLY, G. A. (1955) *The Psychology of Personal Constructs* (New York: Norton).

MCNAMARA, N. (1985) 'Are the Techniques for Behaviour Modification Relevant to Problems of Concern to Teachers in Secondary School?' *Behavioural Approaches with Children*, Vol. 9, No. 2, pp. 34–45.

MERRETT, M. and WHELDALL, K. (1987) 'British Teachers and the behavioural approach to teaching', in Wheldall, K. (ed.) *The Behaviourist in the Classroom* (London: Allen and Unwin) pp. 18–49.

MOORE, P. L. (1987) 'An evaluation of the newly established provision for pupils with adjustment difficulties in two secondary schools', unpublished M.Ed. dissertation (University of Bath).

MUNRO, E. A., MANTHEI, R. J. and SMALL, J. J. (1983) *Counselling. A Skills Approach*, second edition (Auckland: Methuen).

PRESLAND, J. (1980) 'Behaviour Modification and Secondary Schools', *Behaviour Problems in the Comprehensive School* (Cardiff: Faculty of Education, University College).

RUTTER, M., MAUGHAN, B., MORTIMORE, P. and OUSTON, J. (1979) *Fifteen Thousand Hours, Secondary Schools and their Effects on Children* (London: Open Books).

TOPPING, K. (1983) *Educational Systems for Disruptive Adolescents* (London: Croom Helm).

Chapter 10

Reflections and Implications

Tony Charlton
and Kenneth David

Teachers rule, OK?

In Part I of this book it was suggested, on the basis of substantial evidence from research enquiries, that much behaviour at school seems to be independent of home influences. In other words, children's behaviour at school appears to be strongly affected by 'within school' factors. In the broadest context these are concerned with *what* schools offer their pupils and *how* they offer it. While there is little doubt that aspects of school policy and organisation, school ethos and the content of the curriculum make significant contributions to these offerings, we must not underestimate the impact of teachers' classroom behaviour – particularly their management of teaching skills – upon pupil behaviour.

A logical extension of the argument for a 'specific situation' cause of much behaviour, and the importance of 'within school' influences upon pupils' behaviour, is that much of pupils' classroom behaviour is less determined by wider school characteristics than by individual classroom influences. Schools (and homes) *do* influence behaviour in classrooms but we wish to emphasise that the behaviour which occurs in specific situations in the classrooms is largely determined by those very teaching situations. It is difficult not to accept this if we recognise that the same pupils often behave disparately with different teachers.

The reality of the classroom

In stressing the importance of the class teachers' role, and their classroom management skills in particular, we are not merely drawing attention to the good teaching and management skills which are evident in most classrooms, and suggesting that in other classrooms there are less successful colleagues who need to enhance such skills. None of us is perfect, and we do not all share common strengths and weaknesses. Rather, we recognise that:

(a) the great majority of teachers make considerable efforts to succeed in their professional endeavours;
(b) those efforts do not always lead to success; all of us, therefore, to a lesser or greater degree, benefit from continually evaluating and reflecting upon the efficacy of our efforts – this is professionalism;
(c) self-appraisal will most likely lead to success when it has the support of our school and colleagues;
(d) efforts to enhance our management skills will be more likely to achieve success if we have guidelines to good practice for reference or comparison.

Guidelines to good practice

In Part II and earlier in III the contributors considered theories and practices which have relevance for the development of teachers' classroom management skills. It is now our intention to reflect upon, and highlight, some salient points from within those chapters and, with additional pointers of our own, assemble a tentative set of twelve guidelines which may be helpful to practising and student teachers in their efforts to improve their skills in managing pupils' behaviour in classrooms. This checklist is neither comprehensive nor in order of priority, but might be used as a checklist by a teacher, or a school staff, to shape a personal or school plan for the better managment of pupils' behaviour, learning, and development.

1 Using reinforcement skills

A knowledge of the reinforcement concept gives added meaning to much classroom behaviour and, with a healthy degree of self-criticism, we can appreciate the occasional errors of our ways when, for example, our *non-reinforcement of appropriate behaviour* and *reinforcement of inappropriate behaviour* can actively encourage misbehaviour.

While common sense often seems to guide us in our use of *positive reinforcements* it is useful to remember the following.

- We need to be wary of an overzealous use of reinforcements which may lead to satiation.
- Effort should be reinforced as frequently as actual achievements; by doing so we encourage industry and persistence, without which achievement becomes less likely.
- With some individuals it may be necessary to search hard to find behaviours which warrant praise. Perseverance by the teacher in those instances is often crucial for these may be the very pupils most inclined to misbehave because they have been so infrequently reinforced in the past.
- Reinforcements administered publicly to some pupils may, in fact, be construed as punishment. For a variety of reasons (for example shyness, and with older ones a fear of ridicule from peers) some pupils dislike having public attention drawn to their efforts and accomplishments. Praise may need to be given privately.
- We are often misled into believing that reinforcements need to be given immediately following the occurrence of desirable behaviour. While this may be true in some instances, when working with the mentally retarded or the very young perhaps, occasions become more frequent with increasing age and maturity when a delay between behaviour and reinforcement may be not only more convenient, but more effective and desirable. Many of the reinforcements we receive as we grow older (such as assignment grades, degree awards and promotion) are often distant from the acts which earned them. As part of the maturing process youngsters need to learn to appreciate and accept this 'time gap'.
- Reinforcements can be signalled in subtle ways, perhaps a wink or a smile. Where applied within large group situations they not only provide variety but can also be used in a 'confidential' manner. While young children may prefer a hug, it is a sad indictment of the age in which we live that we need to be especially guarded about using such contact.
- What is reinforcing (for example attention and praise) *from one person* may not be so from another. Similarly, what is reinforcing *to one child* may not be so to another. An awareness of these differences gives an indication of the complexity of the reinforcement concept.
- Reinforcements can be given to small and large groups as well as individuals. They can work wonders for group morale.
- On occasions we may need to make clear to pupils what has been reinforced, by drawing attention to behaviour-reinforcement associations. 'Good' may not necessarily indicate to the pupils 'what is good'. It may be more appropriate and beneficial to comment 'Good. You've worked hard this lesson'.

Negative reinforcements also have a contribution to make to teachers' management of classroom behaviour, but they should be used carefully and sparingly. Whereas positive reinforcers are applied to – and so encourage – good behaviour, negative reinforcers (for example, threats) lead to improved behaviour only because pupils behave appropriately in order to *avoid* unwanted consequences. An example of negative reinforcement occurs when a teacher informs a class, at the onset of morning break, that they will remain in the classroom until their rowdy behaviour ceases; so to avoid the unpleasant experience of missing some of their break period, the class behaviour has to improve. However, not all children will regard remaining in the classroom as an unpleasant experience!

While negative reinforcers can make useful contributions to teachers' management skills, an over-reliance upon them can result in the frequent use of threats and warnings; conditions that make little, if any, contribution to a healthy classroom ethos, and are inconsistent with good management practices.

2 Considering punishments

Punishment is a common and often effective occurrence in our lives. Undeniably, a variety of punishments are used in schools and classrooms including:

order-points	loss of privileges
reprimands	suspension
detention	on-report
lines	corporal punishment
time-out from positive reinforcement	sarcasm
	cynicism
disapproval	sanctions

Nevertheless its use in the classroom has aroused some concern and debate. There is evidence available showing that behaviour in some classrooms is controlled by a preponderance of punishments as opposed to rewards (Thomas *et al.*, 1978). It is difficult to envisage a healthy classroom ethos where this type of control prevails.

Opposition against the use of punishment is most frequently based upon the following arguments.

- It often serves only to help prevent a behaviour occurring in the

future; by itself it does not provide alternative acceptable behaviours which should be used.
- It can generate fears and harmful anxieties which may encourage avoidance behaviours (that is, the pupil may avoid places where, or people from whom, punishment has been – or is – given).
- This avoidance of punishment areas (for example a particular teacher, subject or classroom) may generalise to other areas (for example, other teachers, subjects, classrooms, school).
- Its application may serve as an unhealthy model for pupils.

Clearly, where punishment is administered it should be recognised that it may not only prove unhelpful, in the sense that it does not provide positive guidance for miscreants' future behaviours, and may provide unhealthy models for observers and recipients alike, but may also create unhelpful fears and anxieties which actively encourage avoidance behaviours such as truancy.

Nevertheless, it does not seem unreasonable to suggest that intervention attempts restricted to positive or negative reinforcements, building of self-esteem and good modelling may not always be in the best interests of children or teachers. At times it may be both expedient and helpful if pupils experience aversive consequences of their misbehaviour. This does not imply a wholesale usage of punishment, but rather that occasions may demand that it is used, though sparingly and effectively, for the very best of reasons.

Clarizio and McCoy (1983) consider arguments for the use of punishment, and offer the following guidelines for its administration.

- Whenever possible the pupils should be given a signal or warning prior to potential punishment. This, by itself, may deter the misbehaviour. It also provides a degree of fairness where the punishment becomes inevitable (for example 'You were warned!').
- Research evidence has consistently shown it is usually better to punish early, than to delay until the problem has become magnified.
- Attempts should be made in the first instance to remove the rewards which elicit or sustain the misbehaviour.
- It should be made quite clear why the punishment is being meted out.
- It should not be given unfairly and injudiciously.
- It should be employed by teachers in a rational, systematic and 'mood free' manner. Its aim is to improve the pupils' present and future performance, and not provide a cathartic experience for the teacher.

- It should not be administered through, or accompanied by, emotive screaming or yelling conveying an attitude of revenge which may, in fact, serve only to reinforce the very misbehaviour which is being punished.
- It should not be too severe.
- Its use over extended periods of time should be avoided. The length and nature of the punishment should match the offence (for example don't use a sledgehammer to smash a walnut), and the pupil's developmental level.
- The punishment should not take up an inordinate amount of the teacher's time. A detention arranged for after school may be as punishing, if not more so, to the teacher as the pupil.
- Wherever possible, reward related appropriate behaviour either side of the punishment of inappropriate behaviour; thus we reprimand the child when off-task but remember to reward when on-task.

3 Modelling from teachers' behaviour

Modelling is an important way in which children and adults learn 'chunks' of behaviour. From a classroom management perspective modelling theory has much to offer. Children, in addition to that which they learn from the formal curriculum in school, learn much from observing their teachers and peers. It is common knowledge that they often find it easier to learn behaviours which they see practised, rather than only being explained to them: they tend to do even better when the two are combined. They will be more inclined to model the behaviours of those who have prestige: while young children seem intuitively to assign prestige to their teachers, older ones are more discriminative and tend to require their teachers to earn such prestige. In general, teachers who are able to form good personal relationships with their pupils and earn their respect are more likely to earn prestige, and, therefore, have their behaviour modelled.

It seems important, from a modelling perspective, that teachers behave in classrooms in ways which they wish their pupils to adopt. Where inconsistencies exist between the adult's own behaviour and the behaviours asked of the class, pupils can easily become either confused about which 'sets of behaviours' they should adopt, or imitate the wrong ones.

The following give only an indication of the wide repertoire of behaviours which prestigious teachers can demonstrate in classrooms and so encourage their pupils to model.

- Recognising, and respecting, the responsibilities of authority figures such as parents, colleagues, headteachers, and police.
- Respecting other individuals' rights by listening to them, and responding with interest; refraining from using sarcasm and harsh criticism.
- Acknowledging and accepting responsibility for personal errors, and failings, by accepting and responding appropriately to justifiable criticism, and apologising to pupils where situations require it.
- Demonstrating a sensitivity to, and concern for individuals' problems, and feelings (for example concerns, fears, unhappiness, and anxieties), and a willingness to assist where practicable.
- Refraining from over-reactions by practising control of their own emotions.
- By recognising, accepting, and responding responsibly to less, and more, obvious individual differences, such as children with special needs, those from ethnic minority groups and those in care.
- By handling books, equipment and other materials with care.
- By accentuating positive aspects of pupils such as their attributes, achievements, and efforts, rather than negative ones.

4 Enhancing self-concepts

We are now more able, and willing, than in the past, to recognise the role which the self-concept plays in helping to determine behaviour. We know, for example, that children who do not perform well academically tend to hold a more negative picture of their 'self' than their more successful peers. Similarly, there is evidence available suggesting that children experiencing a range of emotional problems such as anxieties, worries and concerns also tend to have low self-concepts. Instances such as these suggest an infinite number of ways in which low self-concepts may be associated with behaviour problems. Pupils who regard themselves as poor achievers, for example, may be conscious of, and sensitive to, their academic inferiority. If their inferior performance fails to attract desired teacher reinforcements then they may resort to misbehaviour in order to 'succeed' in attracting teachers' attention. Equally important, the actual feelings of failure and inferiority may themselves constitute unhealthy emotional states.

What is clear is that classroom experiences may depress, as well as elevate, pupils' self-concepts. Teachers, understandably, have a key role in determining which of these two conditions predominate: their deliberate or unintentional actions help determine their pupils' concepts of 'self'.

Teacher characteristics such as *empathy*, *unconditional positive regard for pupils*, and *genuineness* seem likely to encourage the growth of positive self-esteem in pupils. Empathic understanding implies that teachers can experience their pupils' 'inner world'. They know how they are feeling and, therefore, gain insight into their behavioural responses to those feelings. Unconditional positive regard suggests an interest in, and a liking and concern for the youngster; feelings such as these actively demonstrate that the teacher 'cares' and wants to help. Genuineness is a teacher state which the pupil interprets as an honesty and openness.

In combination these qualities illustrate the 'caring' concern on the teacher's part; one which is both sensitive to pupils' fears, worries and concerns and willing to support, or build up, pupils' skills and self-concepts. Given that such teachers are equipped with other appropriate skills they arrange classroom experiences for pupils which maximise opportunities for personal, social and academic success, yet make failure possible.

More specifically, Canfield and Wells (1976) outline 100 ways to improve children's self-concepts'. They describe in detail a large number of teaching activities and teacher behaviours which can affect pupils' self-concepts in positive and negative directions. While there are too many to describe in detail – or even list – the following provide a cursory glimpse into those activities:

Social silhouettes

Daily, or less frequently, a pupil volunteers to become 'famous'. A full-size head silhouette of the child is drawn on a dark piece of paper, perhaps with the aid of the light from an OHP. It is cut out, mounted on a sheet of different coloured paper and pinned on the wall. For that day, the rest of the class are invited to write *complimentary* comments about that person on a piece of paper, and they attach them to the display. At the end of the day the teacher then reads the comments to the class, after which the 'head' is transferred to another prominent position elsewhere ('Hall of Fame') perhaps in the hall. This type of exercise can work wonders! We would all like to hear the positive thoughts which people hold about us; but only infrequently do we have the opportunities.

Success sharing

Pupils are allocated to small groups and asked to volunteer to share some of their successes, achievements or accomplishments with the group. To give them some needed direction it may be helpful for the teacher to suggest that they first share the experiences they enjoyed, for example, before they started school; then before they were six, then nine and so on. Alternatively, the teacher could encourage them to talk about successes which happened recently, or within the last month, or the last year.

With some children, particularly those with low self-concepts, the teacher may need to draw attention to successes which *they* know the child has experienced – 'Your mother was telling me how helpful you had been in caring for the "new" baby'. This type of activity, correctly managed, can help children to recognise that they will have accomplishments of which they can be proud. In life it is so easy for all of us to become preoccupied with negative, rather than positive, aspects of our 'self'.

On my mind

Pupils each have a silhouette of their own heads. They then cut out pictures, words or sentences which represent their current thoughts and paste them on to the 'profile' to make a collage of their feelings. Later, if pupils are willing, these collages can be shared with others in the class. This activity not only may provide the teachers with helpful information about the pupils' feelings but also may help some pupils to realise that some of their concerns, for example, are shared by others; they are not alone.

Killer statements

Here the teacher gives examples of how people can make comments which cause hurt to others.

> You're a thorough nuisance
>
> She's hopeless
>
> What a stupid boy. Can't you do anything right?

Drawing attention to the fact that other people have feelings that can easily be hurt, can help pupils to become more helpful to, and considerate towards, their peers and others.

The goalpost

The teacher prepares a diagram of a football pitch, complete with a goalpost, on a display board. Children can elect to record their 'goal for the day' on a small piece of card and place it *beneath* the upper bar of the post. On the following day, the teacher invites only those who have achieved their 'goal', to discuss it with the class and then place their 'goal card' above the bar – assuming the 'referees' accept it is a goal.

5 Exploring 'beneath the surface' behaviours

The needs of children (in mainstream as well as special schools) whose behaviour problems are more severe and long lasting may require teachers to be less concerned with changing '*surface*' behaviours than with exploring *beneath* these behaviours to identify, understand and provide for underlying difficulties the children may be experiencing. There is a range of techniques available which teachers can draw upon in order to provide appropriate help. By and large, these strategies and skills are of an order which requires specialist training. In general terms they include establishing classroom climates which provide *security, a degree of predictability, individual help, clear and realistic expectations*, and *safety* for each pupil, in order to enhance individual personal, social and academic competencies, and so help to erase the self-doubts and low self-esteem which often characterise these children.

These strategies and conditions are equally relevant to the needs of children without such serious and long-term problems. However, in more serious instances the use of these strategies requires protracted periods of time within which to develop chances of success.

Where teachers apply long-term strategies, they may well benefit from parallel initiatives which offer them skills to manage more immediate and challenging surface behaviours. Fritz Redl's (1952) contributions to management techniques, rather surprisingly in view of his leaning towards psychodynamic approaches, have proved invaluable to mainstream and special school class teachers time and again. Working with children with severe emotional problems at Pioneer House in America, he stressed the residential community's long-term aims and strategies to assist pupils to establish *'controls from within'*, while recognising that, in the short term, his teachers also needed management techniques which would provide *'controls from without'*.   His response was to construct a set of management skills, which he entitled *The Antiseptic Manipulation of Surface Behaviour*, designed to exercise control over pupils' surface (superficial?) behaviour. Like many effective techniques their apparent simplicity and common sense belies their impact. He talks, for example, about the following.

- *Ignoring misbehaviours* as far as practicable, contending that some misbehaviours have only a limited 'charge' and, if ignored, they lose their charge, and so disappear.
- Using a *sense of humour* to exorcise bad feelings. For example, Jimmy, a petulant and aggressive adolescent, entered the classroom, sat down and placed his feet on the desk and announced to all and sundry that he was going to work at half-pace in future. The inexperienced, yet very sharp, young teacher immediately retorted 'Good; that will be an improvement'. The teacher laughed, the group laughed and Jimmy, somewhat less willing, then joined in; a potentially volatile situation had been defused.
- *Signal interference* exercises quiet (almost confidential at times) yet effective controls over minor misbehaviours – raised eyebrows, a raised finger to the lips or a wink. Some teachers have achieved mastery with this skill. Where the class is working well apart from a single, or small number of culprits, the teacher can practise such signals without disturbing the rest of the class, and without antagonising the individual(s).
- *Hurdle help* is given where a teacher is alert to a situation which can develop unhealthily such as pupils beginning to quarrel or becoming frustrated at not being able to do work. The teacher intervenes before the problem grows and helps the pupils to 'hurdle' or successfully deal with the problem situation.
- *Proximity or touch control* where the teacher controls misbehaviour by physically moving towards it. Approaching the source of misbehaviour and, perhaps, touching a child's shoulder or hand is often sufficient to quell it.
- *Involvement of interest relationships* where a teacher notes that a child is losing interest in his or her work and is about to misbehave. By expressing an interest in that child's work the teacher can refocus the child upon the work and so prevent the misbehaviour.
- *Restructuring*, where the activity being undertaken is beginning to

generate unacceptable behaviour, and the teacher changes the activity to one which precludes 'disturbing' behaviour.
- *Regrouping*; an activity where the teacher transfers the child to another seat, group or – in more extreme situations – another class in order to remove the child from situations in which he or she can either disturb, or become distracted by, others.
- By providing an injection of *hypodermic affection* – giving praise or affection – teachers may encourage a pupil to cope with anxiety or frustration.
- *Antiseptic bouncing*. This occurs when, for a number of reasons, the pupil has to be removed from a situation where he is either causing, or is on the receiving end of, behaviour likely to cause considerable harm to peers or himself. Bouncing, or removal, takes place in order to give help to the pupil, and should not encourage feelings, on the child's part, of rejection or rewarding.
- *Interpretation as interference*, where the pupil has 'misread' or misinterpreted a situation and the teacher intervenes to interpret the situation correctly to the pupil.
- *Direct appeal*; occasions when a direct appeal for appropriate behaviour appeals to a child's sense of fair play or justice.
- Using *promises, rewards, punishments and threats* to encourage appropriate, and discourage unacceptable, behaviour.

Teachers, of course, will know that more severe emotional and behaviour problems demand help which, in terms of time as well as expertise, they are ill-equipped to provide, and perhaps would be ill-advised to attempt. In these instances, if the severity of the problem was previously undetected or unsuspected, the teachers' primary function is to bring the pupil's difficulties to the attention of the relevant referral agencies, in accordance with the school's policy. Guidelines for such action has been reviewed in Chapter 8.

6 Preventive Approaches to Disruption (PAD)

The PAD material (Chisholm *et al.*, 1986) sensibly emphasises a number of basic classroom rules which, though rarely given the recognition they deserve, help to keep pupils to their task, leaving little time for other activities likely to interfere with the smooth running of the class. The philosophy underpinning these 'rules' is as follows:

- Pupils' behaviour is influenced by the teacher's behaviour.

- Teachers with effective classroom control are skilled at avoiding and de-escalating problem behaviour.
- Specific techniques of classroom management and control can be described, practised and acquired by teachers.
- Teachers should take responsibility for developing their skills and should be supported in doing so by their schools.

The 'common-sense' rules draw attention, for example, to the wisdom of teachers practising the following.

1. *Positioning* themselves, particularly at the beginning and ending of lessons, where they have maximal opportunities to oversee and regulate pupils' behaviour. Similarly, when approaching a child to give individual attention there are obvious advantages in assuming a position which requires only an upward glance to monitor other pupils' behaviour.
2. Adequately *preparing lesson content*; making sure that materials and equipment needed are available in sufficient quantity, and are easily distributed.
3. Using unobtrusive and *subtle management skills* such as proximity control by being near miscreants both to quell minor misbehaviours such as talking, unnecessary fidgeting or 'fiddling', and avoiding giving them undue and possibly harmful prominence.
4. Refining and extending their repertoire of *non-verbal skills* in order to:
   (a) avoid teacher behaviours likely to increase the likelihood of pupils misbehaving, such as:
   - speaking in a monotonous way
   - making little eye-to-eye contact with pupils
   - using limited gestures
   - communicating feelings of anxiety or tenseness to pupils

   (b) practise behaviours likely to discourage pupil misbehaviours such as:
   - teachers being at ease with their classes
   - using non-verbal gestures – eye-to-eye contact, rhythm and emphasis in their voices, and changes of posture.
5. Organising their classrooms in ways which motivate children to work well and so leave little time for misbehaviours. In this context the following seem important:
   - Apparatus, materials and furniture should preferably be assembled and arranged prior to pupils' arrival.

- Lesson plans and content are prepared thoroughly, and additional work prepared for those pupils who finish early.
- Work is made appropriate to pupils' age, ability and cultural background.
- Pupils' entrance to classrooms is supervised and orderly.
- Lessons commence in an enthusiastic manner and continue to attract and maintain pupils' attention.
- Instructions are given in a clear audible fashion.
- Where lesson changes take place these are well organised and smooth.
- Vigilance or 'with-it-ness' is practised so as to enable teachers to monitor behaviour, and intervene where potential difficulties arise so as to minimise disruptions.
- Where problems do arise, teachers intervene promptly.
- Teacher actions are perceived by pupils as being fair.
- Classwork and homework is marked promptly and thoroughly, and feedback is helpful and meaningful.
- Effective questioning techniques are developed to check whether pupils have assimilated learning, and to help keep their attention.
- Teaching techniques are varied so as to maintain interest.
- Anticipation of the timing of lessons so that the ending can be efficient and orderly.
- Attention is focused upon the potential dangers of narrow corridors and classroom seating arrangements that offer passageways which impede orderly movement by pupils, and encourage rowdy and boisterous behaviours.
- Avoidance of:
  – using physical means of governing pupils' actions, and
  – ridiculing pupils.

7 Considering the curriculum

We know only too well that it is important that pupils receive a curriculum which matches their present and future needs, and arouses their interests and best endeavours. However, even the best tailored curriculum can be made to look shoddy if teachers of sufficient calibre are not available to administer it. Experiences have frequently shown us how one teacher, for example, can inject a 'breath of life' into a lesson, or subject, while another gives it the 'kiss of death'.

Pupils' misbehaviour, therefore, may be a logical and not unreasonable response to a timetable which includes subjects and material which they have little or no interest in, and which are administered to them in a manner which depresses their interest and discourages healthy involvement.

Pupils' behaviour is also affected adversely or otherwise by the various ways in which schools organise their curriculum. Whether they stream, band or organise mixed ability groups, their policy for allocating teachers to classes, and the range of options they offer, and truly make available, seem to be important considerations.

The main consideration, however, may not be *how* they organise the curriculum but *why*. Schools with similar organisational patterns and intakes often have differing impacts upon their pupils' behaviour as well as learning. An important factor in determining levels of success may be the extent to which senior management have adequately considered, and made informed responses to, the real needs of all their clients; have consulted with staff, parents and pupils, and consequently have made sincere and successful overtures to convince staff, parents and pupils that what they offer and how they offer it is aimed to provide the 'best for all'. While perfection may not be practicable, and compromise may be necessary, *consultation, involvement, sincerity* and *informed decisions* work wonders.

Most good schools have sound policies for internal and external consultations and scrutinies when considering and implementing changes. While disparities will be evident in the ways in which they undertake such action the types of questions which concerned parents may ask, on behalf of their children, could include the following:

1. How is the curriculum organised (for example, setting/banding/mixed ability)? How is this arrangement justified in terms of meeting needs of pupils who are high fliers, average or low achievers?
2. Is the range and content of the curriculum matched to pupils' present and future needs? What arrangements have been undertaken to complete and monitor this match?
3. Are parents, pupils and staff consulted over curriculum matters, particularly where changes are being considered? Are meaningful attempts made to explain to staff, pupils and parents the rationale for the organisation of the curriculum, as well as its content?
4. Are the sexes separated for certain subjects? How is this justified?
5. Is there a homework timetable? Are pupils and parents given copies of this? Is there a school policy about staff adhering to it?

6   Is homework, and other work, marked regularly, adequately and promptly? Is feedback appropriate and adequate?
7   If children are absent what revision arrangements are available on their return?

8   Using the Life Space Interview

The term Life Space Interview originated by Redl (1959) uses principles of psychodynamic theory, and Morse (1963) suggests methods which teachers and others can use. The intention is to develop effective therapeutic support for pupils at a time and in a place where the child's problem is most relevant – in the child's normal life space, not in more distant and strange expert referral settings. It is seen that problems are better dealt with, at least in the first place, in settings where the immediacy and relevance of the support is obvious to the child. Clearly referral to others outside the school may be necessary later, for teachers have limited time and preparation for a full therapeutic role.

Other writers (particularly Hamblin, 1974) have described such supportive encounters between a troubled pupil and responsive teacher, following the same patterns as the LSI theorists, under the general heading of school counselling. Hamblin provides a clear model for counselling for secondary schools (Chapter 2) and describes life space diagrams (p. 126) of the relationships between a pupil and other people with whom he has to live, including teachers, as part of a mutual diagnosis of a problem shared by a pupil and his or her teacher–counsellor.

The interview may be shaped something as follows.

Gobell (1980, p. 68) in describing a basic framework of LSI writes of a downward or inward first part of the interview, where the teacher listens, attends, clarifies and encourages; and an upward or outward second part, when alternative interpretations are explored, other views argued, and appropriate action planned. He suggests that such a model can be used even when there are only a few moments available; the model of always listening and attending to the child first, then exploring possibilities and perhaps allocating blame later, may well be habitual in all experienced teachers' dealings with children's problems. Longer periods of time are obviously essential when feelings have to be explored more fully, when it is necessary to 'squeeze' guilt issues into open awareness, using Redl and Wineman's (1952, p. 257) phrase. Mutually to sort reality from fantasy, to reduce rage or inarticulate helplessness, and to begin to comprehend the feelings of others involved, takes more

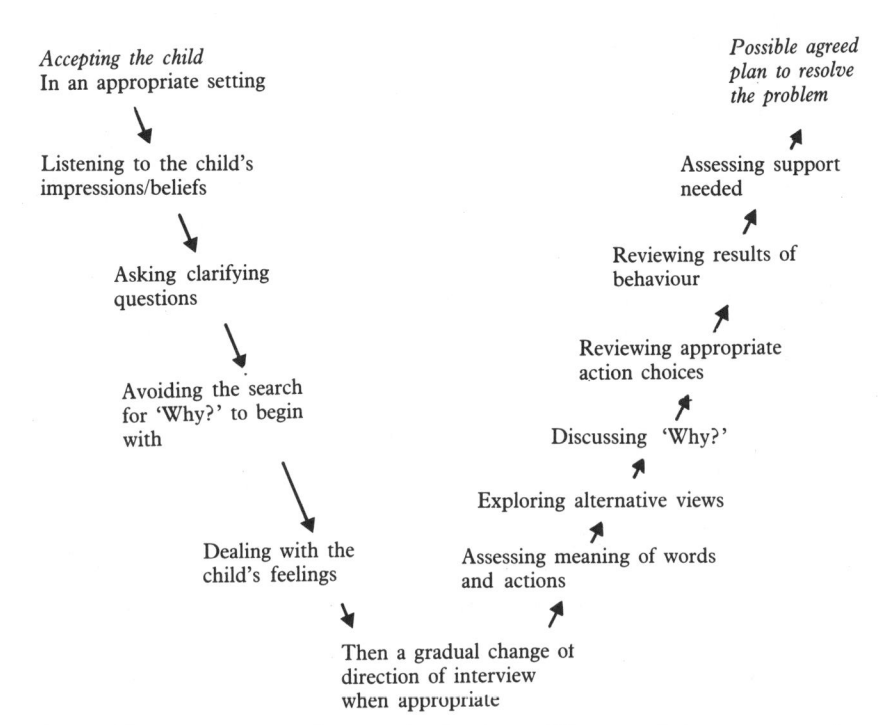

Accepting the child
In an appropriate setting
↓
Listening to the child's impressions/beliefs
↓
Asking clarifying questions
↓
Avoiding the search for 'Why?' to begin with
↓
Dealing with the child's feelings
↓
Then a gradual change of direction of interview when appropriate
↑
Assessing meaning of words and actions
↑
Exploring alternative views
↑
Discussing 'Why?'
↑
Reviewing appropriate action choices
↑
Reviewing results of behaviour
↑
Assessing support needed
↑
Possible agreed plan to resolve the problem

than a few moments of a teacher's time. The need for a pastoral care system which permits time for counselling, both routine and emergency, is clear.

There is a strong case for regular interviews of this sort with all pupils in turn, with an opportunity for teacher and individual pupil to review where they stand in their complementary tasks of teaching and learning. The more therapeutic interview may be a parallel pattern or a development from this.

9 Developing counselling skills and attitudes

A simple form of training in counselling skills and attitudes should be an important part of basic training and in-service work. There are familiar checklists of concepts.

1   The possession or development of :
    - congruence or empathy, even when a pupil is unable to accept reality at times,
    - non-possessive warmth, often undemanding,
    - genuine interest,
    should be part of good teaching as well as counselling.

224 *Managing Misbehaviour*

2   The fundamental ability to listen is not easy for all teachers.
3   Sharing reflective conversation, or counselling or interviewing if we prefer the terms, with a pupil or pupils has various implications.
    • There is a skill in group discussion work. Many problems can be resolved within a class or group by an individual listening to discussion on a theme which has relevance to his particular needs.
    • We need to keep a balance between cold detachment and too emotional an involvement.
    • The rule of parsimony requires us to not labour the obvious.
    • There are limits to confidentiality, and this has to be comprehended by pupils.
    • We must refer to more expert help when reaching the limits of our personally assessed ability to cope with a deep problem. There are different levels of counselling which teachers can sustain – their personal common-sense limits.
    • There are skills of clarifying and summarising what a pupil is saying, used at appropriate times.
    • We should not avoid all silences, and need to study the many forms of questioning.
    • Problems can be cut down to size at times, and pupils can begin to work on a problem in appropriate stages, as part of the 'action plan' worked out in the counselling.
    • There is value in working as part of a pastoral team, for 'shared counselling' is acceptable to many pupils, and answers to problems sometimes lie in the cooperation and understanding of other staff.
    • There is a need for an understanding of personal and social education and study skills.
    • We should consider carefully what personal autonomy means to ourselves and our pupils, and when intervention needs to be weighed against interference.

10   Regularly reviewing pastoral care arrangements

In considering the effect on his classroom management of a school's pastoral care system a teacher might ask the following questions and seek satisfying answers.

1   To whom am I responsible for pastoral and academic matters, and is the support sufficient at my present stage of professional development?

2   Can I share problems and skills with others in a staff team?
3   Do I have the traditional 'tutorial' skills?
    - Listening and discussion skills.
    - Building security and trust in the class.
    - Efficient administrative and recording patterns.
    - Quiet discipline, with occasional referral support.
    - Parental links and cooperation.
    - Overseeing the 'whole person' development of pupils, with an understanding of all his or her activities and work in the school.
    - Relaxed and automatic observation of all that goes on in the class, and in the lives of the pupils, including friendships, quarrels and moods, health signs, welfare needs, and steady development.
4   What in-service development would help me in my work, and how can I seek it?
5   What personal and social education agenda of topics would be appropriate and essential for the age group of my pupils, and do I fully know what this entails?
6   In dealing with behaviour problems have I developed diagnostic skills?
    - When and where does the behaviour occur?
    - Why does it occur?
    - What are the differences in the situations when problems occur and do not occur?
    - What changes might be possible?
    - What support or advice might I need in dealing with this?
7   Am I the cause of some of my classroom problems, and does the school system offer useful advice and guidance?

11   Parent cooperation

Examples were given in Chapter 8 to illustrate how parents, teachers and other professionals can, through a sharing of educational responsibility, respond more effectively to problem behaviours. It was recommended that joint responses might best be developed through four stages of parent–professional involvement. The following questions are designed to help schools reflect upon their current practices within those stages and to consider the need for further developments.

1   *The introductory stage*
    (a) How are parents introduced to, and welcomed into, the work

of the school? Are assemblies, displays, coffee mornings, concerts, information booklets, and personal interview useful?
(b) Is there an agreed school policy for introductory events, or are teachers given a 'free hand'?
(c) Are parents introduced to, and encouraged to become active in, the life of the school *before* problem behaviours have been experienced?
(d) Who introduces new parents to the benefits of closer liaison? Are 'experienced' parents fully involved in this process, perhaps relaying accounts of successful liaison which was of clear benefit to their own child.
(e) How are hidden messages conveyed to parents? Is there a very formalised interview system or ready access via more informal methods? Are parents given a feeling that problem behaviours are 'their fault' and not a shared responsibility?
(f) Is the development of parent–professional liaison seen as a one-way process where the parent has to come to school, or should it be seen as a two-way process where professionals introduce the work of the school through home or community centres?

2   *The informative stage*
(a) How does the liaison process move from the stage of introducing parents to the school into more focused ways of discussing a particular child?
(b) What is the school's policy for giving and receiving information about a child?
(c) Is the process above a procedure of information-giving or one which leads to improved forms of action which benefit the child? Is success consolidated through various complementary forms of controlled praise at home? Is the curriculum adjusted according to specific information regarding the child's interests and motivation?
(d) Is the informative process designed to lead, naturally, to the next stage of joint provision?
(e) Is the informative stage limited to formalised short periods of consultation on parents' evenings, or is this system extended via diary systems and opportunities for discussion at other informal events?

3   *The joint provision Stage*
(a) To what extent do parents and professionals work together with whole classes, groups and individual pupils? Is there a consistent pattern of involvement throughout the school?
(b) How does this process help both partners to develop a better

understanding of their respective roles and intentions towards pupils?
(c) Are there any whole-school initiatives for an active partnership through procedures such as paired and shared reading?
(d) Is advice given through short talks and seminars about particular aspects of the curriculum, and ways of responding to problem behaviours?
(e) How do parents and professionals work together to provide for the particular needs of an individual pupil? Is this work clearly planned and coordinated?

4 *The sharing of responsibility stage*
When problem behaviours have been encountered:
(a) Do parents and professionals keep each other informed at a level which does *not* lead to jointly planned responses?
(b) Do parents and professionals join in the process of shared-information gathering so that they can arrive at a precise description of:
 (i) the behaviour itself,
 (ii) the factors leading up to and surrounding it,
 (iii) the consequences which follow,
 (iv) and expectations about future behaviour?
(c) Is an attempt made by either party to dominate the process by advising the other person about the responses which *they* should make to problem behaviours, or are genuine attempts made to blend the knowledge and skills of both participants in providing for the pupil's needs?
(d) Is there a consistency of response at home and school?
(e) Are attempts made to evaluate the success of shared interventions?

12 Assumptions and expectations

We assume many things about our pupils; they will know, as we do, that hard work brings rewards, we assume. It is a clear and universal fact, we think – but in their particular world all the evidence of family history may have led them to know the opposite, and leads them to a blank incomprehension as to what we are on about. Attitudes and values can be influenced by a respected teacher, and can overcome the built-in assumptions of their neighbourhood and family, but it is skilled and committed work, and requires sensitivity and imagination on the teacher's part. Easy assumptions make life simpler; reflecting on our assumptions and keeping up a questioning and pragmatic attitude about our pupils and their ideas is harder.

When we take the easier path and develop a reputation for not bothering to know their language and world, we alienate some pupils, and behaviour problems easily arise. The disenchanted among our clients are likely to be cynical and watchful, and evidence that we do give thought to understanding (though not necessarily approving) their ideas may bring cooperation, and a growing feeling of interest or curiosity in the teacher's attitudes and demands.

Parallel with this a consistency in terms of behavioural expectations gives a much needed security to pupils, both young and old. They become aware of teachers' expectations and are more able to respond favourably than where there is inconsistency. Arguably the best classrooms – and perhaps homes – have a limited number of essential rules and guidelines, and pupils are free to operate responsibly within these guidelines. Ultimately pupils need to regulate their behaviour from within rather than be controlled from without. If their teachers provide meaningful initial guidelines and provide freedom to exercise increasing control, most pupils benefit from this responsibility.

Conclusion

The recent HMI (1987) report, *Education Observed 5: Good behaviour and discipline in schools*, emphasises many of the management skills and practices mentioned in this final chapter, and its summary provides a useful template for our conclusion.

In their report, HMI emphasise that good behaviour is both a prerequisite for effective learning, and an important outcome of education itself, which society expects from its schools. Good behaviour in school not only minimises the distractions and disturbances which interfere with learning, but also is a crucial part of the learning process within which pupils acquire the attitudes, values and skills which help to prepare them for the future.

HMI refer to the following principles of good practice which are influential in creating and sustaining high standards of behaviour in school:

> A *school policy document* provides a small number of clear and defensible guidelines for behaviour. These guidelines make the school's expectations on behaviour clear, to pupils and parents, and

are firmly, consistently and judiciously enforced. Linked to the formulation and enforcement of these guidelines is the type of *leadership from senior staff* that encourages good behaviour through example, holds healthy professional expectations of colleagues and pupils, is vigilant (and appropriately responsive) to behaviour in the school, and provides positive sources of support for staff as well as pupils.

The *school climate* or ethos both reflects, and influences, the general welfare of the school. The network of relationships and expectations amongst and between pupils, staff, parents and outside professionals, and the overall quality of pastoral care practices, are as influential in determining this climate as the impact of the formal curriculum and teaching skills of those who administer it.

Whilst teachers and their pupils derive benefit from the sparing and flexible application of *sanctions* for certain pupil misbehaviours, their use should be outweighed by the award of *rewards and privileges* for good behaviour. Such a policy actively encourages desirable behaviour whilst discouraging others which are less so.

These basic principles of good practice, and the plethora of highly developed professional skills which contribute to them, provide an insight into the nature of the influences which schools can put to good use to affect their clients' behaviour.

Schools are institutions; they are a microcosm, or inner world, of the larger outside world. As in the outer world, individuals' behaviour is fashioned by, for example, the manner in which they are regarded, valued and rewarded; the nature of the expectations held about them; the quality of the group and individual learning experiences made available to them; the examples set by those with responsibility and authority, and the adequacy of available caring provisions in monitoring and responding to individual and group needs.

The crucial differences between the two 'worlds' lie in areas such as *appraisal, accountability* and *involvement*. In the outside world we are continually having the quality of our lives *appraised* for (if not by) us, and modified where there is a consensus of opinion amongst us that change is necessary, feasible and welcome. Those who are officially appointed to make decisions about our lives are *accountable* to – and often either elected or indirectly appointed by – us. They are also responsive to majority, or particularly strong, opinion. Most major decisions taken about us are made, therefore, with our *involvement*, directly or otherwise, or that of our elected representatives.

In the inner world, however, 'clients' are infrequently permitted to be actively, and effectively, involved in making decisions about matters which have a direct impact upon their lives.

There is a strong wind of change approaching education; one which threatens or heralds, depending upon your particular stance, more appraisal, improved accountability and enhanced involvement. Current discussions relating to teacher appraisal, a national curriculum, the Education Reform Bill in general, and more effective parental involvement, represent a plethora of exciting, innovatory, yet often threatening proposals. Although these proposed changes may not always result in improvements, discussions about them place the 'ball in the schools' court' to await their response. It is not practicable to legislate for good practice. The value of legislation is not that it prescribes good practice, but that *it makes clear where responsibilities lie*.

As this book goes to press the teaching profession, alongside a multitude of other people involved with – and/or concerned for – the educational system, are eagerly awaiting the outcome of a government sponsored enquiry into discipline in schools (the Elton Report). Their deliberations will have paid close attention to the plethora of evidence and comment submitted by professional associations and many others. Undoubtedly, they will have been confronted with conflicting evidence regarding the extent and degree of violence and indiscipline in schools. It is difficult to anticipate how they will sift through, and respond to, disparate claims and suggestions. Hopefully, their findings and recommendations will be influenced by positive, and helpful, recommendations such as those included in the National Children's Bureau's response to the Elton Committee's request for assistance. In response to the question asking what actions relevant organisations and individuals could make to help promote an orderly atmosphere in schools, the NCB (1988) summarised its response (to which one of the Editors contributed) within the following nine major points:

1. General exhortations by the Committee – or by Ministers – to parents or to teachers about the necessity to 'improve standards of behaviour' etc. are unlikely to be effective or of value.
2. The clear message needs to be conveyed to schools (by the Committee in the first instance) that although a number of the familial and other factors which may predispose some pupils to disruption and misbehaviour in school are largely outside the school's control, there is now a great deal of evidence to indicate that the way a school is led and organised and the quality of the relationships which are developed between staff and pupils are of

very considerable importance in determining the behaviour of pupils. Further, this behaviour cannot meaningfully be viewed – nor steps be taken to improve it – in isolation. It is in particular related to the relevance of the curriculum and also to the general ethos of the school. It therefore needs to be tackled in the context of what has come to be termed 'whole school policy'.

3   Local education authorities have an important role to play here in helping their schools to make a rigorous assessment of their problems, procedures and policies; assisting them, where necessary, in the formulation of strategies to tackle any problems; and further assisting and supporting them, as necessary, in implementing and in monitoring such strategies. The LEA's role in this should be supportive and sympathetic. At the same time it should be more proactive and firmer than has often been the tendency in the past. This is, of course, a sensitive issue because, given our system, the effectiveness of headteachers will be under scrutiny and they in particular will need to be consulted and may need professional support in such an exercise. In addition, the teaching unions will need to be consulted. The understanding, co-operation and active involvement of school governors will also be necessary.

4   Two areas of teacher training need to be given higher priority. First is classroom management and control. At the initial training level, for example, recent central directives have once more fuelled a tendency regrettably present in many training institutions to give more time, resources and status to subject studies at the expense of classroom management skills and practical experience. At the in-service level, too, both within schools in their procedures for guiding probationary and younger teachers, and at the local authority level in their INSET priorities, classroom management and skills seem not to be taken very seriously. The other neglected training area, albeit gaining some ground of late, is that of management and organisational development as related to schools as institutions.

5   One specific course of action which we would urge is the encouragement of schools to find ways of listening to and heeding the views of pupils in relation to school procedures, policies and curricula. School Councils are not the only, nor necessarily the best, way of achieving this. Tutorial lessons and House meetings, for example, can also be used for this purpose and questionnaires, especially if they are constructed in consultation with pupils, can be particularly valuable. The experience of schools which have used these and other methods to tap the views of pupils is that

the responses are on the whole frank, honest, perceptive and useful. A working group of the NCB's Children's Policy Review Group is currently gathering evidence on this issue.

6   We have thus far said little about the contribution of parents but we regard it as axiomatic that the more schools can succeed in actively involving parents in formulating and reviewing their policies and procedures, the more understandable, acceptable, and successful they are likely to be. Again, however, we would caution against the presentation of this issue to parents as merely one of rules, regulations and sanctions. Furthermore, if the involvement of parents is seen merely, for example, in terms of a circular letter from the school setting out its rules and procedures and inviting parents' co-operation, it is unlikely to be seen as partnership.

7   It seems to us that sufficient is now known about the nature of the problems in schools and the practical possibilities for promoting institutional change in schools (including the ideas expressed in paras. 2–6), so that a small national development team might usefully be established to help bring about such change. The National Children's Bureau would be happy to discuss this idea further with the Committee, if the Committee wished, and in any event to be associated with any such initiative.

8   One longer term strategy which should be given higher priority by schools is the teaching of personal and social education and preparation for parenthood. This is desirable for a number of reasons and in our view it should be included as a subject area in the core curriculum (NCB, 1987). However, it has particular value in this context because parenting skills in the next generation of parents can help facilitate healthy learning and adjustment in children and can prevent many of the problems which otherwise schools have to deal with.

9   The Government also has an important role to play in this area. We have made it clear that desirable behaviour and appropriate discipline in schools is inextricably bound up with the other important aspects of school life: academic curricula and pastoral care; organisational systems and personal relationships; the perception of the pupils and the morale of the teachers. In our judgement, morale and job satisfaction are rather low in the teaching force at present. The nature and extent of new legislation (with the Education Reform Act still to come) plus the not too distant industrial action, all set against the changing role and status of teachers in society over the past 20–30 years have resulted in an unsettledness which has undermined confidence. The Government

has an important part to play in restoring this confidence and improving job satisfaction. The Government's declared intention of raising the quality of education will not be achieved unless this can be done. And the quality of education is not to be measured simply in terms of pupils' attainment, however well assessed, but also in the quality of respect and regard implicit in the person-to-person behaviour seen in schools.

Many schools and their teachers provide an excellent service for their pupils, but the current climate of opinion, supported by research, is that some schools need to 'try harder to improve', 'pay more attention to', 'concentrate more upon' the range, administration and quality of their offerings. There is another opinion, which is attracting increasing recognition and acceptance; that teachers both individually, and collectively as a staff, can – and do – make a difference; they have considerable opportunities to make positive impacts upon their pupils' behaviour. We hope that the information highlighted, and discussed, in this book will aid discussions as to how teachers can make a positive impact upon pupils' behaviour in school, and elsewhere.

References

CANFIELD, J., WELLS, H. C. (1976) *100 Ways to enhance the self-concept in the classroom: a handbook for teachers and parents* (New Jersey: Prentice-Hall).
CHISHOLM, B., KEARNEY, D., KNIGHT, H., LITTLE, H., MORRIS, S. and TWEDDLE, D. (1986) *Preventive approaches to disruption* (Basingstoke: Macmillan Education).
CLARIZIO, H. F. and MCCOY, G. F. (1983) *Behaviour Disorders in Children* (New York: Harper and Row).
GOBELL, A. (1980) 'Three Classroom Procedures', in Upton, G. and Gobell, A. (eds) *Behaviour Problems in the Comprehensive School* (Cardiff: Faculty of Education, University College).
HAMBLIN, D. H. (1974) *The Teacher and Counselling* (Oxford: Blackwell).
HMI (1987) *Education Observed 5. Good behaviour and discipline in Schools* (London: DES).
LAWRENCE, J., STEED, D., YOUNG, P. (1984) *Disruptive Children, Disruptive Schools* (London: Croom Helm).
MORSE, W. C. (1963) 'Training teachers in life space interviewing', *American Journal of Orthopsychiatry*, 33, 727–30.

NATIONAL CHILDREN'S BUREAU (1988) *Evidence of National Children's Bureau to Committee of Enquiry into Discipline in Schools, Chaired by Lord Elton* (London: NCB).

REDL, F. (1959) 'Strategy and techniques of the life space interview', *American Journal of Orthopsychiatry*, 29, 1–18.

REDL, F., WINEMAN, D. (1952) *Controls from within* (London: Collier-Macmillan).

THOMAS, J., PRESLAND, I., GRANT, M., GLYNN, T. (1978) 'Natural rates of teacher approval and disapproval in Grade 7 classrooms', *Journal of Applied Behaviour Analysis*, 11, 91–4.

Index

ABC analysis, 114–15
absenteeism, 33–4
abuse, child, 27–8, 174
adolescent problems, 31, 140, 174–5
agencies and schools, 173 ff:
   Education Welfare Service, 177
   NSPCC, 179–80
   Other helping agencies, 180–1
   Police, 179
   Probation, 179
   School Health Service, 177–8
   School Psychological Service, 176–7
   Social Services Department, 178–9
AIDS, 17, 146
alcohol abuse, 17
allergic responses, 20–1, 23, 77
Andrew – case study, 98
appraisal, 5, 229
assessment, 42–6, 133:
   and achievement, 82–3
   and cognitive growth, 79–80
   and support teachers, 194–5, 198–9
   continuous, 46–7
   parallel with Social Services, 44–6
asthma, 14, 20, 23–4
auditory disturbance, 17
autism, 19

Barclay Report, 49
BATPAK Scheme, 126–7
behaviour:
   ABC analysis, 114–15
   and classroom management, 127–8
   and environment, 53
   and humanistic viewpoint, 111
   and learning, 67 ff, 74

biological factors in, 11, 16 ff
causation perspectives, 11–13
complexity of, 11, 13
definition, 2–3
development, 93–4
disruptive, 2, 91
exploratory, 99
inappropriate, 92–3
individual/systems and, 56–8
internal/external variables of, 11
management of, 3, 216–8
models in training, 197–8
modification, 50–1, 54–60, 188–9
overt, 98
psychological factors in, 11
'trigger', 95 ff
behavioural, 93:
   analysis, 115–19
   and behaviouristic, 108 ff
   approaches, scope of, 124–5
   BATPAK scheme, 126–7
   intervention, 114–19
   model, 12, 50–51
   objectives approach, 80
   standpoint, 112 ff
   techniques, 125–6
behaviouristic model, 108–111
bereavement, 25–6

child abuse, 27–8, 174
children's needs, 139–42
chromosomes, 18–19
Claire – case study, 13
classroom environment, 101–103, 216–18
classroom reality, 207–8
cleft palate – case study, 13

client centred therapy, 111–12
Cliff – case study, ·109–111
Clive – case study, 13
clumsy children, 17
cognitive growth, 79
community social work, 49
control, locus of, 72–3
counselling, 77–9, 82, 111–2, 133 ff, 137, 145, 200, 222–4
Court Report, 49
curriculum, 56, 142:
   and learning, 82
   inappropriate, 32
   mainstream, 80–81
   pupil's response to, 220–2
   tasks, 71
   unbalanced, 82

delinquency, 32–3
diet, 20–21
disruptive behaviour, 2, 91, 187:
   and pastoral care, 137–8
   low rates of, 188
   preventive approaches to, 218–20
disturbed family, 27
divorce, 26
Down's syndrome, 18–19
drugs and drugs education, 17, 174
dyslexia, 19, 68

eclectic stance, 59–62
eczema, 14, 20
Education Welfare Service, 15, 175, 177, 180, 185
educational psychologist(s), 13, 43, 48, 126, 176, 177, 182–3, 189, 192
Elton Report, 230 ff
encephalitis, 17
endocrine glands, 17–18
environment, 11–12, 18, 53, 68, 101–2
epilepsy, 14, 21–3, 77
evaluation, 201
exploratory behaviour, 94 ff, 216
exploratory learning, 103, 216
expulsion, 137

factors in behaviour, 16 ff
family factors, 11, 27, 53, 57, 59, 77, 138:
   and behaviour problems, 24–30
   and family therapy, 54–5
   in society, 141–2, 175–6
   parent/teacher collaboration, 105–6
food intolerance, 16

genes, 19–20
glands, endocrine, 17–18
Glenn – case study, 96–7
glue ear, 76
group work, 137, 143–5, 200

Health Service and schools, 177–8
Heather – case study, 152–6
heredity, 18
hospitalisation, 25
humanistic psychology, 12, 52–3, 55, 111–12
hyperactivity, 20–1

individuals and systems, 56–8
intervention strategies, 15, 77, 114 ff, 200

Jane – case study, 14
Jean – case study, 185

Kevin – case study, 182
King's Lynn initiative, 162–3

labelling theory, 55–6, 102
learning:
   and assessment, 82–3
   and behaviour problems, 67 ff
   and curriculum, 82
   and emotional/cognitive performance, 71–2
   and emotional problems, 74–6
   and parents, 104–6
   and pastoral care, 81–2
   and self concept, 72–3
   difficulties, 67–9, 92
   effective, 228 ff
   exploratory, 103
   inter-relationships with behaviour, 69–71
   intervention, 77–9, 199
   problems, 67 ff, 124
   social, 104
   third factor variables, 76–7
liaison, agencies and schools, 173 ff, 195
life space interview, 222–3
locus of control, 72–3

maladjustment, 67, 69–72, 75, 99, 187
Mark – case study, 100–101
Mary – case study, 99–100
microcephaly, 19
Meg – case study, 183–4
meningitis, 17

Mike – case study, 122–4
misbehaviour management, 216–18
modelling from teachers' behaviour, 212–13
models, theoretical, 12, 48 ff, 58–62
multi-causal factors, 15
mosaicism, 18

needs, children's, 139–42
nervous systems, 16–17

Oerlinghausen Project, 159, 169–70
otitis media, 76

PAD (preventive approaches to disruption), 218–20
parenting, 26–7
parents, 151 ff:
  and advice, 167–8
  and Heather – case study, 152 ff
  and information, 164–7
  and learning, 104–6
  and shared responsibility, 156 ff
  co-operation, 225–7
  involvement, 105–6, 230
  misunderstandings with teachers, 156 ff
pastoral care, 52, 83, 133 ff, 204:
  and academic progress, 81–2
  and agencies, 173 ff
  and personal and social education, 146
  and primary schools, 142–5
  and support teachers, 195
  and secondary schools, 145–6
  checklist, 133–4
  critical viewpoints in, 136–9
  definition of, 133
  developments/changes in, 142 ff
  effectiveness, 147
  objectives, 174
  reviewing, 224–5
peer group influences, 11, 30–31, 136
personal and social education, 146
phenylketonuria, 19
pregnancy, 17
preventive approaches to disruption, 218–220
problem behaviour:
  definition, 3
  differing between home and school, 48
  eclectic stance, 59–60
  precipitating problems in, 12
  reinforcing problems, 12
  with adolescents, 140, 174–5

phenomenological approach, 55
pollution, 20
poverty, 30
psychodynamic model, 12, 15, 49–50, 61, 93–4
psychological factors in behaviour, 11
psychological factors in learning, 22
Psychological Service, 176–7
psychology, humanistic, 12, 52–3, 55, 111–12
punishments, 210–12

reinforcing problems, 12, 109 ff
reinforcement skills, 116–121, 208–10
relationships, teachers with children, 135–6
Richard – case study, 14
Rubinstein–Tali syndrome, 19
rubella, 17
Ruth – case study, 185–6

school(s), 56, 159, 187–8, 191, 228 ff:
  effect of, 3–4
  factors in behaviour problems, 31 ff
  helping children, 142
  problems, 35–6, 42–3
  systems approach, 54–5
School Health Service, 177–8
Seebohm Report, 49
self-appraisal, 5
self-concept, 72–3, 78, 81, 83, 94, 213–14
self-expectation, 73
separation experiences, 24–6
situations and problem behaviour, 3–4, 47, 207
smoking, 17
social class differences, 28–9
social disadvantage, 29–30, 75
social learning, 104
social learning theory, 113
Social Services Department, 44–6, 49, 178–9, 184–5
special educational needs, 67, 69–71, 140–41
special schools, 61–2, 67, 69–71, 81
Stewart – case study, 14
stress, 25, 200–201
support teachers, 187 ff
syphilis, 17
systems approach, 54–5

teacher(s), 1–2, 32, 35, 56–7, 207–8, 231:

successful/unsuccessful, 36–7
and behavioural problems, 42 ff
understanding of difficulties, 91–2
quality of, 135
and parents, 156 ff
modelling from, 212–13
Terry – case study, 119–121
therapy, client centred, 111–12
toxoplasmosis, 17
Tracy and Garth – case study, 184–5
trigger behaviour, 95–101
truancy, 33–4, 211

tuberous schlerosis, 19
Turner's syndrome, 19
tutorial work, 133 ff, 137, 145–6
Tutt Report, 45

variables of behaviour, 11
visual defect, 16
visual perception, 17

Warnock Report, 45, 67, 69, 140
Wendy, case study, 182–3
Wiltshire support teachers, 187 ff